Leading Issues in e-Government

Edited by

Les Worrall

Leading Issues in eGovernment
Volume One

First edition April 2011
Second Printing July 2012

Note to readers.

Some papers have been written by authors who use the American form of spelling and some use the British. These two different approaches have been left unchanged.

ISBN: 978-1-906638-89-4

Printed by Good News Digital Books

Published by: Academic Publishing International Limited, Reading, RG4 9AY, United Kingdom, info@academic-publishing.org

Available from www.academic-bookshop.com

Contents

About the editor

Les Worrall is Professor of Strategic Analysis at Coventry University. He has published extensively about the UK public sector. He specialises in local government but has undertaken information management and strategic change projects for central government departments. He obtained a PhD from the University of Liverpool in information systems development.

Les was previously employed in UK local government a strategic planner who focussed on the development of information systems and improving the management of information. He was chair of the Local Authorities Research and Intelligence Association and has advised many public bodies – including the then Parliamentary IT Committee - on ICT development. Les has acted as an advisor on projects that have explored how government bodies can better exploit the opportunities provided by web technologies to improve efficiency, service delivery and transparency in local governance.

Les has conducted consultancy on a range of ICT management issues such as improving ICT procurement effectiveness, shared services, outsourcing, training needs assessment, organisational and service redesign and raising senior management and political awareness about the l benefits of ICT.

Les has also been active in management education having been a council member of the British Academy of Management and chair of the Academy's Directors of Research Network.

Contributors

Ömer Faruk Aydinli, *Logica, Public Sector, Arnhem, The Netherlands*
Hisham Alsaghier, *Griffith University, Brisbane, Australia*
Roberta Bernardi, *University of Warwick, Coventry, UK*
Nils Burger, *Utrecht School of Governance, The Netherlands*
Sjaak Brinkkemper, *Institute of Information and Computer Sciences, University of Utrecht, The Netherlands*
Wolfgang Ebbers, *Utrecht School of Governance, The Netherlands*
Marilyn Ford, *Griffith University, Brisbane, Australia*
Rene Hexel, *Griffith University, Brisbane, Australia*
Paul Jaeger, *University of Maryland, USA*
Marijn Janssen, *Delft University of Technology, The Netherlands*
David Landsbergen, *Ohio State University, Columbus, Ohio, USA*
Miriam Matteson, *University of Maryland, USA*
Albert Meijer, *Utrecht School of Governance, The Netherlands*
Anne Nguyen, *Griffith University, Brisbane, Australia*
Abdelbaset Rabaiah, *ETRO Research Group, Virje Universitiet Brussel, Belgium*
Pascal Ravesteyn, *Research Centre for Process Innovation, University of Applied Sciences Utrecht, The Netherlands*
Richard Schwester, *City University of New York, New York USA*
Jeroen Stragier, *Ghent University (UGent) – Interdisciplinary Institute for Broadband Technology (IBBT), Belgium*
Eddy Vandijck, *ETRO Research Group, Virje Universitiet Brussel, Belgium*
Anne Fleur van Veenstra, *Delft University of Technology, The Netherlands*
Pieter Verdegem, *Ghent University (UGent) – Interdisciplinary Institute for Broadband Technology (IBBT), Belgium*
Gino Verleye, *Ghent University (UGent) – Interdisciplinary Institute for Broadband Technology (IBBT), Belgium*

Introduction to Leading Issues in e-Government Research e-Government - Where is it taking us and our Governments?

The last decade has seen a massive growth in e-Government at the local, national and international levels. While there is much hyperbole surrounding e-Government, there has also been a considerable transformation in the ways that government and the governed interact with each other. We are all now encouraged to register to vote, tax our cars, submit our tax returns and report problems via the Internet. We can check on the level of crime in our neighbourhood (http://police.uk) and contact our local police through the web. We are able to blog and twitter and establish our own social networks or become followers of other peoples' (often inane and inconsequential) digital utterances. We can access our local council's documentation over the Internet and engage our local councillors in new forms of conversation. Our local hospital will even remind us by SMS not to forget that we have a hospital appointment tomorrow and we can book an appointment with our doctor over the Internet (even though we sometimes still have to wait an inordinate amount of time to see him/her). Ten years ago, we could do very little of this but is our life any fuller or better because of it? As a person with reasonably developed ICT skills, I would say "yes" but there are still large swathes of any population who exist outside "the web". Paradoxically, it is often those who do not have access to new technologies that are most dependent on publicly provided services.

Grant and Chau (2006, p80) develop a useful definition of e-Government that adequately summarises the various dimension of e-Government that will be examined in this book. They define e-Government as "A broad-based transformation initiative, enabled by leveraging the capabilities of information and communication technology; (1) to develop and deliver high quality, seamless, and integrated public services; (2) to enable effective constituent relationship management; and (3) to support the economic and social development goals of citizens, businesses, and civil society at a local, state, national, and international levels". So, e-Government is about transformation, it's about delivering service far more effectively and seamlessly, it's about developing new forms of communication between government and the governed and it's about enhancing the quality of our lives through economic development and enhancing civil society.

Not only has e-Government transformed aspects of our lives, it has significantly increased the pressure on government to reform and restructure, to improve its performance, to improve public access and to open itself up to greater scrutiny (voluntarily or involuntarily through newly emergent media such as WikiLeaks...although WikiLeaks is itself hardly an e-Government initiative). E-Government is clearly not about carrying on with business as usual: it is also not just about technology. While e-Government does involve using technology to do things not only better but differently, it also enables all us (or is that many of us?) to do things in a way that was not possible before. E-Government is also about increasing transparency, sharpening accountability, increased scrutiny, taking out hierarchies, changing working practices, changing cultures, changing behaviours and about radically changing power structures by making power more diffuse and less concentrated among a small political and administrative elite. It is in these areas where inanimate technology causes conflict as it collides head on with the many sociological, political, institutional and psychological barriers to change that exist in all organisations.

e-Government is also situated in a wider societal context: not only do wider forces for change in society affect e-Government, e-Government affects society as it is, of itself, a force for change. Disentangling this complex reciprocal relationship has proved very challenging because it makes it very difficult to separate out the effects of external barriers to e-Government implementation from e-Government's own internal constraints, limitations and contradictions. Why do some groups use web-based services more intensively than others? Is this because they are more trusting? Is this because the technology provided in some areas is more effective and sensitive to user needs? Why is technology accepted in some contexts and not in others? How can we structure e-Government strategies so that it is more socially inclusive and does not reinforce, reify and perpetuate existing societal divides? How can we develop more multi-channel approaches that will enable a wider cross-section of society to engage with e-Government? Given that the disadvantaged, the old, the unemployed and those who have disabilities tend to be more reliant on public services, how can we structure our approaches to e-Government to meet their needs rather than the needs of the more vocal, more articulate, more advantaged members of society? All these are huge challenges that need to be addressed as e-Government becomes more mature, more pervasive and more institutionalised and embedded within society and its structures.

Citizens are not likely to use e-Government provided services unless they have trust in the systems, unless they feel that their privacy and security are not at risk and unless they feel that there is some compelling reason for them so to do (or because they have to because other means of service delivery are withdrawn). The picture is rather different from a government perspective. Following the boom times in the middle of the last decade we are now faced with an era of austerity in which government in the USA and across Europe are seeking to shrink the public sector by taking out (primarily labour) costs by making government more "efficient". I am often left wondering just how much Orwellian Doublespeak (defined as the deliberate and calculated misuse of language) emanates from government these days and how this has become embedded in "Webspeak" - the modern equivalent to Newspeak (which was, according to Orwell, the official language of Doublespeak). Governments are increasingly seeing e-Government as a means of shrinking the public sector employment base by encouraging (or is it coercing?) citizens (or is it customers?) into filing their tax returns, paying their taxes, applying for licences and doing all manner of administrative task electronically rather than using more traditional and more labour-intensive means. Government bodies themselves are also being forced (by political directives) to develop shared service arrangements and to integrate their back office functions – again, primarily to reduce costs. These initiatives have already had a profound effect on government – but we are still at the beginning of a long journey. Organisational cultures, work practices, client and citizen attitudes and behaviours are gradually changing. The organisational silo mentality is breaking down, structures are becoming flatter, communication is becoming more two-way and less hierarchical but we still have a long way to go.

It is in this context that I set about selecting the papers for inclusion in the book. Each of the papers addresses some of the issues I have raised above. The paper by Rabaiah and Vandijk is based on a study of the e-Government strategies of twenty national governments in which they found that all had experienced problems in implementing their strategies – often the same problems. Their paper showed that all of the strategies had relatively weak foundations and, consequently, had failed to deliver against many of their aims and objectives. Of particular importance was the degree of disconnect between wider government strategies and their e-Government strategy: misalignment is a common problem in strategy making. It is also amazing that strategist still do not seem to realise that implementation changes strategy especially in a field that is as dynamic and as fast moving as e-Government. The one line message here is that strategically, governments could do better!

The truism that the robustness of any strategy is determined by its ability to stand the trials of implementation is pursued in the chapter written by Schwester. Schwester charts the development of e-Government arguing that e-Government has evolved from simple information provision, through transaction processing to more complex forms of citizen communications engagement (or constituent relationships management to use a phrase from the Grant and Chau definition). Schwester argues that effective government is defined by its ability to deploy technological innovations and its awareness of the barriers to the implementation of e-Government. Perhaps not surprisingly, Schwester reveals, from his study of US municipalities, that the extent of e-Government adoption was a function of the financial, technical and human resources that a municipality was prepared to deploy. Most important, he comments on the need for municipalities to make "sustained human capital investments" and to ensure that they have a firmly established ICT capability if their e-Government strategies are to succeed. Additionally, he argues that e-Government is not achievable without strong political and senior management commitment. Essentially, Schwester reveals that effective e-Government cannot be done "on the cheap" and without strong top level commitment.

If we are to understand e-Government, we need to see it as being embedded within the context of the changes that are affecting public management more widely. Since the 1980s, waves of change have passed over public management resulting in the evolution of the "new public management" (or NPM - which might also be a breeding ground for Orwellian Doublespeak). Within NPM, emphasis has moved away from the direct provision of services to enabling and outsourcing. Emphasis has also moved away from a view of government as having centralised power to more diverse and diffuse models of governance with higher levels of citizen engagement and less pronounced information asymmetries between government and the governed. Bernadi's chapter discusses how health information systems have been developed in Kenya and how these developments reflect wider changes in how public management is viewed and how NPM has evolved. She contends that the relationship between NPM and e-Government development is far from straightforward arguing that many ICT and e-Government initiatives have failed because models of NPM have been uncritically adopted and have not be moulded to reflect local institutional settings. Interestingly, Bernadi argues that it is important to understand the "institutional logic" of organisations and that a failure to do so can undermine the potential impact of e-Government. Bernadi reveals that understanding the local context for e-Government development is critical and that "one size fits all" approaches are not portable from one setting to another: attention to local detail is critical.

Similar issues to those in the Bernadi chapter are pursued in the chapter by Verdegem et al who suggest that the knowledge base needed to underpin e-Government strategies has been less than adequate in the majority of cases. They address the question of how governments can systematically measure the progress of their e-Government strategies and, more important, learn from this process. The authors argue that current approaches to evaluating e-Government strategies are too often based on supply-side measures and they argue that a more user-centric, bottom up, data-driven approach is needed. In their evaluation of developments in Belgium, the authors identify a major shift from efficiency to effectiveness in the evaluation of the delivery of public e-services. Perhaps most important is that the authors develop sets of variables that focus specifically on defining inputs, outputs, outcomes and impacts as well as developing a set of measures(such as skills, infrastructure, access and attitudes) that can be used to contextualise their analysis. The essential message from this chapter is that organisations need to develop better structured measurement and monitoring systems to evaluate their e-Government initiatives and put in place the learning loops to ensure that continuous improvement takes place.

The business processes that are embedded within government practices have evolved over decades: many of these processes have been confronted by the discontinuous change caused by the adoption of new technologies. The chapter by Aydinli et al describes, and draws lessons from, a business process and organisational redesign project undertaken in a government department in the Netherlands. The authors adopt, adapt and integrate a range of tools and techniques and use these to bring about the business process redesign and organisational restructuring needed to enhance service delivery and organisational performance. Aydinli et al demonstrate the advantage of using suites of methods that will assist senior managers better to define business strategy, identify critical business processes and make information architectures explicit. The authors admit the exploratory nature of their project and raise issues about whether their approach is scalable and portable to different organisational settings. An important message from their study is that business processes - and organisational structures - need to change to reflect the new realities of e-Government even if these changes are the subject of (often considerable) resistance from within the organisation.

In the current era of austerity, e-Government is increasingly been seen as a means of delivering cost-reduction and improving efficiency and effectiveness. To achieve these ends, Veenstra and Janssen argue that government agencies are increasingly implementing multi-channel service provisioning (MCSP – a means of providing services by means of a number of different channels). The rationale of MCSP is that individual citizens or businesses can use different channels to interact with government based on their preferences, needs, abilities and circumstances. Additionally, citizens or businesses can change their channel if their preferences, needs, skills or circumstances change. Increasingly, new channels are being created and existing users are being encouraged, incentivised or coerced into using channels which enable government departments to save money. The authors reveal that if these strategies are to work effectively then organisational change, the dismantling of silos within organisations, changes to business and work processes, the deployment of new technologies and culture change within the organisation are all pre-requisites.

The theme of channel development is pursued in the Landsbergen chapter which reveals that in the last five years there has been an explosion in the use of social media. He argues that social media are being hailed as "paradigm shifting" because of the new opportunities they provide for the future development of e-Government. Hyperbole aside, Landsbergen argues that social media provide government with an opportunity radically to change "how it does things" and to change business processes "in a way that improves government". Landsbergen emphasises the improved communications potential of social media in that they are interactive and multimedia, they can exploit or facilitate the development of human networks and they are non-hierarchic. Perhaps the most important lesson that government has to learn here is that social networks are not broadcasting tools but two-way communications tools which have the potential to blur boundaries between government and the governed. Given this blurring, Landsbergen emphasises that developing trust is essential in enabling networks to operate effectively and he also argues that government bodies will need to develop the skills of administrators so that they become more responsive to citizens while maintaining the public's trust in the probity and responsiveness of government. Without doubt, social media provide government with a "window of opportunity" but government still, clearly, has many lessons to learn and many structural, procedural, attitudinal and behavioural issues to address.

The new technologies that have emerged over the last ten years have had a massive impact on the social, cultural, economic and political practices that are embedded within society. Understanding the relationship between emerging technology and the changing shape, structure and operation of social interaction is critical if we are to develop more effective and more inclusive e-Government. So too, is understanding what shapes citizens' desire and ability to engage with political processes. Meijer et al develop the notion, using structuration theory, that technology and how it is used are shaped by existing social practices but, importantly, technology has a major role to play in transforming these social and political processes. Consequently, developing an understanding of how technology shapes and is simultaneously shaped by social practices is important if we are to successfully develop e-Government. The authors argue that we need to rethink many aspects of public participation as new models of citizen participation are being constructed "to fit then new routines of the information society".

Several of the papers included in book explicitly identify trust as an issue of concern in e-Government. Those that don't refer to trust explicitly almost invariably contain some implicit reference to trust. Alsaghier et al argue that trust plays a vital role in helping citizens overcome any issues they may have with perceived risk and, consequently, they argue that we need to develop a much clearer understanding of the role of trust and that we need systematically to build public trust if society more widely is to benefit from the further development of e-Government. Enhancing citizen acceptance of e-Government will depend on governments' ability to build trust and if governments want to build trust they need to understand what trust is. The authors develop an eclectic view of trust and seek to integrate concepts drawn from the disciplines of psychology and sociology and from the domains of e-commerce and HCI (Human Computer Interaction). The authors refer to a large body of literature that emphasises the importance of impersonal trust in making social networks work and argue that the absence of trust will preclude the growth of the forms of cooperative behaviour upon which the further development of e-Government depends. The authors argue that if the public do not have trust in e-Government then e-Government will not work: trust is thus a necessary condition for e-Government.

Alsaghier et al identify a number of important constructs that impinge upon a citizen's level of trust in e-Government: these include an individual's disposition to trust (some people are naturally more trusting than others); their familiarity with the "online world"; their trust in institutions; the quality of, for example, websites; the ease of use of e-Government web-based facilities; and a user's perceived sense of risk. The authors admit that their research is still being developed but it provides a useful insight into trust in e-Government and a potential methodology to help us understand what needs to be done to build user trust as a basis for the wider used of e-Government.

When accessing a government website to find information or to conduct a transaction, how many of us stop to think what assumptions web site developers have made about the skills and abilities of the members of the public that will be accessing those sites? This is a critical issue in the public sector given that the public sector tends to cater most intensively for people with specific needs, specific problems and skill sets that may limit their ability to make as good a use of the Internet as more skilled people. Jaeger and Matteson discuss recent developments in the USA where the rapid growth in e-Government has affected the nature of the relationship of the government and its citizens. Here they use the Technology Acceptance Model (TAM) to explore if e-Government has become more accessible to those citizens with disabilities. While their paper focuses specifically on e-Government accessibility for the disabled, they argue that their model and methodology is equally applicable for assessing e-Government accessibility either more widely or for other "marginal" groups in society. Worryingly, the authors reveal that most of the e-Government websites they examined did not comply with the requirements of Section 508 of the Rehabilitation Act: this rendered most e-Government websites inaccessible to some or all citizens with disabilities. Perhaps more important, they found that the organisation's own assessment of the accessibility of their own websites was substantially more positive than the authors' assessment. Perhaps we need to be even more diligent in the development of e-Government strategies that are inclusive and reflect the needs, skills and abilities of all citizens rather than the interests of the technologically capable.

While there has been considerable progress in e-Government, there is still a long way to go before e-Government reaches its potential and all aspects of the Grant and Chau definition of e-Government are effectively delivered. A number of the chapters in this book draw attention to flaws in the e-Government strategies of many public bodies: silo structures and silo thinking still exists; many governments are still living in the age where top-down communications is what government did; despite much delayering hierarchies still pervade; many business processes remain to be re-engineered; power is still strongly concentrated within government; and, many public officials do not have the skills, attitudes and abilities needed to cope with a less hierarchic, faster, more transparent, more accountable world. Many e-Government strategies seem to be under-resourced and not to have had the necessary foundations put in place from which they can be effectively developed. Many public bodies seem more focused on copying from other public bodies rather than learning from other public bodies by the more effective tailoring of apparently generic solutions to local conditions, needs and institutional structures. Trust still seems to be an issue of concern as does developing more inclusivity, accountability and transparency. But despite these problems, there still has been considerable progress. E-Government is all about radical change and transformation and yet a recent publication from within UK local government argues that the track record of government in delivering radical transformational change is poor "as organisations struggle with issues of leadership, capacity and methodology" and, increasingly, resource availability (Socitm Insight Briefing No25, January 2011). We hope that this book will provide some lessons and examples of how transformational change can be more effectively delivered so that e-Government can deliver more of what it promises.

Reference

Grant, G. and Chau, D. (2006) Developing a generic framework for e-Government. Chapter 4 in G. Hunter and Tan F (eds) Advanced Topics in Global Information Management, Volume 5, 72-101. Idea Group: London

Les Worrall
Director, Axiom Research Ltd
Professor of Strategic Analysis
Coventry University, UK
worrall.l@sky.com
March 2011

A Strategic Framework of e-Government: Generic and Best Practice

Abdelbaset Rabaiah and Eddy Vandijck
ETRO Research Group, Virje Universitiet Brussel, Belgium
aabdelgh@vub.ac.be
Originally published in EJEG (2009) Volume 7, issue 3.

Editorial Commentary

The growth in e-Government initiatives over the last decade has been considerable and governments, national and local, have had to make informed choices about how to develop strategies for e-Government implementation that will satisfy generic and more context-specific needs. This paper argues that while there are many commonalities among the programmes that governments have developed, there are also some interesting differences. Rabaiah and Vandijck argue that while the strategies of the twenty national governments they examined were well developed, all had problems with the implementation of their strategies. More important, the authors argue that many of the strategies they examined had weak foundations and consequently, had failed to add as much value as they could. In many cases the links between wider government strategies and their e-Government initiatives were well developed.

To address these issues, the authors develop a generic framework for e-Government which can be used as a benchmark for the evaluation of extant government strategies. Rabaiah and Vandijck argue that even though countries differ in terms of their political, governance and legal systems, their levels of literacy and the extent of Internet penetration, they could add value by focusing on commonalities and identifying best practices. The authors do some interesting work on identifying what the "guiding principles" of different country's e-Government initiatives actually were: interestingly, efficiency emerged at the top of their list followed by enhancing participation. The authors argue that their review of best practices and commonalities will enable governments to make more informed choices about how to design an e-Government strategy that is more clearly linked to the delivery of wider government objectives and less prone to the inevitable problems that arise in implementation.

Abstract: e-Government has become a global phenomenon. There have been some great innovations in e-Government over the last decade. Some governments compete for leadership in offering online services. Others do not want to be left behind. Most governments have developed detailed strategies for realizing their e-Government programmes. Although the goals behind these programmes vary across countries, there are still many commonalities among them. Such commonalities result from the application of best practices. Governments have the tendency to learn from each other. We could identify certain trends in e-Government application. e-Government strategies per se are generally well developed. Yet the problems are mostly associated with implementation. This paper studies the strategies of (21) countries in addition to the European Union to put together a generic strategic framework of e-Government. We found most of these strategies to be lacking a strategic framework - a framework that stems from the e-Government strategy itself. The ultimate purpose of this paper is to introduce a best practice framework that is generic enough to be adopted by any given strategy. The paper argues the missing benefits of such a strategic framework. The proposed framework incorporates very important elements and principles. It has desirable characteristics and features that can add value to the e-Government strategy. Unlike previous studies, the proposed framework defines strategic building blocks of e-Government based on real-life e-Government implementations of the countries reviewed. Our strategic framework possesses modular design. It is flexible, customisable and extensible. In putting this framework together, we took into consideration commonalities, trends, and best practices in addition to relevant work of other scholars.

Keywords: e-Government, framework, strategy, best practice, generic, strategic

1. Introduction

World governments have achieved substantial progress in their e-Government initiatives during the last decade. e-Government has become a world phenomenon. Each government has developed its own strategy to meet the challenges of e-Government development. Nonetheless, e-Government realisation in its full potential is still far from complete. Since it is still a work in progress, e-Government is constantly developing. e-Government strategies are updated fairly frequently. What was valid a few years ago in terms of services delivery, efficiency, etc. may not be satisfactory today. This is mainly due inter alia to rapid debuts of newer technologies and ideas. Since an e-Government strategy serves as a general guide to e-Government realisation, it is crucial to keep it clear and simple.

There are, however, no commonly established guidelines to write clear and simple strategies. Only few research studies (e.g. Heeks, 2006) have provided guidelines for writing e-Government strategies. Still though, no previous studies have been recorded to attempt conceptualising e-Government strategies in order to build a generic and structured one that incorporates the necessary basic elements for a successful development. This article delves into an exploratory study of real-life e-Government strategies. It investigates the possibility of creating a typical e-Government strategy.

An e-Government strategy is a 'plan for e-Government systems and their supporting infrastructure which maximises the ability of management to achieve organisational objectives' (Heeks, 2006). This plan is described in a top-level document that addresses strategic directions, goals, components, principles and implementation guidelines. The strategy should be understandable without any ambiguities. Such a strategy is considered a baseline and thus will be referred to quite often. Different versions of e-Government strategies of (20) countries, in addition to that of the European Union, have been the subject of this study. These countries are: Australia; Belgium; Denmark; Austria; Japan; Finland; France; Canada; Germany; Korea; Singapore; Jordan; Egypt; UK; India; New Zealand; USA; Malaysia; Brazil and The Netherlands.

Choice of the list of countries was based on the availability of relevant published documentations. The countries with best-practice records were among the list. Many of the countries reviewed topped the score of e-Government maturity. To make the list even more representative, we added some of the developing countries. Geographic variation was also taken into consideration. Thus, the list includes countries from all continents. This diversity is meant to provide a generalised perspective of these strategies during the study.

2. Importance of a strategic framework of e-Government

A primary aim of this article is to construct a strategic framework of e-Government. This framework serves as a generic abstraction of an e-Government strategy. Despite its simplicity and necessity as we shall see shortly, an e-Government strategic framework is missing from many of the national e-Government strategies reviewed in this study. At lease not in the way this article is advocating.

The majority of the e-Government strategies of sample countries are lacking a strategic framework. Some countries had included some relevant diagrams but they do not qualify as strategic e-Government frameworks based on our description later on. Only Singapore has included a strategic framework of e-Government. Yet this framework is far from being an adequate abstraction of the country's e-Government strategy. Its components are the vision, action points and key enablers of e-Government. These meagre contents are characteristic of Singapore alone, of course.

Bundling of an e-Government strategic framework could have certainly added value to the strategies of these countries. Today, there is a lot of replication of efforts on the part of governments who look forward to incept e-Government programmes. A comprehensive, well-designed framework and implementation methodology would save governments a lot of time, research, money and disappointments.

Sometimes a picture can convey more information than many pages of text. An e-Government strategic framework is not meant to replace the detailed text of the e-Government strategy but rather to enhance it. It can also serve as a quick alternative. This graphical representation gives a lot of information at a glance, especially when drawn well to stress the main messages of the strategy.

This makes it a perfectly useful tool in the hands of decision-makers. It is more convenient for politicians who are normally non-technical. It is always easier for them to handle graphical representations than huge tables, lengthy texts...etc. Furthermore, a strategic framework gives a simplified yet a comprehensive conceptualisation of what the e-Government strategy is all about. It immediately shows the trends in e-Government realisation. This is particularly important during discussions about e-Government initiatives among stakeholders. Whenever the need arises to consult the strategy it might just be satisfactory to consult the framework first. In case further details are required then the complete strategy is always available. This can, in many cases, save the time and effort of delving into the full text of the strategy.

Being a comprehensive abstraction of the strategy, a strategic framework shows how different basic components fit together. It shows each component in relation to others. This makes planning and foreseeing of discrepancies a lot easier. Contradictions, misalignments, and out of orchestration with the general policies can be spotted easily.

For transparency reasons, people should know about their government's initiatives and intentions. It is also important for a government to publish its accomplishments. The framework is easier to disseminate in brochures and handouts than the complete strategy. This also saves publishing costs.

The e-Government strategic framework should convey the main message of the strategy (i.e. the strategic intent). The framework is very convenient for this purpose. This is because it is top-level representation of the strategic orientation in graphical format. Being a graphical visualisation, the strategic framework of e-Government should be neither cluttered nor too complicated. Simplicity and easy interpretation is the power behind such a framework. Moving towards complexity decreases its usability and value. It is important, though, that the framework highlights the most important aspects of the e-Government strategy. For example, it must include the government's focus and basic components of the e-Government programme.

An e-Government strategic framework has a relatively long-term scope and validity. In order to stay valid, it must respond to changes in the environment. Technology is ever changing at an accelerating pace. It is also frequent that simplification of procedure results in process re-engineering. Organisational structures within the government can also take place. These and many other changes in the environment must not invalidate the framework. It should be flexible enough to cope with them. One way to make a strategy more responsive is to make it as technology neutral as possible.

The proposed framework is "customisable". It is generic in nature and not constrained in some country-specific characteristics. Any country can utilise the proposed framework by populating it with its own visions, objective, initiatives and priorities. Layout and the relationships within and among its different components can also be customised. In this way, individual governments can still reflect their own focus and strategic agenda through local customisation of the framework.

A strategic framework should serve as the bridge between regional and local strategies. In addition, it should also be extensible through detailed sub-strategies. For example, there could be a dedicated strategy for client centricity (e.g. Citizen Centric Government: Electronic Service Delivery Strategy for the Western Australian Public Sector...etc.) Obviously all these requirements are challenging. Extra care can be taken to structure the framework. Before going any further, let us check any previous research that might have tackled the issue.

3. Literature review

We have noticed a relative neglect of this strategic part of e-Government despite its extreme importance. Soundness of an e-Government strategy can be the difference between success and failure of the whole endeavour. Even in practice, many public authorities do not have any e-Government strategy at all (Heeks, 2006).

There have been a number of studies related to e-Government strategies (e.g. Aichholzer, 2004; Bhatnagar, 2004; Chen et al, 2006; Heeks, 2006; Shahkooh and Abdollahi, 2007). Most of these studies, however, shed some light on what e-Government strategies should be like or how to plan them. Some other contributions sought to produce frameworks aimed at better understanding of e-Government as a concept. Each attempt tackled the complexity of e-Government from a certain perspective.

Methodologies and basis for these studies also varied. Grant and Chau (2006) and Wimmer (2002), for example, introduced frameworks to help understand e-Government in its entirety. The framework of Sharma and Gupta (2003) was based on the work done be Heeks (2001), observation of few practical implementations by some countries (exclusively: USA, Canada, Singapore and India), and their own experience. The basic components of e-Government Sharma and Gupta (2003) stated were actually based on maturity levels of e-Government implementation. Others (e.g. Miranda, 2000) thought of building blocks to be purely technical components (e.g. ERP, CRM...etc).

Wimmer (2002) on the other hand, perceived her framework as hodgepodge of different views of e-Government, abstraction layers, and progress of public service. She argued that these perspectives provide better understanding and visualisation of e-Government. Grant and Chau (2006) developed their e-Government framework to help assess, categorise and classify e-Government efforts. They started from few workable definitions of e-Government to figure out the building blocks.

The drive behind developing e-Government frameworks is the lack of mature documentation in literature (Sharma and Gupta, 2003). What is particularly noticeable about these previous studies is the intention behind building the frameworks as well as their domain of application. Most of these frameworks were developed to provide a better understanding of e-Government as mentioned above. No one study was aimed at developing a framework that abstracts the e-Government strategy. Furthermore, none has discussed the importance of embedding a strategic framework in an e-Government strategy. This is where our contribution fits. Our study comes in to fill a gap in literature concerning e-Government strategies. This article advocates the inclusion of a strategic framework in all e-Government strategies in order to realise the benefits stated earlier. Thus, the contribution is distinct. We are building a strategic framework of e-Government that is both generic and based on best practice.

The word "strategic" in the title refers to the facts that it stems from the e-Government strategy. Hence, our approach is rather different. We primarily relied on real-life strategies of e-Government of many countries to produce the proposed framework. Thus, the end product merits as both generic and best practice. In addition, we took the relevant work of researchers mentioned above into consideration in structuring the framework. Particularly, their efforts have helped us examine all possible dimensions of our framework. It is true that e-Government strategies are driven by vision, political and economic factors and requirements of each individual country (Grant and Chau, 2006), yet we found a lot in common in all these facets. Having seen the relative neglect of this vital research on this strategic level, let us now discuss the research methodology followed. This is the subject of the next section.

4. Methodology

Figure 1 below gives an overview of the research methodology followed to structure the framework.

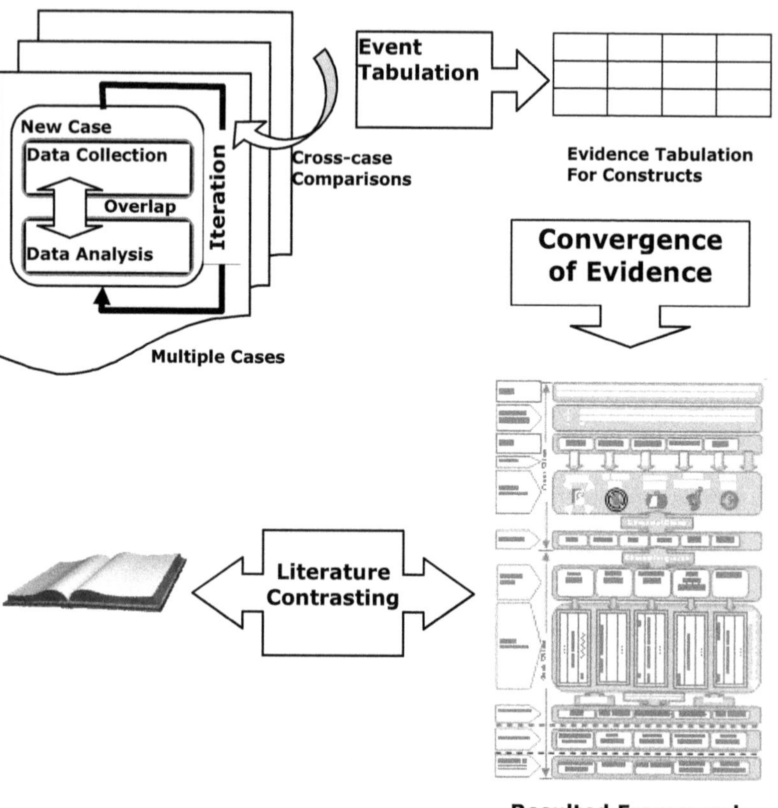

Figure 1: Overview of our research methodology

As the figure shows, we resorted to the *structured case approach* by Plummer (2001). Plummer (2001) suggested that the structured case study approach has the powers of interpretive (during data analysis) and positivist (through conceptual framework) epistemologies. Riedl et al (2007) advocated and implemented the structured case approach to build theory in e-Government. They argued that this methodology draws the linkage between data and conclusion. They concluded the validity of the approach for theory and knowledge building. We estimated that this scientific research methodology fits well the nature of our research. We overlapped data analysis with data collection as Van Mannen (1988) and Glaser and Strauss (1967) suggested. This allowed us to make adjustments during the data collection process. The added flexibility of data collection was important since we were not sure what data collected will become important in the course of our research. We were building a framework out of textual (qualitative) data. In the process, we conducted intensive and iterative cross-case comparisons.

We did not set in advance the number of cases to consult. We added new cases whenever we were in doubt about some construct or component in the framework. We kept adding cases until the addition of a new case produced minimal effect on the emergent framework. In other words, we stopped adding cases once we witnessed a convergence of evidence. We tried to balance the intensity of data collection of the case studies. Too many constructs could have led to a complex framework. Inadequate volume of data or sparse variation on the other hand might have failed to capture the whole picture in its entirety. We were aware of these potential risks and worked to avoid them.

To counteract the possible effects of our initial impressions on data collected we searched for cross-case patterns. We used a mesh of (21) cells for each group of data to generate accurate and reliable constructs. To have a better understanding during comparison analysis we fell back on lens or keyhole comparisons (Walk, 1998). This comparison methodology has produced new perspectives. It allowed us to gather quality data. This was not easy, however. We had to do keyhole comparisons not between two cases but rather among (21).

To validate each construct in the sought framework we tabulated evidence (data) from which each construct has evolved (Miles and Huberman, 1984; Sutton and Callahan, 1987). The reason to follow this technique was the relative variation of evidence across cases. The technique followed made it easier to aggregate a qualitative evidence.

Components and layout of the framework have converged from accumulated evidence (qualitative data). Gradually, a generic framework began to emerge. We compared systematically the emergent framework with evidence collected from the multiple cases one at a time. We continued this iterative process until the data corroborated well the evolving framework. Finally, we consulted literature for contradiction or agreement. In many cases this helped form more perspectives.

The following sections describe in detail the steps taken to structure the framework.

4.1. Best-practice based methodology

This study takes into consideration diverse nations in many respects. Trying to build a generalised framework was first thought to be challenging. It seemed that one-size would not fit all. There are many differences across the different governments. Countries differ in one or more of the following characteristics:

- Political system
- Legal system
- Economic situation
- Available technological infrastructure
- Internet and PC penetration
- Availability of skills and human resources
- Literacy rate
- Computer literacy
- Level of poverty
- Leadership
- Ethnic diversities in terms of norms, languages...etc
- Training capacity
- etc...

Other contextual differences include nationally specific benchmarks such as e-readiness, legal restrictions and existence of a nation-wide e-Government strategy (Becker et al, 2004). With these differences, it is impossible to copy a good example of implementation from one country for another. Yet despite all the differences, there are commonalities too. Governments face similar challenges in planning and implementing e-Government. Infrastructure solutions are very much the same. In general, e-Government principles are similar. In fact, we found much in common.

During this study, the focus was on commonalities and best practice. We immediately came into the dilemma of what best practice was. What was bad practice then? What counts as best practice? We reviewed a number of definitions. In the end, we settled on a workable definition that fits our research intention. Most of the definitions mention the fact that best practice is the best or optimal solution for a problem. BusinessDictionary.com defines best practice as 'Methods and techniques that have consistently shown results superior than [sic] those achieved with other means, and which are used as benchmarks to strive for. There is, however, no practice that is best for everyone or in every situation, and no best practice remains best for very long as people keep on finding better ways of doing things'. Since there is no ultimate knowledge in e-Government, best practice has to be based on experience. We define best practice as a "concept, technique, methodology, or solution that has proven reliable in achieving desired objectives, through experience, research and best available knowledge or technology and that has proven effective through replication".

With this definition in mind, our interest has been on common visions, strategic objectives, priorities, components and applications etc. Commonality can generally indicate repeated successes. This is particularly true if witnessed for a lengthy period. Indeed, we have consulted data from the late nineties through future plans targeting the late twenties of this century. We considered replication across this period. Constructs with more replication records were given higher attention. Throughout this article, evidence was sorted based on this criterion.

5. Structure and contents of e-Government strategies

Analysing e-Government strategies was the first step in structuring the framework. This analysis has set a rough delimiter of framework. It was necessary at this point to have a general idea about the components of the framework. This analysis has actually given us the opportunity to form an impression of the common elements in national strategies.

In the research methodology we mentioned that it was necessary for us to start with no preconceptions. This, we believe, was necessary for letting data collection guide us through the process of compiling evidence. Preconceptions may have limited our focus. We wanted to start from the most abstract form of the e-Government strategies. Thus, we began by studying the major components of the e-Government strategies. These components have provided us with an initial guidance of what to look for during our quest. It was only logical to start from here. Furthermore, we suggested earlier that the proposed framework should reflect the e-Government strategy it stems from. The proposed framework should somehow summarise the e-Government strategy. We studied the most prominent contents of numerous e-Government strategies of our sample countries. Figure 2 (below) shows both the common contents as well as the sequence of appearance in the national e-Government strategy.

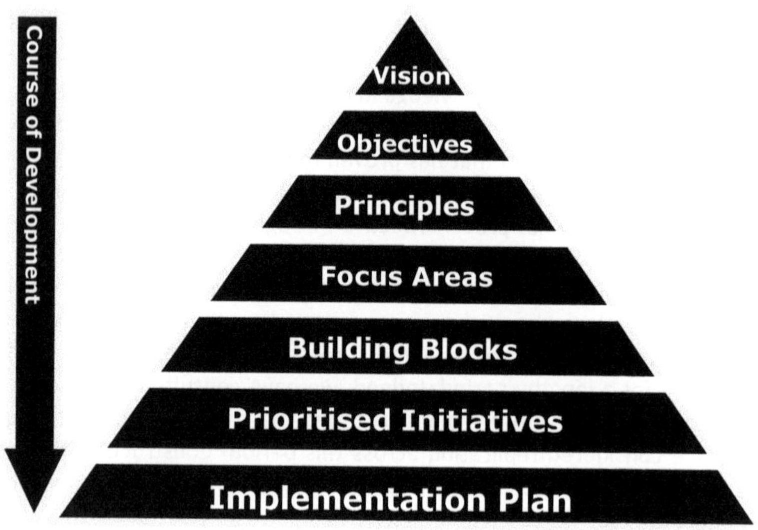

Figure 2: e-Government strategy development based on our findings

Figure 2 above already gives us some hints about the layering of the proposed framework. Since the above components were found to be present in all strategies then they should be basic constructs in our framework.

We studied each of these components in detail in an effort to structure the sought generic strategic framework of e-Government. We were particularly motivated to know the basic elements of each of these components as well as the relationships among them. It must be said at this point, that our research was not limited to the components found in Figure 2 above. These components, however, have provided a starting point of what to look for next. The following sections present the findings.

6. Vision

All e-Government strategies reviewed have included a vision right at the beginning. Vision and political will are indispensable to launch the e-Government project. Vision is necessary, as it will be always the motto of the e-Government committee, which is normally responsible for planning and spearheading implementation (Heeks, 2006). It will always be referred to during implementation later on. The vision is important because it reflects the policy of the government. From this vision, the committee is held accountable to lay out the mission statement, which is normally more expressive than the vision and contains further details. During analysis, there were only two instances (UK and Jordan) where a mission statement was mentioned together with the vision in the e-Government strategy. In most cases, only the vision was included. Therefore, we did not study the mission statement as we were only seeking commonalities and repetitions.

An e-Government vision is driven by the unique setting of social, political, and economic factors and requirements (Park, 2008). One should note that the vision might change for the same country upon the introduction of a new e-Government strategy.

7. Strategic objectives

Each government sought to achieve certain objectives from the development of its e-Government programme. These objectives are extremely important. They justify the huge resources often dedicated to e-Government initiatives.

Unlike in business, governments must make sure that money is spent extremely wisely. In a democratic system, the government needs to get approval of the national parliament to authorise the budget. People responsible for the inception and development of e-Government must work hard to convince decision makers about the necessity for e-Government. Without support from the leadership, e-Government is doomed for failure as many studies suggested (e.g. OECD, 2003; United Nations, 2003; BBeGov, 2007). Justification is critical for the success of e-Government initiatives. The strategic objectives of e-Government play an important role in this justification. Thus, greater care must be put to devise them in coherent manner.

Strategic objectives should provide a complete package for what the government is going to achieve. They must not be totally unrelated or completely disconnected. For a viable implementation, they must provide some sort of a universal focus that reflects a general direction behind the initiative. For example, some strategic objectives are focused around providing more citizen satisfaction (e.g. Singapore). Others seek to achieve more citizen participation or democracy (e.g. Korea, Egypt...etc.) and so on. This focus might come in response to existing deficiencies or shortcomings.

Because of the absolute importance of the strategic objectives behind e-Government implementation, they are highlighted in the national e-Government strategy. They are referred to as strategic here because they stem from the e-Government strategy. They also show a long term and high impact intent. They guide an important investment. It is a transparency imperative for these objectives to always be a coherent part of any e-Government initiative.

We analysed and compared the strategic objectives found in each of the e-Government strategies of the sample countries. To see exactly what strategic objectives the majority of governments sought, we studied all e-Government strategies of this group of countries. Figure 3 shows strategic objectives based on their popularity among countries. We started by tabulating each country's vision and strategic objectives. We studied each objective to find out what meanings it held. We panned through the mesh of objectives looking for similarities. Afterwards, we were able to introduce a list of objectives that can fairly represent each of the original individual objectives. This way, 31 representative strategic objectives were identified. The objectives were then examined for commonality.

For each common objective, we counted the number of countries that adopt a similar one. For instance user-centric operation/orientation scored 17. In other words, out of 20 countries, 17 of them declared in their e-Government strategy that user centricity was a strategic objective. The same methodology was applied to each common objective.

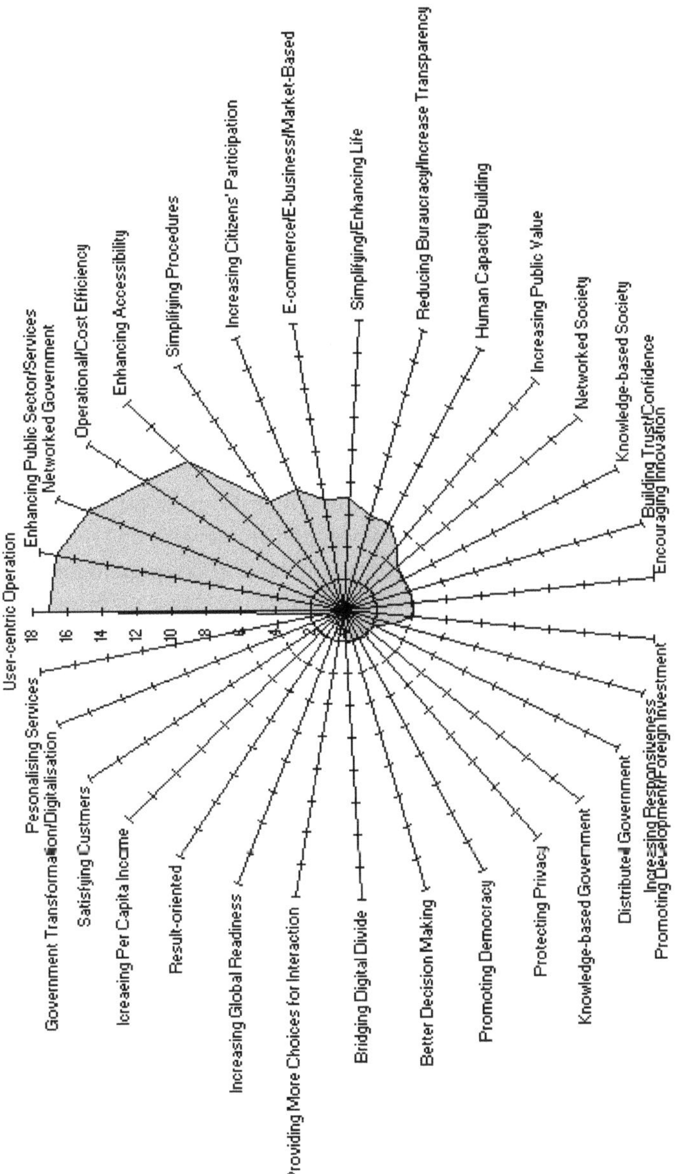

Figure 3: Popularity of strategic objectives as evidenced in the e-Government strategies of the sample countries

This study revealed that the number one strategic objective sought after by governments was "user-orientation". In fact, some studies have accentuated the importance of client-centricity (e.g. CceGov, 2007, Dutil et al, 2007, ECOTEC, 2008). Practically, to achieve cost-effective, relevant and personalised services, e-Government needs to be client-centric as revealed by a new study (CceGov, 2007). The study also concluded that customer focus and addressing customers' changing needs enhances democratic dialogue.

Enhancement of public sector capacity for better services, networked government, efficiency, simpler procedures, to boast citizen's participation, business facilitation, simplification of life, increasing public value and human capacity building are respectively among the most prominent strategic objectives that appeared in the e-Government strategies.

These objectives have affected the design of the strategic framework of e-Government. For example, the developed framework has manifested client-centric design. This was because client centricity was found to be the number one strategic objective. The other strategic objectives have at times forced a particular layout of some relevant parts of the framework.

7.1. Guiding principles - trends

Common guiding principles of e-Government were explored. These principles define the general themes of e-Government projects. We managed to capture the trend in these guiding principles from a global perspective. These trends show where world governments are heading in their e-Government programmes. The findings tell us about what qualities can be expected from e-Governments in the coming few years.

Common trends in e-Government strategies play an important role in designing a strategic framework. They delimit the possible constraints. In addition, they provide focus and control over design and implementation.

We collected the guiding principles through delving in to the strategies at hand in a similar manner to what we did previously for the strategic objectives. Table 1 below lists these principles sorted in terms of adoption by the different countries in a descending order.

Table 1: Common guiding principles of e-Government by country

Guiding Principle	**Adopting Countries**
Efficiency/capacity	India, Jordan, The Netherlands, Egypt, Australia, New Zealand, Finland, Austria
Participatory government/Considerate administration	Korea, The Netherlands, Egypt, Brazil, New Zealand, UK, Finland, Austria, Denmark
Universal Accessibility	India, Japan, Brazil, UK, Austria, New Zealand
User-oriented	Japan, Egypt, Australia, UK, Denmark
Convenience/Satisfaction	India, The Netherlands, New Zealand, Austria
Interoperability	Finland, France, Denmark, Austria
Knowledge-based government	Korea, Finland, Brazil, UK, Belgium, Germany
Transparency	India, The Netherlands, Austria
Reliability	India, The Netherlands, Jordan
Trust	Finland, The Netherlands, New Zealand
Networked/integrated government	Korea, Brazil, New Zealand
Quality	The Netherlands, Jordan, Denmark
Open source/standards	Brazil, France, Austria
Redundancy Control	Jordan, The Netherlands
Flexibility	Jordan, Denmark
User-friendliness	Japan, Austria
Rationalisation of resources	Brazil, Denmark
Shared services	Australia, Denmark, New Zealand, Korea
Mutualism & Cooperation	France, Austria
Privacy	The Netherlands, Austria
Orchestration/standardisation	Brazil
Channel of choice	The Netherlands
Personalisation	The Netherlands
Accountability	The Netherlands
Balanced Social development	Finland
One-stop-shop	India, Korea, Austria
Responsiveness	The Netherlands
Value for money	Australia
Security	Jordan
Scalability	Jordan

Guiding Principle	Adopting Countries
Manageability	Jordan
Continuity	Jordan
Creativity	Japan
In conjunction with the European Commission	France
Shared software development	France
Competitiveness	Finland
Sustainability	Austria
One-time information entry	Australia
No wrong door	New Zealand, Australia
Service packaging	New Zealand
Attract Employees	New Zealand

The most recurring guiding principle is to always consider efficiency while devising solutions. The second guiding principle is to design e-Government in such a way as to allow greater participation from the constituents. Clearly, this is a social requirement that also calls for government to become more responsive and considerate vis-à-vis its users. A responsive government aims at offering better services. To achieve this, we need to achieve internal efficiency.

The third most important guiding principle for e-Government is to achieve universal access. Throughout our quest, we have seen that accessibility was given amplified attention. This is actually, quite logical. There is no point in designing state-of-the-art services (online or otherwise) at high costs without being accessible to every one. Services should be accessible to all, indiscriminately, regardless of their financial abilities, language, geographical locate etc.

User-centricity was found earlier to be the most sought after strategic objective. Appearing here at position number four, has surprised us. This means that governments do not give it the necessary attention when developing e-Government. We expected a guiding principle that enforces client centricity on the design of every system or service. This is especially because we have used the same group of countries to generate both the common guiding principles and the common strategic objectives. Still though, it is in an advanced position among the guiding principles.

The fact that each government in this study has created a portal means that they made a great step forward towards one-stop shop. Still, not all of them have explicitly adopted the one-stop service delivery model. The portal per se does not guarantee a one-stop shop. It requires designing all the e-Government systems to be *connected* in such a way that no matter where the user starts his or her quest, he or she will always be pointed to the right service. This clearly needs collaboration among all government units. Therefore, this guiding principle should receive more attention for a better user experience.

The proposed framework should incorporate the major guiding principles listed above. They affect the general layout of the framework, particularly the relationships among the components. The common guiding principles of Table 1 above were found to target three areas of e-Government: *service delivery*, *internal efficiencies* and *government networking*. These three areas were found to capture most attention of world governments, as we shall see in the next section.

7.2. Focus areas of e-Government

In the previous section, it was mentioned that there are three main areas targeted by certain guiding principles. These areas were service delivery, internal efficiencies and government networking. We wanted to certify this fact by measuring another construct.

To do this, we looked for the key areas targeted by e-Government strategies. We relied on the focus areas declared by governments themselves in the strategies. Similar to the methodologies described above, we tabulated the findings in Table 2 below. The left column lists the common focus areas sorted by replicatability. The right column squeezes in for each focus area the countries that have declared it as a focus area in their national e-Government strategies as well as probably other official documentation. Again, the findings are sorted top-down based on the number of countries (replication).

From Table 2, one can see that the number one focus area is service delivery. This piece of finding shows that the majority of governments pay the greatest attention to service delivery. A government service can be either informational, interactive or transactional (United Nations, 2001). Governments seek better service delivery.

Table 2: Focus areas of e-Government

Focus Area	Countries
Service Delivery	India, Egypt, Canada, Germany, Austria, The Netherlands, Denmark
Internal Efficiency	India, Brazil, UK, The Netherlands, Denmark, Egypt
Government Networking	Germany, Finland, Denmark, Austria, Brazil, Belgium
Infrastructure Development	India, Japan, Egypt, Brazil, Germany
Accessibility/Interface	India, Canada, UK, Finland
Administrative Reform	Korea, Finland, The Netherlands, Belgium
Knowledge/Information Management	Korea, India, Brazil, Germany
Legislation/Regulations	India, Egypt, UK
e-Commerce/business adaptation	Japan, Egypt, UK
HR Development	India, Japan
Cooperation	Austria, Belgium
PPP	Austria, UK
Simplifying procedures	The Netherlands, Belgium
Engagement of people	Austria, Finland
Building confidence/trust in online services	Canada
Standardisation	Germany

However, intensities of effort in these focus areas are not equal. The list in Table 2 is sorted according to the intensity of work from top to bottom. The more the number of countries in a particular focus area the more work is being carried out in this area. The table reflects the priorities of action for governments. The top four focus areas of e-Government, which involve the highest number of countries, are service delivery, internal efficiency, government networking and infrastructure development. However, work on infrastructure will not continue to be a major action area of e-Government for two reasons:

- Government investments in infrastructure are not as eager as that of business
- This domain is important at the starting phase of e-Government. Many governments have already achieved mature IT infrastructures.

This leaves us with three major areas of action: service delivery, internal efficiency and government networking.

8. Building blocks of e-Government

A similar approach was followed in order to discern the common basic building blocks of e-Government. Not all governments have explicitly stated the building blocks in their strategies. For such cases in particular, we had to have a look at the major projects carried out during implementation of e-Government. This allowed us to figure out the basic blocks implicitly.

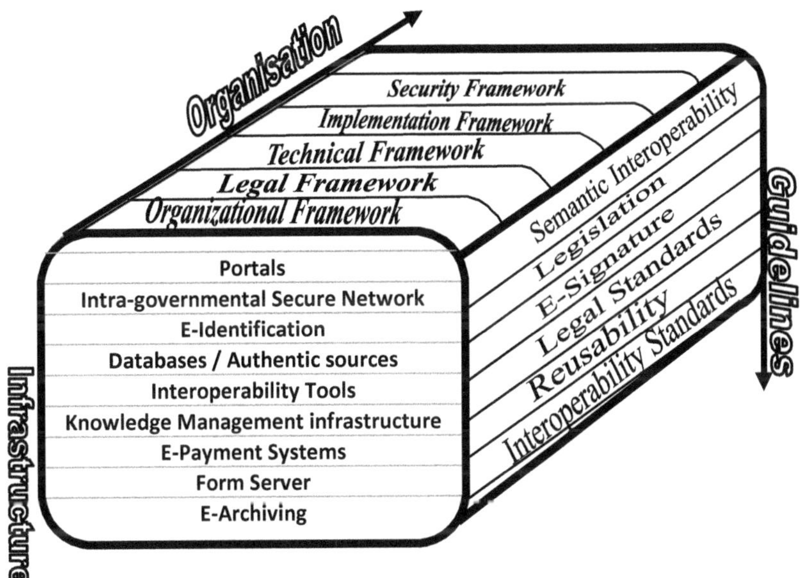

Figure 4: e-Government components cube

Figure 4 shows the different components of e-Government. This cube of components of e-Government depicts the organisation of e-Government from a practical perspective. It shows how governments visualise the basic elements of their e-Government programmes. The cube is based on commonalities in describing the building blocks as evidenced in the national strategies of e-Government of the samples countries.

9. Modularity

As mentioned earlier, newer versions of e-Government strategies are very common. This comes as a response to changes in the environment. Even some parts of the e-Government strategy can be fixed, updated, or changed. The proposed strategic framework of e-Government must thus exhibit a flexible design. Rigid frameworks will fail to survive in a world where technology advances rapidly. In addition, reform can result in many organisational and even possibly functional changes.

Modularity allows flexibility. Therefore, the proposed framework is modular. It is easy to add new modules to the framework. It is also convenient to update a certain module without messing up the whole framework. As such, the proposed strategic framework is fully extensible and customisable. It can be augmented with all kinds of sub-frameworks and architectures.

Modularity serves another purpose set forth as one of the basic characteristics of the sought framework. It makes the framework layout less cluttered and more legible. It was also found to be one of the trends in some e-Government strategies (e.g Austria, The Netherlands, Jordan). These strategies have been planned to be modular. The strategic framework of e-Government presented in this article is a core framework that needs local customisation.

At this point, all the bricks and mortar to structure the strategic framework of e-Government are ready at hand. The next section introduces this framework and elaborates on its components.

9.1. The strategic framework of e-Government

Figure 5 presents the proposed strategic framework of e-Government. This is the generic and best-practice based framework that we were seeking to put together.

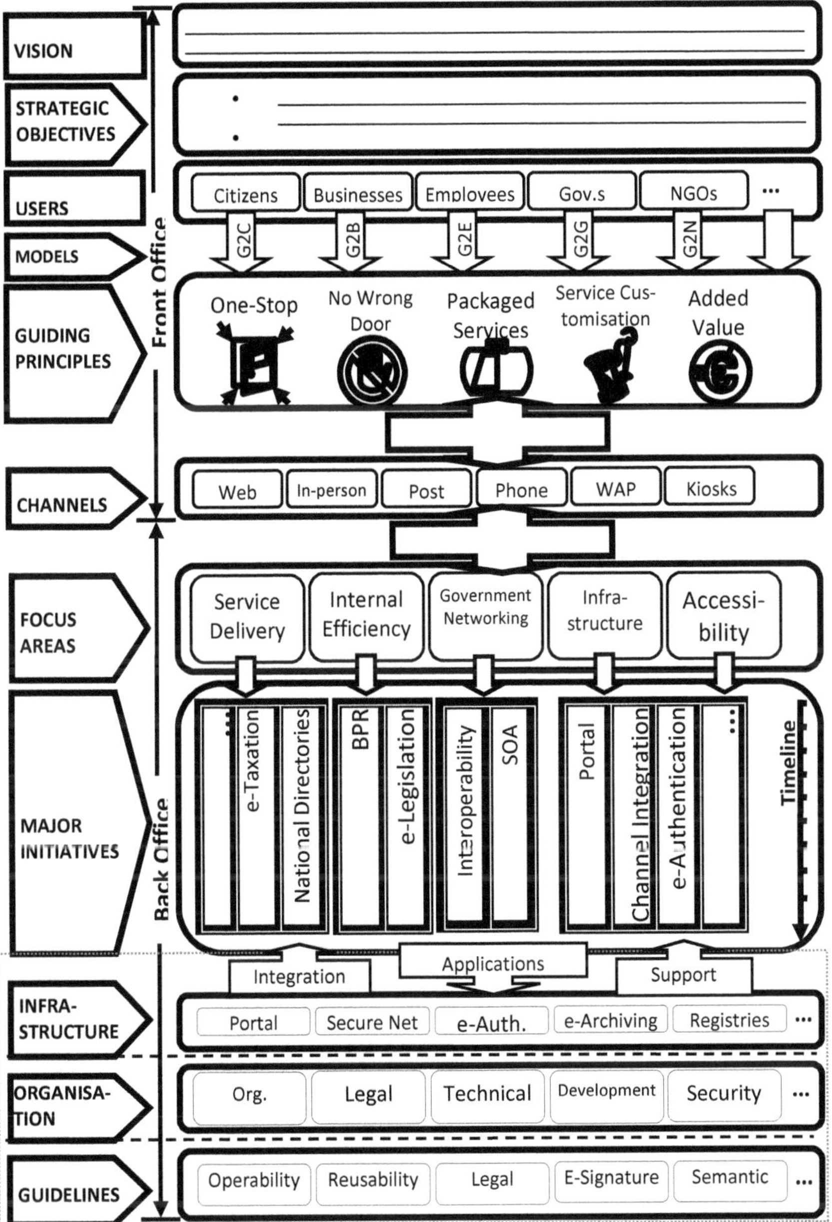

Figure 5: The proposed strategic framework of e-Government

As we can see, layering reflects the common components of the strategic frameworks of e-Government reviewed. The general flow of the layout matches up roughly the general layout of e-Government strategies described in a previous section.

The framework is obviously modularised. Each component is a module in itself. Figure 5 shows these modules and the relationship among them. One can see that there are more modules than the basic common components of the generic e-Government strategy described above. The reason is this framework shows more than just the common components of an e-Government strategy. The modules are:

- Vision
- Strategic objectives
- Users
- Delivery modes
- Guiding principles
- Channels
- Priority areas
- Major initiatives
- Infrastructure
- Organisation
- Guidelines

The framework is subdivided into two main parts: the front office pane and the back office pane.

10. Conclusions

We have introduced a generic strategic framework for e-Government. This framework is very useful to incorporate in e-Government strategies. It simply adds value to an e-Government strategy. Not only does this graphical representation recap the basic elements of the strategy, it also visualises the relationships among the basic components within the strategy. It has been found that no such framework was present in most e-Government strategies reviewed in this study. This gives rise to the importance of the proposed framework.

The proposed framework offers a comprehensive view of the e-Government programme. It incorporates very important components of front office and back office views. It has been modularised for flexibility, extensibilities and customisability.

Unlike other frameworks, the proposed one is best practice based. It comes as result of a comprehensive study of e-Government strategies produced by (20) countries in addition to the European Union. We hope that the proposed framework will help practitioners and researchers for better implementation and understanding of e-Government.
One of our prominent findings in this research is the noticeable concentration on the technical components of e-Government. We found out the following components labeled as "Basic Components" in the majority of strategies reviewed:

- Electronic access to government
- Electronic authentication
- Unique identification numbers for citizens and businesses
- Key registers/Authentic sources
- Electronic personal identification (chip cards)
- Electronic information exchange
- Fast connections among government organisations

Although these technical components are crucial for building the basic infrastructure, yet a holistic view of e-Government must be depicted in the strategy. Since there has been a shift from e-Government to e-Governance (e.g. Marche and MacNiven, 2003; Dawes, 2008) other socio-technical components must receive proper attention.

Although the framework was created based on practice (using federal e-Government strategies), yet interviews with practitioners for feedback on the findings might prove insightful. This mostly qualitative research has revealed the important constructs to building a framework. Quantitative research in the form of surveys targeting practitioners responsible for the development of federal e-Government would reveal their impressions on the developed strategic framework. This however, can be challenging because of the difficulty in making contacts and arranging for such a study with a large number of countries in order to prove statistically feasible. From our experience, getting cooperation from government officials is not an easy task.

References

Aichholzer, G. (2004) 'Scenarios of e-Government in 2010 and implications for strategy design', *Electronic Journal of e-Government*. Volume 2, Issue 1.

Agence pour le développement de l'administration 1 électronique, (2004) *Enjeux stratégiques de l'administration électronique*. France.

Australian Government Information Management Office, (2006) *Responsive Government - A New Service Agenda*. e-Government Strategy. Australia.

BBeGov (2007). *Breaking Barriers to e-Government* study, [Online], Available: http://www.egovbarriers.org/. [7 August, 2008].

Bhatnagar, S. (2004) E-Government: From Vision to Implementation : a Practical Guide with Case Studies. ISBN 0761932607, 9780761932604. SAGE.

Cabinet Decision, (2002) *Implementation Plan for the E-Government Initiative 2005. Progress Report on Implementation*. Dated 11 December 2002.

Cabinet Office, (2006) *Transformational Government Enabled by Technology*. UK.

Cabinet Office, (2005) *Transformational Government Enabled by Technology*. Cm 6683. UK.

CceGov (2007) *Citizen-centric e-Government* study, [Online], Available: http://www.ccegov.eu/ [1 September, 2008].

Central IT Unit, (2000) *e-Government - A Strategic Framework for Public Services in the Information Age*. ISBN 0 7115 0394.X. Cabinet Office. UK.

Chen, Y., Chen, H. Huang, W., Ching, R. (2006) 'E-Government Strategies in Developed and Developing Countries: An Implementation Framework and Case Study', *Journal of Global Information Management*. Idea Group.

Civil House of the Presidency of the Republic (2002). *2 years of Electronic Government Review of Achievements and Future Challenges*. Ministry of Planning, Budget and Management . Presidency of the Republic. Council of Government. Executive Committee of Electronic Government. Brasilia.

Dawes, S. (2008) 'Governance in the information age: a research framework for an uncertain future', *Proceedings of the 2008 international conference on Digital government research*. Montreal, Canada.

Commission of the European Communities, (2006) *i2010 e-Government Action Plan: Accelerating e-Government in Europe for the Benefit of All*. SEC(2006) 511.

Department of Information Technology Website. Ministry of Information and Communication Technology, [Online], Available: http://www.mit.gov.in [5 May 2008].

Dutil, P., Howard, C., Langford, J., Roy, J. (2007) 'Rethinking Government-Public Relationships in a Digital World: Customers, Clients, or Citizens?', *Journal of Information Technology and Politics*. Volume 4, Number 1.

ECOTEC (2008) Organisational change for citizen-centric e-Government: Issues, Policy and Strategy. ECOTEC Research and Consulting Ltd. UK.

e-Government 2.0. Das Programm des Bundes (2006). Bundesministerium des Innern | IT-Stab Alt-Moabit 101D | 10559 Berlin. Available: http://www.verwaltung-innovativ.de [1 September 2008].

e-Government Overview, [Online], Available: http://www.american.edu/initeb/ym6974a/e-Government.htm#E-Government%20Overview [15 January 2008].

e-Government Programme, (2007) *Jordan e-Government Architecture Vision*. Government of the Hashemite Kingdom of Jordan.

e-Government Programme, (2007) Jordan *e-Government Target Architecture (Central Platform)*. Government of the Hashemite Kingdom of Jordan.

E-Government Unit of the State Services Commission, (2003) *The e-Government Component Architecture*. Version 1.1. New Zealand.

e-Government Unit, (2005) *e-Government Interoperability Framework*. Version 6.1. Cabinet Office. UK.

e-Government Unit. *Transformational Government – Implementation Plan*, [Online], Available: http://archive.cabinetoffice.gov.uk/e-Government [3 May 2008].

Enterprise Operations Division, (2000) Texas Electronic Government Framework. USA.

ePractice.eu (2008) *e-Government in Austria*. E-Government Factsheets. European Commission.

ePractice.eu, (2008) *e-Government in Belgium*. e-Government Factsheets. European Commission.

ePractice.eu, (2008) e-Government in Finland. e-Government Factsheets. European Commission.

ePractice.eu, [Online], Available: http://www.epractice.eu [17 February 2008].

Europen Commission, (2004) *Framework to Reinforce the Exchange of Good Practices in e-Government A contribution to eEurope 2005*.

Federal Enterprise Architecture Programme Management Office, (2007) *Value to the Mission*. FEA Practice Guidance, OMB. USA.

Federal Planning Bureau Economic Analyses and Forecasts, (2002) *Towards E-Gov in Belgium*. Situation in August 2002. Working Paper. Belgium.

Federal Information and Communication Technology (FEDICT), (2007) *Fertile Soil for Customer-Friendly e-Gov*. Activity Report 2001-2006. Belgium.

Glaser, B. and Strauss, A. (1967) The discovery of theory: Strategies of qualitative research. London: Wiedenfeld and Nicholson.

Government of the Netherlands (2006) *Progress Report 4 e-Government*. The Netherlands.

Government of the United States of America, (2002) *Implementing the President's Management Agenda for E-Government - E-Government Strategy. Simplified Delivery of Services to Citizens*. Version 60. USA.

Grant, G. and Chau, D. (2006) 'Developing a Generic Framework for e-Government' in Felix, B. (ed.) *Advanced Topics in Global Information Management*. Idea Group Inc (IGI). ISBN 1591409233, 9781591409236.

Guido Bayens (2006). *e-Government in the Netherlands - An architectural approach*. Available: http://www.via-nova-architectura.org [1 September 2008].

Government On-Line, (2006) *From Vision to Reality and Beyond*. Government of Canada.

Government On-Line, (2005) *From Vision to Reality and Beyond*. Government of Canada.

Government On-Line, (2004) *From Vision to Reality and Beyond*. Government of Canada.

Heeks, R. (2001). 'Understanding e-Governance for development'. *i-Government Working Paper Series*, Institute for development Policy and Management, University of Manchester.

Heeks, R. (2006) Implementing and Managing E-Government: An International Text. ISBN 0761967923, 9780761967927. Sage.

International Economic Affairs Division, (2007) Japan's New IT Reform Strategy and u-Japan. Deputy Director. Telecommunications Bureau. Ministry of Internal Affairs and Communications of Japan. Japan.

ICT Strategy Unit, (2007) *Administration on the Net - An ABC Guide to E-Government in Austria*. Federal Chancellery. Austria.

ICT Strategy Unit, (2008) *i2010 Austria – Strategic Framework*. Federal Chancellery. Japan

IT Strategy Headquarters, (2001) *e-Japan Strategy*. January 22, 2001. Japan.

Japanse Ministry of Internal Affairs and Communications, [Online] Available: http://www.soumu.go.jp [1 August 2008].

Kenniscentrum bouwt mee aan de e-overheid, (2007) *NORA 2.0 Netherland's e-Government Reference Architecture*. The Netherlands.

Joint Research Centre, (2004) *e-Government in the EU in the Next Decade: the Vision and Key Challenges*. Technical Report Series. EUR 21376 EN. European Commission. Directorate General.

Joint Research Center, (2006) *Towards the e-Government Vision for the EU in 2010: Research Policy Challenges*. Directorate General. European Commission.

Marche, S. and MacNiven, J. (2003) 'E-Government and e-Governance: The Future Isn't What It Used To Be', *Canadian Journal of Administrative Sciences*. pp. 74-86.

Miles, M., and Huberman, A. (1984) Qualitative data analysis: A source book of new methods, Beverly Hills, CA: SAGE.

Ministry of Telecommunication and Information Technology, (2005) *The National Strategy of Telecommunications and Information Technology 2005-2008*. Final Edition. Palestine.

Ministry of Government Administration and Home Affairs, (2006) *Annual Report for e-Government*. South Korea

Ministry of Government Administration and Home Affairs (MOSTI), (2007) *Korea E-Government*. Ministry of Government Administration and Home Affairs. Korea.

Ministry of Communication and Information Technology, (2004) *The Egyptian Information Society Initiative for Government Services Delivery*. e-Government Programme. 7/3/04 AD-1/11.

Ministry of Communications and Information Technology, (2006) *Information Technology Annual Report 2005-2006*. Government of India.

Ministry of Communications and Information Technology, (2007) *Information Technology Annual Report 2006-2007*. Government of India.

Ministry of Communications and Information Technology, (2008) *Information Technology Annual Report 2007-2008*. Government of India.

Miranda, R. (2000) The Building Blocks of a Digital Government Strategy. *Government Finance Officers Association*. Volume 16. Issue 5. Page 9.

Modernisation.gouv.fr, (2006) *Le Schéma Directeur de l'administration électronique 2006-2010*. Principes. France.

Murakami, T. (2005) *Japan's National IT Strategy and the Ubiquitous Network*. No. 97. Government of Japan.

OECD (2003), *Challenges for E-Government Development, 5th Global Forum on Reinventing Government, Mexico City*, [Online], http://unpan1.un.org/intradoc/groups/public/documents/un/unpan012241.pdf [17 August, 2007].

Office of e-Government, (2008) *Citizen Centric Government Electronic Service Delivery Strategy for the Western Australian Public Sector*. Department of the Premier and Cabinet Government of Western Australia. Australia.

Office of the Chief Information Officer, (2003) *e-Government Plan, 2004 – 2007*. Ministry of Management Services. British Colombia.

Park, R. (2008) 'Measuring Factors That Influence the Success of E-Government Initiatives', *Proceedings of the 41st Hawaii International Conference on System Sciences*. 1530-1605/08, IEEE.

Plummer, A. (2001) 'Information systems methodology for building theory in health informatics: the argument for a structures approach to case study research', *Proceedings of the 34th Hawaii International Conference on Systems Sciences*. Maui, Hawaii, USA.

Project Steering Committee, (2006) *From Integrating Services to Integrating Government. Report by the iGov2010*. 2006 Report on Singapore e-Government. Ministry of Finance. Singapore.

Projekt Digital Forvaltning Den Digitale Taskforce, (2002) Towards e-Government – Vision and Strategy for the Public Sector in Denmark. Denmark.

Public Works and Government Services Canada. Audit and Ethics Brach, (2005) *Evaluation Framework for the Government On-line (GOL) Initiative*. 2004-613 Final Report.

Riedl, R., Roithmary, F. and Schenkenfelder, B. (2007) 'Using the structured case approach to build theory in e-govenrment', *Proceedings of the 40th Hawaii international Conference on Systems Sciecnes*. 1530-1605/07. Hawaii, USA.

Secrétariat d'État à la Réforme de l'État, (2004) *Plan d'Action de l'Administration Electronique (P2AE)*. Ministère de la Fonction publique, de la Réforme de l'État et de l'Aménagement du territoire. France.

Shahkooh, K., Abdollahi, A. (2007) "A Strategy-Based Model for E-Government Planning. International Multi-Conference on Computing in the Global Information Technology (ICCGI'07).

Sharma, S, Gupta, J. (2003) 'Building Blocs of an E-Government—A Framework', *Journal of Electronic Commerce in Organisations*. Volume 1 Number 4. pp. 1-15. Article No. ITJ2487.

State Services Commission, (2006) *Enabling Transformation A Strategy for e-Government 2006*. November 2006. ISBN 978-0-478-30302-5. New Zealand.

State Services Commission, (2006) State of the Development Goals Report 2006. ISBN 0-478-24473-8. New Zealand.

Sutton, R., and Callahan, A. (1987) 'The stigma of bankruptcy: spoiled organizational image and its management', *Academy of Management Journal*.

Technical Committees, (2004) *Strategic Planning Workshops*. Consolidated Report. Executive Committee of Electronic Government.

The Danish Government, (2004) *The Danish e-Government Strategy 2004-06*. Denmark.

The Danish government, Local Government Denmark (LGDK) and Danish Regions, (2007) *The Danish e-Government Strategy 2007-2010 - Towards Better Digital Service, Increase Efficiency and Stronger Collaboration*. Denmark.

The Official Web Site of the President's e-Government Initiative, [Online], Available: http://www.whitehouse.gov/omb/egov [23 April 2008].

The Open Group (2007), *The Open Group Architecture Framework (TOGAF)*. Version 8.1.1, Enterprise Edition. Exeter: Author.

The National Knowledge Society Strategy, (2006) *A renewing, human-centric and competitive Finland 2007–2015*. Finland.

The Norwegian Ministry of Government Administration and Reform, (2006) *An Information Society for All*. Norway.

Treasury Board of Canada Secretariat, (1999) *Strategic Directions for Information Management and Information Technology: Enabling 21st Century Service to Canadians*. Catalogue No. BT53-10/1999. ISBN 0-662-64526-X.

United Nations (2001) Benchmarking E-Government: A Global Perspective - Assessing the UN Member States. United Nations. Retrieved 1 August, 2007 from http://www.park.cz/soubory/egov-un2001.pdf.

United Nations (2003) *World Public Sector Report: E-Government at the Crossroads, New York: United Nations*, [Online] http://unpan1.un.org/intradoc/groups/public/documents/un/unpan012733.pdf [19 June, 2008]

US Department of the Interior, (2007) *e-Government Strategy FY 2008 – FY 2013*. USA.

Van Mannen, J. (1988) Tales of the field: on writing ethnography. Chicago: University of Chicago Press.

Vanvelthoven, P. (2003) *Note stratégique du Secrétaire d'Etat à l'Informatisation de l'Etat*. Belgium.

Walk, K. (1998) How to Wite a Comparative Analysis, Writing Center, Harvard University. Retrived 12 December, 2007 from http://www.fas.harvard.edu/~wricntr/documents/CompAnalysis.html.

Wimmer, M. (2002) *Towards Knowledge Enhanced E-Government: Integration as Pivotal Challenge*. *Johannes Kepler Universitat*, [Online], Available: http://www.iwv.jku.at/aboutus/wimmer/habilschrift.pdf [14 August 2008].

Examining the Barriers to e-Government Adoption

Richard Schwester
City University of New York, New York USA
rschwester@jjay.cuny.edu
Originally published in EJEG (2009) Volume 7 issue 1

Editorial Commentary

The robustness of any strategy is determined by its ability to stand the trials of implementation. All strategies are full of good intentions but any strategy that does not have embodied within it an understanding of the factors that will delay, retard or prevent implementation is not a good strategy. Schwester's paper on the barriers to e-Government adoption complements Rabaiah and Vandijck's paper in that they argued that all the national e-Government initiatives they had explored had experienced problems during implementation. Schwester charts the development of e-Government arguing that e-Government has evolved from simple information provision, through transaction processing to more complex forms of citizen communications (see the paper by Susanto) and engagement (see the papers by Meijer and Landsbergen). The author argues that effective government is defined by an administration's ability to accept, apply and creatively deploy technological innovations: he also argues that if a government is to achieve effectiveness it has to be fully aware of the primary barriers to the implementation of e-Government.

Schwester develops a model to explain the pattern of e-Government deployment among municipalities in the USA. His analysis revealed that the extent of e-Government adoption was a function of the financial, technical and human resources that a municipality was prepared to deploy. Most important, he argued that municipalities that wish significantly to expand their e-Government presence must realise the importance of making "sustained human capital investments" and investing in having a firmly established ICT capability. However, none of this is achievable without strong political and senior management commitment to the belief that investment in ICT and e-Government can make a sustained contribution to effective and efficient government.

Abstract: e-Government initially began as process where government entities developed websites and began populating these sites with information. After mastering this information dissemination aspect, government units moved toward processing online transactions. Subsequent to mastering transaction processing, governments moved across a continuum and engaged citizens online in a participatory framework; that is, offering Internet applications that connect citizens with public administrators, decision-makers, and perhaps elected officials. While the subsequent progression and potential benefits of e-Government applications are without limits, there are a number of barriers that impede the implementation of such applications. Using survey data collected by the International City/County Management Association (ICMA), this paper examines the factors that most impede the adoption of e-Government applications. Central research questions include: what are the differences between municipalities that have comprehensive e-Government platforms and those that do not, and to what extent do certain barriers explain these differences? Multiple regression results indicate that e-Government adoption is a function of financial, technical, and human resources. Holding all other factors constant, municipalities with higher operating budgets, more full-time IT staff, and technical resources are more likely to implement a comprehensive e-Government platform. Political support is a key and fairly robust determinant of municipal e-Government adoption as well.

Keywords: e-Government adoption, municipalities, barriers, service delivery, information dissemination, citizen participation

1. Introduction

e-Government initially began as an intra-governmental communication tool. Soon thereafter, government organizations developed websites and began populating these sites with information. After mastering information dissemination, government units moved toward processing online transactions -- which mirrors the private sector's focus on electronic commerce. Subsequent to mastering transaction processing, agencies moved to engage citizens online in participatory frameworks; that is, providing Internet applications that connect citizens and decision-makers (Calista and Melitski 2007; Holzer at al. 2004; Moon 2002). While the subsequent progression and potential benefits of e-Government applications are without limits, there are several potential barriers that impede the implementation of such applications (Carrizales 2008). This paper, therefore, examines the factors that most impede the adoption of Internet-based applications. Central research questions include: what are the differences between municipalities that have comprehensive e-Government platforms and those that do not, and to what extent do certain factors explain these differences? The Internet as a service delivery and participatory medium has taken hold. Governments throughout the world are relying on the Internet to provide services, make information more accessible, and afford citizens an alternative means of connecting with government officials (Holzer and Kim 2003; 2005). However, the further growth of e-Government is predicated on practitioners having a better understanding of the factors that create a disincentive for governments to implement innovative e-Government applications.

2. Components of e-Government

2.1. e-Service delivery

According to Moon (2002), e-Government was initially envisioned as a means of enhancing intra-governmental communications via an intranet system. Cloete (2003) argues that effective government is a function of accepting and applying technological innovations, and as such, the notion of e-Government expanded to include web-based information dissemination and service delivery applications. Some of the most fundamental developments included posting policy or regulatory information online. Soon thereafter, government forms were made available for download from municipal websites, and citizens were able to request municipal information via e-mail or electronic request forms. More recent examples of e-Government progression include more interactive service delivery. Residents or proprietors can now apply for permits or licenses online. Municipal taxes, utilities, and fines can be paid online. In many instances, citizens can now report violations or submit service delivery complaints via government websites. In short, individuals are able to fulfill day-to-day needs via the Internet (D'Agostino et al. forthcoming; Carrizales et al. 2006).

More advanced developments in e-Government services have received significant attention from municipal governments, such as allowing residents to make service requests online as part of non-emergency 311 systems. In the municipality of Hampton, Virginia, residents can request a trash pickup or that a pothole be filled by completing an electronic service request form that is forwarded to Hampton's 311 call center (see Figure 1). Residents are guaranteed a reply within one business day, and they are able to track the status of their requests online as well. Hampton's Internet applications further allow an individual to search the 311 call center's frequently asked questions (FAQs). That is, if one were to type "trash collection" into the FAQ question description box, that individual would be given a list of 25 FAQs sorted by relevancy. This type of emphasis on e-service delivery can be attributed, in part, to citizens transferring their expectations of commercial websites to government websites (Schwester et al. forthcoming).

Figure 1: Electronic service request form, Hampton (Virginia) Call Center

2.2. Digital democracy

A second component of e-Government deals with changing the way governments interact with citizens (Korac-Kakabadse and Korac-Kakabadse 1999). The emphasis is on fostering transparency, communication, and participation (Pascual 2003). The use of technology in this regard can be traced to the 1960s. Scholars, activists, and politicians were envisioning technological utopias whereby the communicative distance between citizens and government officials is effectively reduced (Nugent 2001; Bryan, Tsagarousianou and Tambini 1998). This component of e-Government is sometimes referred to as digital democracy. Public realm theorists such as Habermas (1989) emphasize the importance of social mechanisms that allow private individuals to pass judgment on public acts. Habermas provides a historical description of European social institutions throughout the 17th and 18th centuries, namely the English coffee houses, German literary societies, and the salons of France. These institutions brought together generic intellectuals and created forums for debate regarding the state of society. According to Habermas (1984), the ideal public arena fosters inclusive and voluntary citizen participation within the context of influencing how government power is wielded. The notion of digital democracy has been championed by some as a means of realizing Habermas' conceptions of the ideal pubic sphere.

In the context of a democratic system, citizens have a measure of influence over the policies impacting their lives. The relationship between government and citizens is foremost within a democratic system. With digital democracy, emphasis is placed on the processes and structures that define the relationships between government and citizens and between elected officials and appointees. According to Hacker and van Dijk (2000, 1), digital democracy refers to "a collection of attempts to practice democracy without the limits of time, space and other physical conditions, using ICTs [information and communications technologies] or computer-mediated communication instead as an addition, not a replacement for, traditional 'analogue' political practices." Nugent (2001, 223) refers to digital democracy as "processes carried out online -- communicating with fellow citizens and elected representatives about politics." Digital democracy may be defined as all practices to improve democratic values using the Internet. O'Looney (2002) compares the interaction between citizens and government within the context of traditional and digital democracy. He notes that while communications are filtered through representatives and the media in a traditional democracy, direct communications among citizens, public managers, and elected officials are now possible in a digital democracy. Communications with citizens involve a one-message-fits-all approach in a traditional democracy. Within a digital democracy, official communications may be personalized based on an individual's interests and needs, and citizens can potentially track and influence decision-making at every step in the policy making process, ranging from agenda setting to a final vote.

According to Kakabadse et al. (2003), digital applications may alter the dynamic of representative democracy, affording citizens a direct means of influencing the public policy-making process. Some early examples of such applications include information disclosure pertinent to government decision-making, as well as some potential for two-way communication (Docter and Dutton 1998; O'Sullivan 1995). Newsletters posted on municipal websites represent information dissemination, while providing feedback and comments to elected official is another. More advanced applications include online discussion boards and online policy forums (Holzer et al. 2004). Proponents of these types of applications argue the end result will be greater government transparency and openness. Increased government openness can then lead to increased accountability and reduced government corruption. Seoul, South Korea's Online Procedures Enhancement for Civil Application (OPEN) system exemplifies a successful practice of transparency and decreased corruption in government via the use of the Internet (Holzer and Kim 2003). Online discussion boards are another example of an opportunistic use of technology. Online discussion boards provide for political discussions without requiring participants to share space and time. The subsequent result is an increase in access to political debate (Malina 1999). The potential for online participation by citizens in decisions and policy-making is growing through initiatives such as "Regulations.gov" (Skrzycki 2003). Through Regulations.gov, citizens can view descriptions of proposed and final Federal regulations and read the full text of the regulations for 75 agencies. In addition, citizens can submit their comments to the Federal agency responsible for the rulemaking action through the Regulations.gov website.

The Government Information Agency (GIA) in Korea is a department of the central government that is considered a best practice. GIA websites are portal sites for disseminating information from all departments in the central government, and for discussing major policy issues among citizens. The Agency collects information on government policies from all departments in the central government and updates the site several times a day, giving citizens an opportunity to keep abreast of day-to-day developments. Via the GIA's websites, citizens are able to ask public officials for specific information. When citizens request information on specific government policies, public officials then collect the information and post the results within a week (Holzer et al. 2004)

Hoogeveen Digital City is considered one of the more advanced community networks in terms of engaging citizens in digital-based politically oriented discussions. Hoogeveen experimented with three specific Internet-based discussions: (1) the digital consultation hour, (2) digital debate, and (3) digital discussion platform. The digital consultation hour is a bimonthly discussion of community issues. It is a synchronous, real-time exchange between Hoogeveen elected officials and citizens, and it is facilitated through a question and answer format. The digital debate was a real-time event used during the 2002 municipal elections wherein citizens were able to deliberate policy issues and pose questions to candidates and party representatives. Finally, the digital discussion platform is an online public space that allows citizens registered within the network to discuss predetermined community issues (Jankowski and van Os 2002).

In the context of digital democracy, there are two viewpoints regarding the use of the Internet to transform the relationship between government and citizens. First, there are the technological optimists who believe the Internet is easier, faster, and offers qualitatively better ways of existing, working, communicating, and participating in public life. McConaghy (1996) argues that publicizing information used in the development of government policies would allow citizens to be more fully involved in the democratic process. Further, in terms of representativeness, the Internet can alert policy makers as to the needs and preferences of the citizenry regarding potential policies, and they make citizen participation more possible by overcoming the problems of large, dispersed populations.

The alternative view is less optimistic, and is centered on the premise that bringing about change in institutions and behavior patterns is a sluggish and problematic process. Unless carefully moderated, digital-based forums can become chaotic. Unmediated forums can potentially become abusive and disjointed. Politicians and other community leaders with whom citizens wish to interact may be reluctant to participate in digital forums for fear of being "flame." (Conte 1995). Then, there is the problem of dealing with the overload of undifferentiated and uncategorized information. In spite of the increasing amounts of information now available, its wide distribution, and the speed with which it is transferred, there is little if any evidence to suggest that the quality of decision-making has improved or that decisions are more democratic given the integration of Internet-based applications.

Skeptics further note the digital divide. This divide draws a distinction between those with Internet access and Internet-related skills and those without. It weakens the Internet as a mainstream and inclusive medium to the extent that it disproportionately impacts lower socio-economic individuals who have historically played a less significant role within the public policy process (Norris 2001). A parallel criticism is that Internet-based applications are skewed towards technical experts fluent in the jargon of public policy, which will alienate average citizens. While experts largely influence public policy dialogues, this may be more pronounced through Internet-based conduits. In addition, the Internet as a communications medium favors individuals with strong writing skills, and these individuals tend to have greater access to financial resources and education.

2.3. e-Government barriers

Without question, e-Government is a reality. Governments are using the Internet to deliver services, disseminate information, and facilitate a more open dialogue between citizens and government. Internet-based applications show great potential for democratic renewal, especially with regard to reconnecting citizens to government. The Internet ideally broadens participation in the policy process, and citizens and public agencies save time and paperwork through electronic service delivery. However, there are a number of barriers that potentially impede e-Government adoption. By barriers we mean any factor that creates a disincentive for governments to develop new or further develop existing e-Government applications i.e., supply side barriers (Enyon and Dutton 2007).

One potential supply side barrier is organizational or staff resistance, and the source of this resistance is the perception that technology replaces the need for people. In other words, if services can be provided via the Internet, the need for conventional office workers may decrease, thus resulting in fewer jobs. If individuals are fearful of being replaced by Internet applications, it is likely that these individuals will resist. Lack of support from politicians and high level bureaucrats is another possible barrier. Luke warm support from high level decision-makers often leads to "stop and go" e-Government progress and sustainability problems. The result is underdeveloped e-Government platforms. Similarly, a lack of public support may create a disincentive to pursue e-Government. Financial and human capital investments need to be made if e-Government is to flourish. This underscores a need to demonstrate tangible gains from e-Government -- i.e., return on investments (ROI). ROI associated with e-Government may include cost and time savings related to service delivery requests (Enyon and Dutton 2007). Technical know how and proper hardware and software are supply side barriers (West 2004). Security and privacy issues exist as well. Government must ensure that personal information is kept confidential and secure (Gilbert et al. 2004). The aforementioned factors are possible impediments to e-Government adoption, and the purpose of this research is to determine which of these factors most impede the adoption of e-service and digital democracy applications.

3. Method

The unit of analysis is U.S. municipalities with less than 100,000 in population. Smaller municipalities are the focus given that previous empirical work is somewhat skewed toward larger cities (Holzer and Kim 2003; Carrizales et al. 2006). The dependent variable is a composite measure consisting of 17 e-Government applications, 13 of which relate to service delivery and information dissemination applications and four relate to digital democracy (see Table 1). Each composite measure item was coded 1 or 0, whereby 1 indicates that the municipality has adopted this application as part of its website. The e-Government applications were weighted equally so as to avoid value-laden judgments regarding the importance of one application compared to another. These 17 coded items were added to form a composite e-Government score. A score of 0-8 indicates low e-Government adoption, while a score of 9-17 indicates high adoption. The composite measure reliability coefficient is .80, which indicates a high degree of reliability. One possible constraint of the composite measure is its exclusion of critical e-Government applications.

The independent variables include: municipal population, number of full-time employees within each municipality's IT department, municipal operating budget, lack of staff, lack of knowledge about e-gov applications, lack of support from elected officials, difficulties justifying return on e-Government investments, staff resistance to change, privacy issues, security issues, technology needs, and lack of community interest. Data were collected via mail survey in 2004 by the International City/County Management Association (ICMA), whereby 7,944 municipalities were sampled and 3,410 responses were obtained (42 percent response rate). The specific content of the survey was developed by ICMA and is available via their website (http://icma.org).

Table 1: Municipal e-Government applications

1. Online payment of taxes
2. Online payment of utility bills
3. Online payment of fines/fees
4. Online completion and submission of permit applications
5. Online completion and submission of business license applications/renewals
6. Online requests for local government records
7. Online delivery of local governments records to the requestor
8. Online requests for services, such as pothole repair
9. Online voter registration
10. Online property registration, such as animal, bicycle registration
11. Forms that can be downloaded for manual completion (e.g., voter registration, building permits, etc.)
12. Employment information /applications
13. Ordinances/codes
14. Council agendas/minutes
15. Electronic newsletter sent to residents/businesses
16. Streaming video
17. Online communication with individual elected and appointed officials

4. Findings

4.1. Summary statistics

Summary statistics presented in Table 2 indicate that the mean e-Government score is 5.1 (SD = 3.0) out of a possible 17. This indicates that the level of e-Government adoption is low. The barrier to e-Government adoption identified most frequently was a lack of staff, as 55 percent of municipalities encountered this barrier. Nearly 33 percent cite difficulties justifying return of investments as a barrier to e-Government adoption. Thirty-six percent and 28 percent of municipalities cite security and privacy issues, respectively. Twenty-four percent of municipalities feel that residents have lukewarm feelings toward e-Government and thus the demand for more applications is somewhat modest. Residents may be resisting movement from a government structure where services are provided electronically rather than face-to-face. Finally, 21 percent of respondents feel that technology needs dictate how comprehensive a municipal e-Government platform will be. This ties into staff needs as well.

Table 2: Summary statistics for variables used in analysis

Variable	Mean	Std. Dev.
e-Government score	5.09	2.99
Population	18,417	19,829
IT full time employees	1.00	1.28
Budget	1,282,083	7,215,734
Lack of staff	.55	.50
Lack of knowledge	.15	.36
Lack of support elected officials	.12	.33
Difficulty justifying ROI	.33	.47
Staff resistance	.18	.38
Privacy issues	.28	.45
Security issues	.36	.48
Technology needs	.21	.40
Lack of community interest	.24	.43

N=1813

A comparison of high e-Government adopters (e-Government score 9-17) and low adopters (e-Government score 0-8) shows that the mean score for high adopters is 10.3, while mean score for low adopters is 4.4, thus indicating a significant gap between high and low adopters. High adopters are far more likely than low adopters to use the Internet for the completion of day-to-day transactions. For example, 37 percent of high adopters allow its residents to pay taxes online. This compares to only seven percent of low adopters. Forty-seven percent of high adopters allow for completion and submission of permits online. This compares to only seven percent of low adopters. Service requests further differentiate high and low adopters, as 83 percent of high adopters allow residents to request services online (e.g., request for trash pickup, pothole repair). Only 25 percent of low adopters have incorporated this service application as part of their websites. There appears to be a disparity from an information dissemination perspective, as 79 percent of high adopters allow residents to make online requests for government records. Of this 79 percent, 66 percent will delivery such records electronically. Only 23 percent of low adopters allow for electronic record requests, and only 15 percent will deliver via the Internet. In terms of applications that have a communicative focus between residents and public officials, 70 percent of high adopters and 26 percent of low adopters distribute electronic newsletters to residents and businesses. Further, 97 percent of high adopters and 69 percent of low allow for online communication with individual elected and appointed officials, and 100 percent and 82 percent of high and low adopters respectively disseminate municipal council agendas and minutes via the Internet. Forty percent of municipalities with an advanced e-Government platform provide streaming video feeds of council meetings, public hearings, and other public affairs. A mere seven percent of low adopters do the same. Table 3 provides a summary of high and low e- adopters.

Table 3: e-Government applications provided by high and low adopters

	Mean (Std. Dev.)	
Application	High (n=213)	Low (n=1,600)
Online payment of taxes	.37 (.48)	.07 (.26)
Online payment of utility bills	.45 (.50)	.06 (.25)
Online payment of fines/fees	.36 (.48)	.05 (.21)
Online completion and submission of permit applications	.47 (.50)	.07 (.25)
Online completion and submission of business license applications/renewals	.36 (.48)	.03 (.17)
Online requests for local government records	.79 (.41)	.23 (.42)
Online delivery of local governments records to the requestor	.66 (.47)	.15 (.36)
Online requests for services, such as pothole repair	.83 (.38)	.26 (.44)
Online voter registration	.14 (.35)	.02 (.14)
Online property registration, such as animal, bicycle registration	.21 (.40)	.01 (.10)
Forms that can be downloaded for manual completion	.98 (.15)	.62 (.48)
Employment information/application	.98 (.15)	.65 (.48)
Ordinances/codes	.95 (.21)	.71 (.45)
Council agendas/minutes	1.0 (0)	.82 (.39)
Electronic newsletter sent to residents/businesses	.70 (.46)	.26 (.44)
Streaming video	.40 (.49)	.07 (.25)
Online communication with individual elected and appointed officials	.97 (.17)	.68 (.46)

On average, high adopters have more full-time IT employee than low adopters (2.1 compared to .87). High adopters have more population (20,088 compared to 18,194) and far greater operating budgets ($4,426,264 compared to only $863,515). In terms of specifically identified barriers, 37 percent of high adopters indicated that a lack of staff is a barrier to e-Government. This compares to 57 percent of low adopters. Difficulties justifying returns on e-Government investments were cited almost equally among high and low adopting municipalities, 34 percent among high adopters and 33 percent among low. Security issues were cited as well, as 40 percent of high adopters and 36 percent of low adopters believe that Internet security concerns impede the advancement of e-Government. A lack of knowledge about e-Government applications, lack of support from elected officials, staff resistance to change, security issues, technology, and lack of community interest are cited as barriers, albeit less frequently. Table 4 provides summary statistics that compare high and low e-Government adopters, with emphasis on barriers to adoption.

Table 4: Comparison of high and low e-Government adopters: variables used for analysis

		Mean (Std. Dev.)
Variable	High (n=213)	Low (n=1,600)
e-Government score	10.30 (1.52)	4.40 (2.40)
Population	20,088 (20,916)	18,194 (19,676)
Budget	4,426,264 (4.83 e+07)	863,515 (3,601,404)
IT full time employees	2.01 (1.69)	.87 (1.16)
Lack of staff	.21 (.41)	.57 (.49)
Lack of knowledge	.09 (.29)	.16 (.36)
Lack of support elected officials	.03 (.18)	.13 (.34)
Difficulty justifying ROI	.34 (.47)	.33 (.47)
Staff resistance	.21 (.41)	.17 (.38)
Privacy issues	.31 (.46)	.27 (.46)
Security issues	.40 (.49)	.36 (.48)
Technology needs	.14 (.34)	.22 (.41)
Lack of community interest	.16 (.37)	.26 (.44)

4.2. Inferential statistics

Multiple regression was used to determine which factors best predict e-Government adoption. The regression results seem to tell a somewhat different story than the summary statistics. According to regression model 1 (Table 5), the following independent variables are statistically significant predictors ($p < .05$) of a municipality's e-Government score: municipal population, number of full-time IT department employees, municipal operating budget, lack of staff, lack of support among elected officials, difficulty justifying returns on e-gov investments, and technology needs. The number of full-time IT department employees is the most robust predictor of e-Government adoption. The positive coefficient suggests that the addition of one full-time IT employee would increase a municipality's e-Government score by .82 ($t = 14.98$). In more practical terms, the model suggests that an additional employee nearly predicts the adoption of one additional e-

Government application. Similarly, the barrier lack of staff is negatively related to e-Government adoption. Consistent with previous research (Holden, Norris, and Fletcher 2003; Moon 2002; Norris and Demeter 1999), greater municipal population predicts a higher level of e-Government adoption, as does a municipality's operating budget.

Model 1 further indicates that a lack of support among elected officials is a robust determinant of e-Government adoption. In other words, if elected officials do not subscribe to e-service delivery, the dissemination of information via the Internet, or Internet applications that better connect residents and government officials, then that municipality is much less likely to have a comprehensive e-Government platform. It should be noted that the elected official coefficient is fairly robust (t = -4.77). There is a significant and positive relationship between difficulties justifying returns on e-gov investments and e-Government adoption. One might expect the sign of this coefficient to be negative rather than positive. Municipalities may be willing to invest in e-Government applications, the technical know how, and human capital so long as there will be tangible gains -- e.g., cost savings, improved service delivery, greater resident satisfaction with services and access to municipal information. These tangible gains are not likely to be immediate, and presumably this may dissuade elected officials and decision-makers from investing scarce resources in the hopes of future returns. Based on the results here, however, returns on investments are not driving e-Government adoption. Finally, technology needs predict e-Government adoption, as greater technology needs predict a lower e-Government score.

Note that lack of knowledge about e-Government applications was not a statistically significant predictor of a municipality's e-Government score. This is perhaps attributable to the widespread dissemination of e-Government best practices. This does underscore the importance of keeping abreast to technological innovations that may enhance existing application or foster the implementation of new applications. Of additional importance is recognizing the demands of residents -- in other words, knowing what applications are most important to people is key to establishing an e-Government platform that is utilized frequently. Furthermore, the fact that staff resistance was not a predictor of e-Government adoption is encouraging. All too often, change is met with resistance for fear of unknown consequences. From an administrative standpoint, e-Government could be viewed as a first step toward the automation of municipal services, thus reducing the need for people. The results here, however, suggest that e-Government may not be perceived as a means of replacing current workers. In fact, e-Government applications may enhance work environments by freeing up staff to work on more critical aspects of municipal governance rather than attending to more routine requests.

In regression model 2 (Table 5), independent variables not significant in model 1 were removed. There results of model 2 mirror those in model 1.

Table 5: Barriers to e-Government adoption: OLS multiple regression results

Model 1		
e-Government score	Coefficient	*t*-value
Population	8.26 e-06	2.61 **
IT full time employees	.82	14.98 **
Budget	2.91e-08	3.11**
Lack of staff	-.48	-3.58 **
Lack of knowledge	-.29	-1.54
Lack of support elected officials	-.95	-4.77 **
Difficulty justifying ROI	.35	2.51 *
Staff resistance	.30	1.75
Privacy issues	.13	0.75
Security issues	.25	1.61
Technology needs	-.49	-3.02 **
Lack of community interest	-.03	-0.23
Constant	4.31	30.30
n=1813 R^2=.21		
Model 2		
e-Government score	Coefficient	*t*-value
Population	8.40e-06	2.65**
IT full-time employees	.847611	15.87 **
Budget	2.85e-08	3.05 **
Lack of staff	-.48	-3.61 **
Lack of support elected officials	-.92	-4.68 **
Difficulty justifying ROI	.40	2.97 **
Technology needs	-.45	-2.82 **
Constant	4.38	31.91
n=1813 R^2=.21		

5. Conclusion

Multiple regression results indicate that e-Government adoption is a function of financial, technical, and human resources. Holding all other factors constant, municipalities with higher operating budgets, more full-time IT staff, and technical hardware are more likely to have a comprehensive e-Government platform; that is, they have higher e-Government scores. There is an important caveat as it relates to human capital. Municipalities implementing new or significantly expanded e-Government platforms must realize the importance of making sustained human capital investments. In other words, municipal leaders that view e-Government related IT staff as part-time consultants -- individuals brought in primarily at the development and implementation phases or individuals who are tapped only periodically -- are not likely to have comprehensive and fully dynamic e-Government applications. Technology is ever changing, and thus keeping pace requires a commitment to maintaining full-time IT staff. This is consistent with Norris and Kraemer (1996) who maintain that the adoption of cutting edge information and communications technologies is a function of having a firmly established IT department.

Political support is a key determinant of municipal e-Government adoption as well. This underscores the importance of winning over the "powers that be." This is consistent with Carrizales' (2008) study of municipal managers. Specifically, Carrizales found that if a municipal manager held a positive view of e-Government, then that municipality was more likely to have an advanced e-Government platform. Winning over the powers that be could be done by stressing the benefits of e-Government. This may include cost and time savings due to reduced paperwork and the reduced need for face-to-face interactions, which over time may increase municipal performance. In other words, by giving people the option of filing permits, paying fines, or making service requests via the Internet, administrative staff may be able to dedicate more energy to other endeavours.

Privacy and security issues and a lack of community interest were not statistically significant barriers to e-Government scores. This is perhaps attributable to the proliferation and widespread acceptance of e-commerce. Private goods and services are requested and purchased via the Internet and communications with service providers and customers are enhanced through online forums and instant messaging. Thus, the proliferation of such applications throughout the public sector represents a natural transition. Also, the fact that lack knowledge about e-Government was not a statistically significant barrier is encouraging. It signals that municipalities are likely aware of best practices and what types of applications exist. Although we must continue to disseminate information as it relates to new e-Government applications and feasibility studies that guide the implementation of such applications.

In total, while e-Government is happening, there is significant distance between high and low adopters -- and even many high adopters have room to enhance their e-Government platforms. It should be noted that some municipalities may knowingly choose to be low adopters. There are presumably socio-cultural factors that are not captured in this analysis that predict e-Government adoption. For instance, some communities may view e-Government as too technocratic and potentially isolating, thereby fostering greater detachment between government and its citizens. Communities embracing this viewpoint are seemingly less likely to have comprehensive e-Government platforms. A better understanding of the socio-cultural barriers that impede e-Government adoption is ultimately needed.

References

Bryan, C., Tsagarousianou, R., & Tambini, D. (1998). Electronic Democracy and the Civic Networking Movement in Context. In *Cyberdemocracy: Technology, Cities, and Civic Networks*, edited by Roza Tsagarousianou, Damian Tambini, and Cathy Bryan, 1-17. New York: Routledge.

Calista, D., & Melitski, J. (2007). e-Government and E-governance: Converging Constructs of Public Sector Information and Communications Technologies. *Public Administration Quarterly,* 31(1).

Carrizales, T., Holzer, M., Kim, S.-T., & Kim, C.-G. (2006). Digital Governance Worldwide: A Longitudinal Assessment of Municipal Websites. International Journal of Electronic Government Research, 2(4), 23-30.

Carrizales, T. (2008) Critical factors in electronic democracy: A study of municipal managers. Electronic Journal of e-Government, 6(1), 2-30.

Cloete, F. (2003). Assessing Governance With Electronic Policy Management Tools. *Public Performance and Management Review* 26(3), 276-290.

Conte, C.R. (1995). Teledemocracy -- For Better or Worse. *Governing*.

D'Agostino, M., Schwester, R., Carrizales, T., & Melitski, J. (forthcoming). A Study of e-Government and E-governance: An Empirical Examination of Municipal Websites. *Public Administration Quarterly*.

Docter, S. & Dutton, W.H. (1998). The first amendment online: Santa Monica's public electronic network. In R. Tsagarousianou, D. Tambini, & C. Bryan (Eds.), *Cy-*

berdemocracy: Technology, cities, and civic networks (pp. 125-151). London: Routledge.

Enyon, R., & Dutton, W.H. (2007). Barriers to networked governments: Evidence from Europe. *Prometheus,* 25(3), 225-242.

Gilbert, D., Balestrini, P., & Littleboy, D. (2004). Barriers and benefits in the adoption of e-Government. *International journal of Public Sector Management,* 17(4), 286-301.

Habermas, J. (1989). *The Structural Transformation of the Public Sphere*. Cambridge: Harvard University Press.

Habermas, J. (1984). *The theory of communicative action. Vol. 1, Reason and the rationalization of society*. Boston, MA: Beacon Press.

Holden, S.H., Norris, D.F., & Fletcher, P.D. (2003). Electronic Government at the Local Level: Progress to Date and Future Issues. *Public Performance and Management Review* 26(3): 1-20.

Holzer, M., Melitski, J., Rho, S.-Y., & Schwester, R. (2004). *Restoring Trust in Government: The Potential of Digital Citizen Participation.* Washington, DC: IBM Endowment for the Business of Government.

Holzer, M., & Kim, S.-Y. (2005). *Digital Governance in Municipalities Worldwide: An Assessment of Municipal Web Sites Throughout the World.* Newark, NJ: National Center for Public Productivity.

Holzer, M., & Kim, S.-Y. (2003). *Digital Governance in Municipalities Worldwide: An Assessment of Municipal Web Sites Throughout the World.* Newark, NJ: National Center for Public Productivity.

Jankowski, N.W., & van Os, R. (2002). *Internet-based political discourse: A case study of electronic democracy in the city of Hoogeveen.* Paper Presented at the Prospects for Electronic Democracy Conference, Carnegie Mellon University, Pittsburgh, Pennsylvania.

Korac-Kakabadse, A., & Korac-Kakabadse, N. (1999). Information Technology's Impact on the Quality of Democracy: Reinventing the 'Democratic Vessel.' In Reinventing *Government in the Information Age: International Practice in IT-Enabled Public Sector Reform*, edited by Richard Heeks. London: Routledge.

Malina, A. (1999). Perspectives on Citizen Democratisation and Alienation in the Virtual Public Sphere. In *Digital democracy: Discourse and Decision Making in the Information Age*, edited by Barry N. Hague, and Brian D. Loader, 23-38. London: Routledge.

McConaghy, D. (1996). "The Electronic Delivery of Government Services." *Comments on the UK Green Paper* (unpublished).

Moon, M.J. (2002). The evolution of e-Government among municipalities: Rhetoric or reality? *Public Administration Review*, 62(4), 424-433.

Norris, P. (2001). *Digital divide: Civic engagement, information poverty, and the internet worldwide*. Cambridge: Cambridge University Press.

Norris, D., & Demeter, L.A. (1999). Computing in American City Governments. In *The 1999 Municipal Yearbook,* 10–19. Washington, DC: ICMA.

Norris, D. F., & Kraemer, K.L. (1996). Mainframe and PC Computing in American Myths and Realities. *Public Administration Review* 56(6): 568–76.

Nugent, J.D. (2001). If e-democracy is the answer, what's the question? *National Civic Review,* 90 (3), 221-223.

O'Looney, J.A. (2002). *Wiring governments: Challenges and possibilities for public managers*. Westport: Quorum Books.

O'Sullivan, P.B. (1995). Computer networks and political participation: Santa Monica's teledemocracy project. *Journal of Applied Communication Research,* 23(2), 93-107.

Pascual, P.J. 2003. *e-Government*. Asia-Pacific e-Primers Series. United Nations Development Programme, Asia-Pacific Development Information Programme.

Skrzycki, C. (2003). U.S. Opens Online Portal to Rulemaking; Web Site Invites Wider Participation in the Regulatory Process. *The Washington Post*, January 23, E01.

Schwester, R., Carrizales, T., & Holzer, M. (forthcoming). An Examination of the Municipal 311 System. *International Journal of Organizational Behavior and Theory.*

Tsagarousianou, R., Tambini, D., & Bryan, C. (1998). *Cyberdemocracy: Technology, Cities and Civic Networks*. London: Routledge.

West, D.M. (2004). Equity and accessibility in e-Government: A policy perspective. *Journal of e-Government,* 1(2), 31-43.

IT Enactment of new Public Management: the Case Study of Health Information Systems in Kenya

Roberta Bernardi
University of Warwick, Coventry, UK
Roberta.Bernardi06@phd.wbs.ac.uk

Editorial Commentary

If we are to develop a better understanding of e-Government, we need to have a clear understanding of the forces affecting public management more widely. Over the last thirty years there have been considerable changes in the nature of government and in how public management has been conceptualised: these debates have been encapsulated in the evolution of the new public management (NPM). Within the development of NPM, emphasis has moved away from the direct provision of services to enabling and outsourcing. Emphasis has also moved away from a view of government as having centralised power towards more diverse and diffuse models of governance based on higher levels of citizen engagement and less pronounced information asymmetries between government and the governed. Bernadi's paper provides an example of how health information systems have been developed in Kenya and how these developments reflect wider changes in how public management is viewed and how NPM has evolved. Bernadi develops a strong link between new public management (which focuses on service rationalisation, decentralised management structures, performance-based management systems, clearer and devolved accountability and high levels of citizen engagement) and developments in information and communications technologies. She argues that the relationships between NPM, ICT deployment and e-Government development are far from straightforward, arguing that many ICT and e-Government initiatives have failed because models of NPM have been uncritically adopted in the Third World and they have not been moulded to reflect local institutional settings. Interestingly, Bernadi argues that it is important to understand the "institutional logic" of organisations and that a failure to do so can undermine the potential impact of e-Government. She goes on to show that misalignments between macro-level policy and the ground-level enactment of these policies can result in serious failures. The Bernadi paper provides useful insights drawn from a detailed case study which complement the more macro-level findings of the papers by Rabaiah and Vandijck and Schwester.

Abstract: In the last 20 years most African governments have embarked on health sector reforms sponsored by international partners. Conceived under New Public Management (NPM), the majority of these reforms leverage information technology to decentralise hierarchical structures into more information efficient organizations. The paper illustrates the case study of health management information systems in Kenya in order to better understand how the enactment of information technology has influenced the organisational outcome of New Public Management reforms within the health sector in Kenya. The case study provides a longitudinal account of how the adoption and usage of information technology within two health management information systems of the Kenyan Ministry of Health has affected the implementation of NPM reforms. Data collection and analysis have been framed within an institutionalist perspective viewing different agents acting under the pressure of competing logics (New Public Management and Old Public Administration) at three main levels of action: the macro or policy level (e.g., formal policies), the meso or organisational level (e.g., professional norms and management), and the user or agency level (e.g., IS users' routines). The case study has shown that NPM institutions were not supported by coherent actions unifying all actors involved in the restructuration of health information systems in Kenya so that IT enactment was not consistent across the health information system giving way to structural changes that were not aligned with what was envisaged in the reforms. Findings point to the rhetoric behind certain reform discourses by the main actors involved, particularly at the macro-policy level. The paper calls for a stronger source of political legitimacy to support discourses around public sector reforms so that through the right competences and systems of values at the meso level information technology can be used as a catalyst for a more consistent implementation of the reforms. New discourses around the potential of IT should be more aligned with certain institutions underpinning the practices of policy makers at the macro level inducing Government echelons to legitimize IT at the macro-policy level.

Keywords: information technology, health information systems, e-Government, new public management, institution theory, Africa, developing countries

1. Introduction

In the last 20 years most African Governments have embarked on health sector reforms sponsored by international partners (Lambo and Sambo, 2003). Usually conceived under New Public Management (NPM), the majority of these reforms leverage information technology to decentralise and integrate health management and information systems (HMIS) structures to improve health care delivery (Kimaro and Nhampossa, 2005).

Yet, available studies on the restructuring of HMIS in Africa show that goals of decentralisation and integration are rarely achieved (e.g., Kimaro and Sahay, 2007). On the contrary, in most cases the health sector scenario is still characterised by weak district health management systems (Odhiambo-Otieno, 2005) storing information into vertical programmes' databases that are not accessible by district managers (Chilundo and Aanestad, 2004).

Challenges to the achievement of expected results were identified, including the resistance of recipient local actors to import New Public Management reform models. Such resistance was stemming from a tension between the managerialist principle underpinning the restructuring of HMIS for more efficient evidence-based management practices and health workers' and data managers' routines shaped by the local bureaucratic culture (Smith et al., 2008). Similar tensions have been identified in relation to the adoption of Western information technologies as well. Usually these technologies are software solutions designed in Western countries and adapted to the local contexts by international consultants with little participation of final users (Kimaro and Nhampossa, 2005).

Hence, challenges to restructure management information systems to implement NPM reforms in the health sector are mainly linked to the institutional complexity of the African health sector contexts, characterised by the divide between imported reforms and IT designs at the macro level and expectations and actions of implementers at the micro-level (Madon et al., 2007).

Based on the case study of two health management information systems of the Ministry of Health in Kenya, this paper aims to shed light on this divide by focusing on *how new public management reforms are enacted in the restructuration of health management information systems in Kenya*.

In order to answer this research question, the case study will be analysed under an Institutional Theory perspective, in particular by taking an institutional logics approach. "Institutional logics" determine the way institutions shape individual identities, organisations, organisational fields and sectors of society (Friedland and Alford, 1991). In particular, the tension between opposing logics is viewed as a source of cultural resources through which actors may either reinvent or resist the meanings of imported logics (Thornton and Ocasio, 2008, pg. 101).

Under this perspective, the context of the health sector of an African country like Kenya has been conceptualised as being influenced by two main sets of logics: managerialist logics belonging to NPM reforms imported by international donor partners, and bureaucratic logics belonging to the traditional Old Public Administration (OPA) model inherited from the British colonial domination. The analysis of the case study will focus on how and why different actors such as international donor partners, national decision makers and main health information system users enact behaviours that reproduce (or re-invent) either NPM or OPA logics and what consequences these different enactments have in the restructuring of health management information systems in Kenya. More specifically, the case study analysis will focus on how the enactment of competing logics influences the design of information channels, monitoring indicators, and information technology investments.

In addition, information technology designs are also viewed as embedding "technical norms" (Czarniawska 2008), which have also been institutionally shaped during their designs and, therefore, may shape users' practices and social structures in their context of usage. Whereas institutions or social structures influence the enactment of the material properties of IT, the design of the latter may promote new meanings and practices, thereby reshaping the institutional order infused in public sector structures (Orlikowski, 2000; Orlikowski and Barley, 2001). Thus, the case study presented in this paper will also take into account how the IT-artefact influences the enactment of NPM and OPA logics across the spatial and temporal distance between its development and usage.

2. The New Public Management

New Public Management is one of the major public sector reforms adopted by African and other developing countries under the pressure of multilateral financial institutions such as the World Bank. NPM supports increased efficiency and accountability for public administrations through the adoption of market-oriented management mechanisms used in the private sector (e.g., result-based management, outsourcing, etc.). Initiated in the 1980s in the United States as an alternative to bureaucracies, NPM soon acquired a global dimension (Hood 2000). One of the lead arguments of NPM supporters was that bureaucracies failed to be those efficient and rational forms of organization as was postulated by Weber (1946). In particular, NPM was thought to enable the Governments of developing countries to take advantage of the growth opportunities of the market economy (Larbi, 2006; World Bank, 2002).

In particular, given the NPM focus on the rationalisation and decentralisation of management structures and performance-based accountability, information technology assumes a strategic role in the implementation of the new reforms (Osborne and Gaebler, 1992). However some studies have linked the failure of IT initiatives within the Government administrations of developing countries to the use of pre-packaged NPM reforms (Ciborra and Navarra, 2005). In particular, the disaggregation tendencies of NPM (Dunleavy et. al., 2006) matched with the inconsistencies of foreign development programmes (Therkildsen, 2006) have contributed, in most cases, to the fragmentation of information systems (Kimaro and Nhampossa, 2005) which increases, rather than reduces, complexity (Bellamy and Taylor, 1992).

Such failure has been related to the top-down approach of IT-led public sector reforms (Ciborra, 2005) which do not account for the constraints posed by existing institutional settings. The main features of the local context, such as socio-economic conditions, weak organisational capacity (Marikanis, 1994), informal systems of values (e.g., tribal norms) (Higgo, 2003), incompatible legal frameworks and poor political legitimacy have actually inhibited the success of NPM reforms. These same factors distorted the post-colonial bureaucratic model by supplanting transparency and inclusiveness procedures with patrimonial, clientelistic and rent-seeking practices (Batley and Larbi, 2006). Other institutional factors such as power relationships (Dada, 2006), political change and budget processes, and different labour contexts and markets (Bozeman and Bretschneider, 1986; Kraemer and Dedrick, 1997) have influenced the impact of information technology within public organisations.

The challenges posed by institutional contexts to the effect of information technology in implementing public sector reforms support arguments on the lack of a linear causal relationship between information technology and organisational structures (Kraemer and Dedrick, 1997). On the contrary, there have been either cases where integrated information systems and network technology seems to have supplanted bureaucracies with centralised and networked structures (Dunleavy et. al., 2006) or cases where IT use - information exchange in particular - has not been successful in converting traditional hierarchical structures of public administration into networked forms of organisations (Bretschneider, 2003).

Therefore, a deeper consideration of the institutional context and its influence on technology adoption and usage could represent the missing link between public sector reforms and the attainment of expected performance. Fountain (2001), for example, refers to "technology enactment" as the process by which organisational forms, both affecting and being affected by existing institutional arrangements, influence the adoption of IT. The "enacted technology" can send feedback that directly creates changes in the organization and indirectly in policy institutions. Thus, the effects of information technology in relation to public sector reforms can be better understood by situating IT-enabled organisational change in the actual institutional context of a public organisation.

This is particularly true in the case of health sector reforms in most African countries aiming to decentralise and integrate health care and health management information systems. These objectives are envisaged in a series of international and regional agreements. One of these is the Alma Ata Declaration on Primary Health Care of 1978 (WHO 1978), putting emphasis on decentralised health management systems (Kimaro and Sahay, 2007) for a more efficient and inclusive health care delivery. Another significant reform was started in 1996 by the United Nations Special Initiative on Africa which led the way to Health Sector-Wide Approaches (SWAps) to coordinate health interventions among international and national development actors (Lambo and Sambo, 2003).

Yet, the implementation of such reforms through Government IT innovation involves multiple stakeholders (international organisations, foreign consultants, governments, public employees, etc.), all acting according to different sets of rules, norms, and interests. In addition, rules and norms embedded in exogenous reforms and information technology designs may enter into conflict with values and norms shaping the actions of local public sector employees.

3. Theoretical framework

The case study presented in this chapter has been analysed through an institutional logics perspective. "Institutional logics" are "sets of 'material' practices and symbolic constructions which constitute a field's organising principles and which are available to organisations and individuals to elaborate" (Friedland and Alford, 1991). They represent the content and meaning of institutions (Thornton and Ocasio, 2008), defined as socially constructed systems of rules, norms, and meanings (Berger and Luckmann, 2004), which shape human action into regularities of behaviour and interaction patterns (Barley and Tolbert, 1997).

Institutional logics determine the way institutions shape individual identities, organisations, organisational fields and sectors of society (Friedland and Alford, 1991). Yet, actors are embedded within institutional logics (Thornton and Ocasio, 2008) and social structures do not prevail over action (DiMaggio and Powell, 1983). On the contrary, institutional logics can either constrain and enable individuals in advancing their interests and increase their political, social, and economic advantages by granting them partial autonomy (Thornton and Ocasio, 2008).

Following an extensive literature review of public and health sector and management information systems reforms in Africa, and in other developing countries (e.g., Kimaro and Sahay, 2007), the health sector of African countries can be viewed as characterised by two main logics: the managerialist logic imported through "New Public Management" reforms (Hood,

2000) and the bureaucratic logic of "Old Public Administration" (Lynn, 2006), namely the traditional post-colonial bureaucracies. These two logics are believed to produce variation in the main institutions (Thornton and Ocasio, 2008 p. 113) characterising the different dimensions of organisational structures (e.g., Child, 1972) (Table 1).

Table 1: Main Institutions of an Organization's Structural Dimensions Under New Public Management, Old Public Administration, and "Hybrid" Logics.

Structural dimensions	NPM Institutions	OPA Institutions	Hybrids
Control systems	Accountability	Non-evidence based management	-
Decision making	Decentralisation	Centralisation	-
Integration	Disaggregation (agencification)	Functional / vertical integration	Horizontal integration

These different institutions characterise the institutionalisation of information processing practices or routines of an information system user's sustaining a particular type of organisational structure. Variation of content and meanings of these different institutions is shaped by the institutional logic that users enact.

Under the logic of NPM, the *institution of accountability* underpins management practices meant to account for results through outcome-based and performance measurement mechanisms (Osborne and Gaebler, 1992). The *institution of decentralisation* points to the de-concentration of authority to front-line managers (Olowu, 2006). De-concentration, however, has also brought fragmentation or agencification of the public service into independent implementing units (Therkildsen, 2006), such as in the case of the verticalisation of health programmes underpinned by the *institution of disaggregation*.

In opposition to these stand institutions identified under the OPA logic. Firstly, the *institution of non-evidence based management* stemming from a patronage system resisting efforts to implement result- and performance-driven systems (Kiragu and Mutahaba, 2006). Secondly, the *institution of centralisation* involving the concentration of decision-making at the highest ranks of the hierarchy. The latter is strongly connected with the *institution of functional or vertical integration*, whereby actions are controlled through uniform and rigid administrative procedures (Grindle, 1997).

An additional institution identified in the literature review is the *institution of horizontal integration* referred hereafter simply as the *institution of integration*. This institution falls neither under the NPM logic nor under the OPA logic. It represents international partners' intentions to integrate data management practices across all levels of the health system in order to reverse the trend of donor-driven fragmentation and verticalisation of HIV/AIDS programmes and their information systems. Hence, the institution of integration can be considered as being characterised by a hybrid logic between the NPM and OPA logics.

Thus, the objective of the case study is to identify and distinguish those institutions that are actually enacted as taken-for-granted institutionalised information processing practices and those that, in contrast, occur only in the form of policy accounts. The latter, therefore, are not reflected in IS users' institutionalised behaviours.

More specifically, the acceptance of NPM reforms are expected to give way to the adoption and institutionalisation of information processing practices that encode institutions underpinned by the managerialist logic of NPM. In contrast, the resistance to NPM would maintain old institutionalised practices or institutions informed by the bureaucratic logic of Old Public Administration. A third outcome is that NPM is only partially accepted and adapted to the local bureaucratic context, in which case the adaptation of NPM practices in the local context would give way to the creation and institutionalisation of "hybrid" information processing practices.

By analysing which institutions or taken-for-granted information processing practices are either re-invented or replicated, the analysis of the case study takes a multilevel perspective which views the context of health sector reforms and health management information systems in Kenya as characterised by three main levels of action: the macro or policy level (e.g., formal policies), the meso or organisational level (e.g., management structures) and the user or agency level (e.g., IS users' routines). The multilevel perspective helps identify the main motivations or factors that drove main actors (e.g., international donor partners, national decision-makers, public employees, etc.) involved in health sector reforms and the re-structuration of health management information systems to enact specific institutions.

In addition, the enactment of institutions at different levels is associated with the technical features of technology. Depending on how institutionally-embedded actors enact institutional norms embedded in software designs, the technical properties of a technology can also influence the way actors enact institutions characterised by competing logics.

4. Methods

The chapter adopts a case study methodology to analyse a multiplicity of context-embedded processes that are not linked by linear causal relationships (Yin 2003, p. 13). Thanks to its holistic focus, the case study is one of the research methods most widely used and discussed in qualitative IS research, particularly in relation to the analysis of the situated interaction between organisations, information technology, and people (e.g., Dubé and Paré, 2003).

The case of the Ministry of Health in Kenya was primarily selected for its typicality (Yin 2003, p. 41). Like other African countries, Kenya's health sector reforms aim to decentralise and integrate its health management information systems (Figure 1; Figure 2).

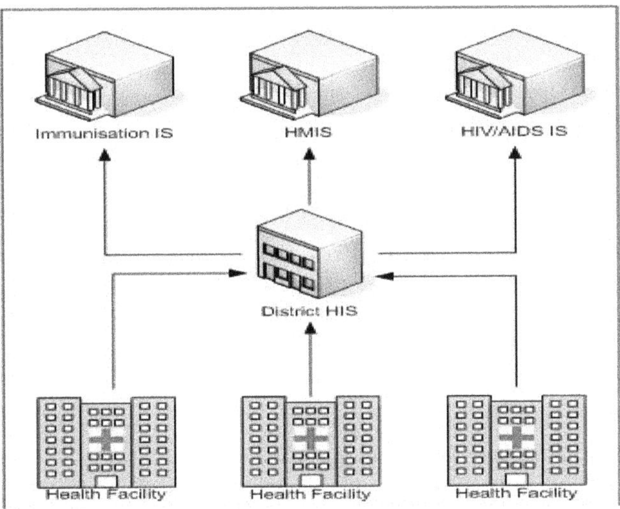

Figure 1: Vertical and Centralised Health Information Systems in Kenya

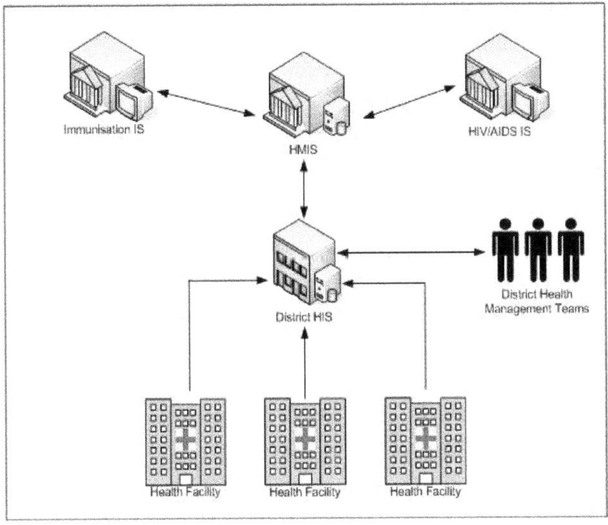

Figure 2: Planned Decentralised and Integrated Health Management Information System

As the purpose of the research is mainly to explain the variation underpinning different enactments of IT-enabled NPM reforms, the case incorporates more than one unit of analysis to provide enhanced analytical insights into the processes under study (Yin 2003, p. 46).

The units of analysis were chosen based on the criteria of "theoretical replication" whereby specific differences between them were known to generate contrasting but significant results, bringing an enriched theoretical understanding of the complex interrelationships the study seeks to unravel (Yin 2003, p. 47). This led to the choice of the following units of analysis: the central Division of Health Management Information Systems (HMIS), the Kenya Expanded Programme of Immunisation (KEPI), and the Division of HIV/AIDS.

This paper illustrates the case of the first two units of analysis, the central Division of Health Management Information Systems and the Kenya Expanded Programme of Immunisation. Each unit has a vertical information system in place. The two units have been chosen based on the ratio between donor and government funding, the status of their information system and their technological maturity. Thus, the HMIS is the least donor funded and the one with the oldest and least efficient and technologically innovative information system in place. The KEPI has seen a gradual phase out of donor funding against an increase in government funding. It also has a mature information system and is the one with the best achievements in the Ministry in terms of technological innovation and information system performance.

Given the longitudinal perspective of the case study, informants with the earliest dates of employment have been selected when possible. They represent not only health records information officers (HRIOs), the direct users of the information system, but also medical management and technicians (Table 2). This sample allows a diversified and comprehensive view of the evolution of the information system, and of how institutional reforms and technological changes have affected roles, working practices, and management structures within the information system.

Table 2: Matrix of Sample of Informants Grouped According to Unit of Analysis, Profession, Date and Length of Deployment in the Unit

Deployment date	No. of years per unit	HMIS				KEPI			
		HRIO	Medical Doctor	IT	Other medical profession	HRIO	Medical Doctor	IT	Other medical profession
Before 1980	30-35	1							
1980-1985	25–30	3							
1985-1990	20-25	1							1
1990-1995	15-20	2	1	1		2			1
1995-2000	0-5								1
1995-2000	5-10					1			
2000-2008	0-5	1	2			2	1		
2000-2008	5-10		1			1	1		
	Totals	8	4	1	0	6	2	0	3

The documents selected comprise: main donor project and policy documents, Government policies, the units' official documents including minutes of meetings, and reports of the information system. The documents cover a period from 1980 to 2008 and have been sampled randomly per time period.

Interviews and relevant documentary extracts were transcribed and coded in NVIVO 8. Starting from a pre-defined set of institutions classified under NPM and OPA logics respectively (see Table 1), new codes were created along the process of data analysis (Miles and Huberman, 1984, p. 58) and organized within time-series.

5. Case study analysis

5.1. Division of Health Management Information Systems (HMIS)

5.1.1. The 1980s and 1990s: Misalignments between Policy Discourses and Enactments

The Division of Health Management and Information Systems (HMIS) were established in the first half of the 1970's under the aegis of the World Health Organisation. Since its establishment HMIS has been the target of sporadic capacity-building interventions within the scope of donor-driven projects. In particular, the lack of a systemic and countrywide approach to the strengthening of the health information system was rooted in the World Bank-sponsored principle of Selective Primary Health Care preferred by most donor partners, as contrasted with the system approach to primary health care advocated by WHO at the Conference of Alma-Ata (Brown et al., 2006).

The selective principle in international aid undermined the legitimacy of policy discourses of integrated planning and management of health care in favour of ad-hoc and small-scale projects. This strengthened the verticalisation of information systems, which supported evidence-based planning and management practices encoding the *institution of accountability* only within the limited scope of donor-funded projects instead of the whole health system. Hence, such activities contributed to reinforce the *institution of disaggregation* encoded in non-integrated processing of separate data sets by stand-alone systems both at national and district level.

Donor partners' legitimacy of a "selective" approach to health care was most likely linked to the limitations of different governance and funding mechanisms across donor agencies in taking long term commitments and pooling financial resources into a common basket. Secondly, donor partners were not motivated to support wide-sector approaches due to the Government's lack of engagement in the reforms. Major supporters for decentralisation were, in fact, donor partners who, faced with the financial mismanagement of the central government, were more willing to fund local projects rather than channel their money through the central administration (Kenya 1997, p. 29).

The Government's resistance towards the implementation of these reforms was due to the strong centralised orientation of its bureaucratic structures. In particular, decentralising more administrative autonomy to local authorities was not seen positively, as it would have meant a loss of power by the national leadership in favour of local political leaders belonging to opposing ethnic factions (Ogot, 1995).

Other reforms, such as the pre-electoral split of districts, were meant to sustain an *institution of centralisation* to fasten political control rather than bringing the legitimacy of new health management practices supporting the institutionalisation of *decentralisation* for better public service delivery. These were, in fact, face-lifting reforms limited to changing the administrative boundaries of districts without empowering health facilities.

Overall, the Government's resistance to reforms was underpinned by *institutions of centralisation* and *non-evidence based management,* whereby decisions and budget allocations were still made centrally without relying on data. The persistence of old institutions created resistance to the creation and institutionalisation of new practices of *decentralisation* and *accountability* in health management. Hence, the poor level of Governmental support for HMIS which, in contrast, was at the centre of reforms of integration and decentralisation of health information and management systems.

Under these circumstances local managers saw information as only addressing the monitoring and planning needs of donor projects, rather than those of the health system overall. This contributed to the lack of local ownership of information reinforcing the *institution of non-evidence based management* encoded into mere data management practices that were not a function of either local planning or management.

5.1.2. The years 2000: a new boost to health sector reforms

The issue of the Second National Health Sector Strategic Plan in 2005 marked a shift of engagement in the strengthening of HMIS. The new strategic plan, in fact, put more emphasis on Monitoring and Evaluation systems in order to assess progress towards the Millennium Development Goals (UN 2000). Donor partners were the major source of funding for the Division.

One donor partner in particular, the Danish International Development Agency (DANIDA), was keen on scaling up its support to HMIS across the country in compliance with the discourses of integration and improved aid coordination entailed in the Paris Declaration on Aid Effectiveness of 2005. In addition, DANIDA's endorsement of a sector-wide approach was also due to increased trust commitment to reforms after the elections of the new President Mwai Kibaki in 2002.

Increases in aid brought about by the reforms and the new political environment constituted a source of new legitimacy of health information. As part of the reforms, the Ministry of Health also planned to integrate and decentralise its health information systems. Yet, the Government did not show much commitment to the strengthening of the health information indicating that central Government action was still underpinned by *institutions of centralisation* and *non-evidence based management.* This contributed to the uneven development of the health information system across districts.

In addition, support received from donor partners was not successful in instilling a culture of evidence-based management underpinning the usage of information for decision making encoded in the *institution of accountability*. The analysis has in fact highlighted the persistence of separate sources of funding and hence accountability shaping data management practices across different information systems.

5.1.3. Poor Legitimacy of Health Records Information Officers (Hrios) and Management

Lack of legitimacy of the health information system by the Government, and donor partners' incapacity in providing sector-wide support, characterised the poor institutional support offered to health records information officers. Their performance was thus undermined, further exacerbating the negative perception of the usefulness of health information, particularly at district level where it was needed for neither planning nor management. The more HMIS did not work efficiently, the more the Department and medical records officers were regarded responsible for the problem.

In order to elevate their status, health records information officers tried to advocate for the utility of health information with the executives of the Ministry of Health: "...we have worked for many years to enable the gurus... in this ministry... to understand what we are... to show them... how we can use that data we have collected and worked on to show incidences, prevalence of the diseases".

Despite lack of support from both donor partners and the Government, health information officers and their managers engaged in discourses of decentralised and integrated computerisation of the health information system from the 1990s. Hence, health records information officers' intentions were supportive of *institutions of accountability, decentralisation, and integration* and constituted the main source of endogenous legitimacy of the health information system, on which their survival and growth depended.

It is only after 2005 and the new health sector reforms of the Second Strategic Plan that HMIS started receiving funds to decentralise and integrate the information system. Yet, management lacked the capacity and vision to negotiate a more integrated, rationalised and gradual approach to the process of computerisation sponsored by donor partners. In addition, the lack of a national ICT strategy at the macro level left HMIS management without any guidance on the technical standards for implementation during the process of computerisation, posing serious threats to the harmonisation of computerised systems across the whole Ministry and other Government departments.

The result was a non-homogenous strengthening of the information system country-wide whereby some districts were still using hard copies for data reporting. The persistence of manual systems in certain districts, lack of storage capacity of Excel that other districts were using, and the usage of a strongly centralised computer system such as Clarion at the national level, contributed to maintaining strongly centralised patterns of information processing practices, thus encoding the *institutions of centralisation and disaggregation*.

5.1.4. Computerisation

Since the late 1980s computerisation has been mainly undertaken to address donor projects' needs with very poor vision of the capacity and information requirements of HMIS. The result was inefficient computer systems and the lack of programmers and other IT professionals that could have advised on how to use the few development resources available for the set up of a more functional computing environment.

The IT system used in the division was a Clarion data base. Clarion is a warranty-free programming tool for the development of Data Base Management Systems supplied by a donor partner project in the early 90s in order to computerise all HIS subsystems and data reports generation. Yet, the Clarion experience showed that IT potential was not fully achieved due to the co-participation of three factors: i) the technical complexity of the system, ii) human capacity and iii) and institutional dynamics.

First of all, the technical complexity of Clarion framed users' perception of the inadequacy of the system in meeting certain information requirements. However, since Clarion was a development tool, its design was flexible rather than rigid. Howeverits flexibility needed enablers to emerge, such as programming skills which were not available in the Division. Most of interviewed users referred to Clarion as an unfriendly and inefficient system: "...it is very cumbersome, it is based on DOS... before you access it there is always a problem... we entered the data and we could not do anything with that, we called a programmer and he is not based here".

Technical complexity has most likely influenced negatively the diffusion of Clarion across the health information system. In fact there was no trace of Clarion being used in the districts, whereas until the introduction of Excel in the years 2000, Dbase III was a core part of the Ministry's computer training. It can thus be assumed that computerised districts were mainly using Dbase. This situation encouraged the co-presence of manual and stand-alone computer systems and a lack of common standards (Grafton and Permaloff, 1991) which, in turn, gave way to fragmented and inconsistent information processing behaviours encoding the *institution of disaggregation*.

One institutional factor that - by interacting with technical complexity - contributed to bogging down HIS computerisation was the low institutionalisation of information technology as evidenced by the language used to refer to computer-related issues both before and after the reforms in the years 2000: "The Ministry as a minimum should endeavour to make as many cadres as possible "computer literate", a term used to express knowledge of what computers are and what they can do.". Poor institutionalisation of IT led to poor planning and management of the IT component including lack of IT expertise within the Ministry of Health which, as well, amplified users' perception of technical complexity.

5.2. Kenya Expanded Programme of Immunisation (KEPI)

5.2.1. The 1980s and 1990s: The Verticalisation of Immunisation and Disease Surveillance Information Systems

The Kenya Expanded Programme of Immunisation (KEPI) in 1980 as part of a ten-year project funded by the Danish International Development Agency (DANIDA). The Programme's mission constituted the national effort towards the achievement of the global immunisation goals set by the World Health Assembly in Geneva in 1974 (WHO, 1974).

Under the pressure of DANIDA, the project put emphasis on the set up of a sound monitoring system for the planning and management of KEPI activities. Facing the inefficiency of the central Health Management Information Systems Division in feeding the Programme data, DANIDA recommended the set up of a vertical immunisation and disease surveillance information system.

The phase out of the DANIDA project in 1990 marked the end of a substantial and consistent flow of funding to the Programme. As well, this was the time when international donors started downsizing their support to immunisation systems all over Africa leading to a decline in immunisation coverage. One of the major causes of this reverse trend was the rise of other health priorities attracting donor interest such as HIV/AIDS (WHO, 1994).

The evidence of a donor-driven pilot District Health Management Information System between 1988 and 1990 assumes a small scale and piecemeal effort towards the decentralisation and strengthening of the health information system initiated in 1985. The inadequacy of such an approach was recognised by the Ministry authority as well: "...the PS is meeting with donors on September 16th [1991] to seek long term funding for HMIS activities in the Ministry including our district work".

Therefore, in contrast with policy discourses of "integration", donor partners preferred the creation of vertical information systems rather than integrating with HMIS. Vertical systems such as the one created for the Programme represented the enactment of the NPM *institution of disaggregation* which is at the core of the fragmentation of the health information systems in the country. This is because the *institution of accountability* was not encoded in the entire health information system, but applied only for the scope of activities of donor-funded projects, given that data management practices were meant to account for resources invested in immunisation activities and not for the whole health system.

In addition, the Government was putting very little effort into the implementation of decentralisation reforms, whereas its contribution to the Programme was very little compared to foreign aid. As reported by official records of the Programme, in 1999 the Programme was in fact receiving only 15% of its funding from the Government budget and 85% from donor partners. In one instance in particular, the Government decided to delegate the procurement of stationary (e.g., data reporting tools) and office equipment to the district offices without granting the districts the necessary financial autonomy: "Medical stationary in the District is in acute shortage. This is as a result of Government's action of decentralising printing of medical stationary". Not only were budgets still approved centrally, but funds were also allocated by the Treasury: "Government funds are controlled initially by the Division of Primary Health Care... and secondly at the district treasury [...] Availability of finances at the facility and district levels is subject to availability of cash at the district Treasury, which depends on reimbursement by the national treasury". Thus, districts lacked the means to enact the new policy of decentralisation. This confirms the reluctance of the central government to hand over power to the local administrations which, by resisting decentralisation, contributed to the persistence of centralised information processing practices encoding the *institution of centralisation*.

Thus, districts were only dependent on the piecemeal approach of donor partners, which contributed to an uneven development of the health information system on the ground, characterised by good- and bad-performing districts. This exacerbated the de-motivation of health workers and district medical officers in charge of the collection and reporting of data. Thus, data management practices on the ground were supportive of the *institution of non-evidence based management* given that local managers were not the direct consumers of information.

5.2.2. The Global Alliance of Vaccines and Immunisation (GAVI)

The end of the 1990s saw the introduction of a new contributor to immunisation in the country, i.e., the Global Alliance for Vaccines and Immunisation (GAVI). GAVI was meant to support the Programme not only through the introduction of new vaccines (e.g., HiB in 2001) but also by contributing to the strengthening of the monitoring and evaluation system through its "performance-based grant programme" (GAVI, 2007). Funds were in fact released against periodic performance measurement through a Data Quality Audit (DQA) (GAVI, 2004). GAVI's emphasis on reliable quality data to justify funding increased the Programme management's support for the strengthening of the information system.

Yet, as the Global Alliance's funding was limited to the financing of vaccines the majority of the remaining expenses on immunisation were covered by the Government, which increased its contributions to immunisation from 49% in 2000 to 53% in 2001 (WHO, 2001). In 2001 GAVI's share of contributions to immunisation was instead 34%, whereas other multilateral and bilateral donor partners were contributing 13% (WHO, 2001). Moreover, the trend of funding from 2003 to 2005 shows an exponential increase of Government contributions to immunisation starting from a 44% share in financial year 2003-2004 and reaching a 91% share in financial year 2004-2005 (Health, 2008, p. 45).

It is therefore possible that the GAVI performance-based grant was not the only reason behind the stronger legitimacy of the information system within the Programme. Increased funding from the Government may also have constituted a strong source of legitimacy for the information system, whose accountability was now important to the Government and not only donor partners, as it was ten years before. Under this perspective the management perceived longer-term benefits from the enactment of the *institution of accountability* through the strengthening of the information system. Through a sounder base of data on its activities, the Programme aimed to gain a more advantageous position in the competition for a share of the national public health funding with other health departments.

Hence, both the start of GAVI and the increase in Government contributions increased the management's awareness of the utility of decentralised health information systems to account for funding. As a consequence, the management started to give more credit to health records information officers' discourses of decentralisation by mobilising donor funding for the set up of a "decentralised [...] multiuser window based programme which can be used in a networking environment". The original design of the proposed system was meant to fully delegate data processing to the lower levels, starting from the provinces all the way down to the facilities. Still, it took almost four years before the implementation of the new system started. Until then, although "...the year [2002-2003] witnessed a continued improvement in data processing" at least in a few provinces, there are reports of misalignment between types of technology and information processing practices on the ground, and inconsistent data processing across the different levels of the information system causing duplications and delays.

5.2.3. Computerisation

Following the decision to create a stand-alone vertical information system for routine immunisation and disease surveillance, around 1990 an IBM computer equipped with a Computerised Epidemiological Information System (CEIS) was procured with donor money. CEIS was a DOS-based and centralised IT system designed for the management and statistical analysis of epidemiological data. Due to its stand-alone architecture, it only provided a single-user environment and hence centralised processing of information.

The acknowledgement of the limitations of a centralised computerised information system was one of the trigger discourses for the installation of a decentralised computerised information system in the late 90s. Despite this, CEIS continued to be used for a long time. Data kept being entered centrally into the system reiterating the *institution of centralisation* which clashed with accounts of decentralisation.

Between 2003 and 2004 CEIS broke down, forcing the programme to rely exclusively on Excel which, although being an efficient data analysis tool, had low data storage capacity posing no little constraint to the maintenance of an updated immunisation and disease data base. The need for a new computerised system became thus more compelling to such an extent that in 2004 the new system EPI-Info was implemented with the support of the U.S. Centres for Disease Control (CDC) in conjunction with WHO. Epi-Info is a public domain (free-of-charge) statistical software for epidemiology developed by CDC. It has been in existence for 20 years. Its first Windows version, Epi-Info 2000, was released in 1999. Until then, it could be run as a DOS programme in a Windows environment (Harbage and Dean, 1999). Its simple programming language allows non-programmers to easily build and customise data-based management systems (Ma et al., 2008).

Epi-Info was rolled out to the provinces but not to the districts as originally planned. Data entry was thus decentralised only to the provinces whereas data analysis was still performed by the central data management unit. Districts would send data to the provinces, which would share data with the central data management unit either by entering them into Epi-Info or by sending data sheets by e-mail.

Therefore, the decentralisation of the information system produced the partial decentralisation of data entry practices. Hence, the new system did not have a substantial impact onto the decentralisation of planning and management structures at the lower levels, given that both districts and provinces were not empowered in decision making since data analysis was still performed at the central level reiterating the *institution of non-evidence based management.*

It is arguable that the slow pace with which the whole process of computerisation was carried out was due to misalignments between the legitimacy of the new IT system driving the supportive action of health records officers and management at the meso level, and the legitimacy of a well functioning monitoring and evaluation system by donor partners and decision makers at the macro level. First of all, although donors recognised the importance for a more efficient information system at all levels, they might not have been ready to commit considerable funding for its automation. Secondly, the central government support to automation was still very poor due to little awareness among decision makers of IT as a powerful control and monitoring tool. In addition, the Government was still privileging a central mode of governance so that policy-makers' actions were still encoding *institutions of centralisation* and *non-evidence based manage-*

ment in contrast with new practices of *decentralisation* and *accountability* envisaged in the reforms and in the new computerised system.

6. Discussion of findings

The case study of the central Division of Health Management Information Systems and the Programme of Immunisation of the Ministry of Health shows different outcomes in the implementation of health sector reforms. This has been mainly due either to the partial enactment of NPM logics, such as in the case of sector-specific accountability underpinning donor projects, or the resistance of OPA institutions such as centralisation enacted by the Government (Table 3).

Table 3: Across-Unit Comparison of NPM and OPA Institutions per Levels of Action

<table>
<tr><th>Levels of action</th><th>HMIS</th><th>KEPI</th></tr>
<tr><td rowspan="2">Macro level:
Donor partners</td><td colspan="2">Decentralisation
Sector-specific accountability
Disaggregation</td></tr>
<tr><td>Poor financial support to computerisation</td><td>Higher financial support to computerisation, but not enough for large scale IT support</td></tr>
<tr><td rowspan="2">Macro level:
National policy-makers</td><td colspan="2">Centralisation
Non-evidence based management
Poor legitimacy of information technology</td></tr>
<tr><td>Poor financial support</td><td>Higher financial support after 2000</td></tr>
<tr><td rowspan="2">Meso-level: HRIOs</td><td colspan="2">Decentralisation</td></tr>
<tr><td>Integration
Sector –wide accountability</td><td>Sector-specific account-ability</td></tr>
<tr><td>Meso-level: manage-ment</td><td>Decentralisation
Sector –wide accountability
Integration
Poor IT vision</td><td>Support decentralised IT system only after GAVI and increase of Govern-ment funding</td></tr>
</table>

Levels of action	HMIS	KEPI
Information Technology	Centralisation Technical complexity (dis-aggregation)	Decentralisation User-friendliness
Micro-level users	Centralisation	Partial decentralisation
	Non-evidence based management	

First of all, the case study has shown how donor support to the decentralisation and integration of the health information system was not strong enough. Given the sector-specific focus of donor initiatives, the accounts of *accountability* underpinning donors' calls for an efficient monitoring and evaluation system on the ground applied only to the scope of activities of donor-funded projects. In other words, donors did not legitimise the decentralisation and integration of the health information system for better performance of the whole health system, thereby the verticalisation of the health information systems reinforcing fragmented information processing practices encoding the NPM *institution* of *disaggregation*.

On the other hand, the central government was reluctant to hand over power to the local administrations so that its governance practices were strongly rooted into the OPA *institution of centralisation*. The gap between the institutional discourses and enactments of decentralisation by the central government has contributed to the persistence of centralised information systems structures and data management practices supporting the *institution of centralisation*.

Thus, health workers' motivation to collect data was very low as they could not see the benefits of the system. Since the main consumers of data were donors and national programme managers, health workers' information behaviour was informed by the *institution of non-evidence based management* underpinning the lack of local ownership of information and the poor perception of the importance of data evidence for health planning and management.

The lack of legitimacy of health information on the ground was a major concern for health information officers in both units of analysis. In fact, their power and legitimacy in the health system depended on the strengthening of the health information system. Under these circumstances health information officers were at the front line to increase the legitimacy of health information among its users. This is why they advocated the upgrading of centralised DOS-based computer systems rather than networked and decentralised IT systems. Thus, in both units health records information officers played a key role in promoting new information processing practices encoding the *institution of decentralisation* and *accountability* across the whole health system. In addition, the division of HMIS was also keen to integrate information processing structures and practices supporting the *institution of integration* to gain a leading role in maintaining the health management information system for the entire Ministry, as was envisaged in the reforms.

Yet, the management support to health information officers' discourses of computerisation came under different circumstances. Whereas the management of HMIS showed immediate interest in supporting computerisation, the management of KEPI showed its support only when it saw the opportunity to leverage increased capacity of the information system to attract funding from GAVI and secure increased Government funding. This can be explained by the fact that KEPI's mission was not completely shaped around the health information system as it was for HMIS.

Still, only the managers of KEPI have been successful in bringing technological and structural changes to their information system. This was because they could count on higher donor support. In contrast, donor support to implement the necessary technological innovation for the restructuring of HMIS came much later, whereas its management lacked the capacity and the vision to negotiate the terms of computerisation with donor partners to better suit IS users' requirements.

Thus, despite the fact that computerisation in both units was slacking due to the piecemeal approach of donor partners and lack of legitimacy of IT by the Government, KEPI was the only successful unit in implementing a new decentralised IT system.

In contrast, HMIS was still relying on a centralised DOS-based system after more than fifteen years of discourses of restructuration of their information systems. Due to its centralised architecture and technical complexity, Clarion could not be easily and cost-effectively adopted by the lower levels of the health system, posing limitations to the decentralization of the division's information processing structures. As a consequence, apart from a few districts sending their reports in Excel sheets, most data entry was still done at the central level enacting the OPA *institution of centralisation*.

On the contrary, a Windows and web-based IT system like Epi-Info was more friendly and easier to adopt by the lower levels. Due to institutional constraints - such as inconsistent donor funding and lack of support from the central Government - Epi-Info was implemented in the provinces but not in the districts as planned, leading to a *partial decentralisation* of the health information systems and data entry practices. Although this was not enough to instil and institutionalise *accountability* in the lower levels of the health information systems, the new computerised system represented a major achievement towards reducing the gap between institutional accounts of decentralisation and their enactment.

Hence, the case study has shown how processes of computerisation and technical complexity are influenced by institutional dynamics. At the same time, it can be argued that more user-friendly systems like Epi-Info can produce different outcomes from more complex systems like Clarion with the same institutional arrangements ... such as lack of legitimacy of IT. This means that different systems with different technical properties may require different institutional arrangements to be optimised. In addition, although professional norms and management's engagement are essential for IT innovation in public administration, they need institutional enablers at the macro-policy level in order to fully exploit the innovation potential of computerisation.

7. Conclusions

The case study has shown that NPM institutions were not supported by coherent actions unifying all actors involved in the restructuration of health information systems in Kenya. Its main sets of meanings were either eluded or reinterpreted so that IT enactment was not consistent across the health information system, giving way to structural changes that were not aligned with what was envisaged in the reforms. In particular, the case has highlighted three main misalignments of political discourses: the clash between NPM institutions such as *decentralisation* with the old public administration institution of *centralisation*; different interpretations and enactments of NPM institutions by different actors (e.g., sector-specific *accountability* in donor projects implementations vs. sector-wide *accountability* in health management by HRIOs and middle-management). This not only unleashed internal contradictions in NPM reforms but gave way to the abuse of the NPM institution of *disaggregation* by being more driven by donors' priorities related to project implementation and monitoring rather than the reforms of the health sector. The consequence was an incomplete implementation of reforms, including partial attempts of decentralisation across the health information system leaving unheard discourses of integration.

Moreover, this case has shown that misalignments between policy discourses and their enactments can be particularly deleterious if they occur at the macro policy level. This highlights the importance of political legitimacy of reforms in the public sector to bring more results in shaping certain behaviours that are meant to be changed at the micro level. This was evidenced, for example, by the partial decentralisation of the immunisation information system brought about by piecemeal donor support and lack of IT legitimacy by the government. As a result, management was not successful in achieving substantive change in health management and planning practices and structures.

Thus, the findings of the study do not question the efficacy of NPM reforms. Rather, they point to the rhetoric behind certain reform discourses by the main actors involved, particularly at the macro-policy level. A stronger source of political legitimacy needs to support these discourses so that through the right competences and systems of values at the meso level, IT can be used as a catalyst for a more consistent implementation of reforms. This new source of legitimacy could stem from the codification of new sets of meanings constituting a valid intermediary between NPM and African OPA models. For example, the institutional discourse of "controlled decentralisation" or "decentralised bureaucracies" could replace more dissonant discourses of "decentralization" or "managerialism". Such new discourses could induce Government echelons to legitimize IT at the macro policy level. Under this perspective IT could be seen as keeping the operational freedom given to peripheral units under control. In the health sector this would facilitate integration rather than disaggregation of health management practices.

Localised policy discourses could also help determine the role of IT in building an interface between informal and formal governance systems characterising most African Governments. Under this perspective, more research of the main value systems characterising these two different levels of governance in relation to IT usage is recommended.

References

Barley, S.R. and Tolbert, P.S. (1997) "Institutionalization and Structuration: Studying the Links Between Action and Institution", *Organization Studies*, Vol 18, No. 1, pp 93.

Batley, R. and Larbi, G.A. (2006) "Capacity to Deliver? Management, Institutions and Public Services in Developing Countries", In Bangura, Y. and Larbi, G.A. (eds.) *Public Sector Reform in Developing Countries,* Palgrave MacMillan, New York.

Bellamy, C.A. and Taylor, J.A. (1992) "Informatization and New Public Management: A new agenda for public administration", *Public Policy and Administration*, Vol 7, No. 3.

Berger, P.L. and Luckmann, T. (2004) "From the Social Construction of Reality: A Treatise on the Sociology of Knowledge", In Dobbin, F. (ed.) *The New Economic Sociology: A Reader,* Princeton University Press, Princeton, NJ.

Bozeman, B. and Bretschneider, S. (1986) "Public Management Information Systems", *Public Administration Review*, Vol 46, No. 6, pp 473-473.

Bretschneider, S. (2003) "Information Technology, E-Government, and Institutional Change", *Public Administration Review*, Vol 63, No. 6, pp 738-741.

Brown, T.M., Cueto, M. and Fee, E. (2006) "The World Health Organization and the Transition from "International" to "Global" Public Health ", *American Journal of Public Health*, Vol 96, No. 1, pp 62-72.

Child, J. (1972) "Organization Structure and Strategies of Control: A Replication of the Aston Study", *Administrative Science Quarterly*, Vol 17, No. 2, pp 163-167.

Chilundo, B. and Aanestad, M. (2004) "Negotiating multiple rationalities in the process of integrating the information systems of disease-specific health programmes", *Electronic Journal on Information Systems in Developing Countries*, Vol 20, No. 2, pp 1-28.

Ciborra, C. (2005) "Interpreting e-Government and development: Efficiency, transparency or governance at a distance?", *Information Technology & People*, Vol 18, No. 3, pp 260-279.

Ciborra, C. and Navarra, D.D. (2005) "Good governance, development theory, and aid policy: Risks and challenges of e-Government in Jordan", *Information Technology for Development*, Vol 11, No. 2, pp 141-159.

Czarniawska, B. (2008) "How to misuse institutions and get away with it: some reflections on institutional theories", In Greenwood, R., Oliver, C., Sahlin, K. and Suddaby, R. (eds.) *The Sage Handbook of Organizational Institutionalism,* Sage Publications, London, pp 769-782.

Dada, D. (2006) "The Failure of E-Government in Developing Countries: a Literature Review", *Electronic Journal of Information Systems in Developing Countries*, Vol 26, No. 7.

DiMaggio, P.J. and Powell, W.W. (1983) "The Iron Cage Revisited: Institutional Isomorphism and Collective Rationality in Organizational Fields", *American Sociological Review*, Vol 48, pp 147-160.

Dubé, L. and Paré, G. (2003) "Rigor in Information Systems Positivist Case Research: Current Practices, Trends, and Recommendations", *MIS Quarterly*, Vol 27, No. 4, pp 597-635.

Dunleavy, P., Margetts, H., Bastow, S. and Tinkler, J. (2006) "New Public Management Is Dead--Long Live Digital-Era Governance", *Journal of Public Administration Research and Theory*, Vol 16, No. 3, pp 467-494.

Fountain, J.E. (2001) *Building the Virtual State: Information technology and Institutional change*, Brookings Institution Press, Washington D.C.

Friedland, R. and Alford, R.R. (1991) "Bringing society back in: Symbols, practices, and institutional contradictions ", In Powell, W.W. and DiMaggio, P.J. (eds.) *The new institutionalism in organizational analysis,* University of Chicago Press, Chicago.

GAVI (2004) *Kenya Data Quality Audit.*

GAVI (2007) "The GAVI Alliance", [online], GAVI, http://www.gavialliance.org/resources/FS_GAVI_Overview_Feb07_web_EN.pdf

Grafton, C. and Permaloff, A. (1991) "Inexpensive Database Management Software", *Political Science and Politics*, Vol 24, No. 2, pp 226-231.

Grindle, M.S. (1997) "Divergent Cultures? When Public Organizations Perform Well in Developing Countries", *World Development*, Vol 25, pp 481-495.

Harbage, B. and Dean, A.G. (1999) "Distribution of Epi Info software: An evaluation using the internet", *American Journal of Preventive Medicine*, Vol 16, No. 4, pp 314-317.

Health, M.o. (2008) *Public Expenditure Review 2008*, Ministry of Health, Kenya, Nairobi.

Higgo, H.A. (2003) "Implementing an Information System in a Large LDC Bureaucracy: The Case of the Sudanese Ministry of Finance", *Electronic Journal of Information Systems in Developing Countries*, Vol 14, No. 3.

Hood, C. (2000) "Paradoxes of public-sector managerialism, old public management and public service bargains", *International Public Management Journal*, Vol 3, pp 1-22.

Kenya, G.o. (1997) *Sessional Paper no. 4 of 1997 on AIDS in Kenya*, Kenya Government Printer, Nairobi.

Kimaro, H.C. and Nhampossa, J.L. (2005) "Analyzing the problem of unsustainable health information systems in less-developed economies: Case studies from Tanzania and Mozambique", *Information Technology for Development*, Vol 11, No. 3, pp 273-298.

Kimaro, H.C. and Sahay, S. (2007) "An Institutional Perspective on the Process of Decentralisation of Health Information Systems: A Case Study from Tanzania", *Information Technology for Development*, Vol 13, No. 4, pp 363-390.

Kiragu, K. and Mutahaba, G. (2006) *Public Service Reform in Eastern Africa and Southern Africa. Issues and Challenges. A Report of the Proceedings of the Third Regional Consultative Workshop on Public Service Reform in Eastern and Southern Africa 2005*.

Kraemer, K.L. and Dedrick, J. (1997) "Computing and public organizations", *Journal of Public Administration Research & Theory,* Vol 7, No. 1, pp 89.

Lambo, E. and Sambo, L.G. (2003) "Health Sector Reform in Sub-Saharan Africa: A Synthesis of Country Experiences", *East African Medical Journal*, Vol 80, No. 6, pp 1-20.

Larbi, G.A. (2006) "Applying the New Public Management in Developing Countries", In Bangura, Y. and Larbi, G.A. (eds.) *Public Sector Reform in Developing Countries,* Palgrave MacMillan, New York.

Ma, J., Otten, M., Kamadjeu, R., Mir, R., Rosencrans, L. and McLaughlin, S. (2008) "New frontiers for health information systems using Epi Info in developing countries: Structured application framework for Epi Info (SAFE) ", *International Journal of Medical Informatics*, Vol 77, No. 4, pp 219-225.

Madon, S., Sahay, S. and Sudan, R. (2007) "E-Government Policy and Health Information Systems implementation in Andhra Pradesh, India: need for articulation of linkages between the macro and the micro", *The Information Society*, Vol 23, pp 327-344.

Marikanis, A.E. (1994) "Public Sector Employment in Developing Countries: An Overview of Past and Present Trends", *International Journal of Public Sector Management*, Vol 7, No. 2, pp 50-68.

Miles, M.B. and Huberman, A.M. (1984) *Qualitative data analysis: a sourcebook of new methods*, Sage, Beverly Hills, London.

Odhiambo-Otieno, G.W. (2005) "Evaluation of existing District Health Management Information Systems. A case study of the District Health Systems in Kenya", *International Journal of Medical Informatics*, Vol 74, pp 733-744.

Ogot, B.A. (1995) "Transition from Single-Party to Multiparty Political System 1989-93 ", In Ogot, B.A. and Ochieng', W.R. (eds.) *Decolonization & Independence in Kenya 1940-93,* James Currey, London, pp 203-241.

Olowu, D. (2006) "Decentralisation Policies and Practices under Structural Adjustment and Democratisation in Africa", In Bangura, Y. and Larbi, G.A. (eds.) *Public Sector Reform in Developing Countries,* Palgrave MacMillan, New York.

Orlikowski, W. (2000) "Using Technology and Constituting Structures: A Practice Lens for Studying Technology in Organizations", *Organisation Science*, Vol 11, No. 4, pp 404-428.

Orlikowski, W. and Barley, S.R. (2001) "Technology and Institutions: what can Research on Information Technology and Research on Organizations Learn from each Other?", *MIS Quarterly*, Vol 25, No. 2, pp 145-165.

Osborne, D. and Gaebler, T. (1992) *Reinventing Government: How the entrepreneurial spirit is transforming the public sector*, Addison-Wesley, Reading, MA.

Smith, M., Madon, S., Anifalaie, A., Lazarro-Malecela, M. and Michael, E. (2008) "Integrated Health Information Systems in Tanzania: experience and challenges", *Electronic Journal on Information Systems in Developing Countries*, Vol 33, No. 1, pp 1-21.

Therkildsen, O. (2006) "Elusive Public Sector Reforms in East and Southern Africa", In Bangura, Y. and Larbi, G.A. (eds.) *Public Sector Reform in Developing Countries,* Palgrave MacMillan, New York.

Thornton, P.H. and Ocasio, W. (2008) "Institutional logics", In Greenwood, R., Oliver, C., Sahlin, K. and Suddaby, R. (eds.) *The Sage Handbook of Organizational Institutionalism,* Sage Publication, London, pp 99-129.

UN (2000) *Millennium Declaration. General Assembly Resolution 55/2*, United Nations, New York.

Weber, M. (1946) *The theory of social and economic organization*, translated by Henderson, A.M. and Parsons, T., Free Press & The Falcon's Wing Press, Glencoe, Ill..

WHO (1974) *Expanded Programme on Immunisation*, Resolution WHA 27.57 adopted by the 27th World Health Assembly, 7-23 May 1974, Geneva.

WHO (1978) *Alma Alta Declaration.*

WHO (1994) *Expanded Programme on Immunization Bulletin*, No. 001, June.

WHO (2001) "Kenya's immunization costing and financing situation 2001", [online], World Health Organization, http://www.who.int/immunization_financing/countries/ken/about/en/index.html

World Bank (2002) *World Development Report 2002: Building Institutions for Markets.*

Yin, R.K. (2003) *Case study research: design and methods*, Sage Publications, Thousand Oaks, Calif.

Measuring for Knowledge: A Data-Driven Research Approach for e-Government

Pieter Verdegem, Jeroen Stragier and Gino Verleye
Ghent University (UGent) – Interdisciplinary Institute for Broadband Technology (IBBT), Belgium
Pieter.Verdegem@UGent.be
Jeroen.Stragier@UGent.be
Gino.Verleye@UGent.be
Originally published in EJEG (2010) Volume 8, Issue 2.

Editorial Commentary

Most governments have developed e-Government strategies but Verdegem et. al. suggest that the knowledge base needed to underpin the future development and improvement of such strategies is less than adequate in the majority of cases. The question of how governments can take the steps needed systematically to measure the progress of their e-Government strategies and, more importantly, to learn from this is addressed in this chapter. In particular, the authors argue that current approaches to measuring and monitoring progress with e-Government strategies is too often based on supply-side measures and naive benchmarking: they argue that a more user-centric, bottom up, data-driven approach is needed. The authors have conducted a large-scale research project looking at the contextual variables that affect the availability of, and user satisfaction with, a range of services in Belgium. Interestingly, the authors argue that they have identified a major shift from efficiency to effectiveness in the evaluation of the delivery of public e-services.

A critical issue in any research problem is to be clear about what is being measured and what is the most valid and reliable way of measuring the dependent and independent variables selected. Verdegem *et al.* discuss these issues in some depth as they develop their framework for analysis. Interestingly, they develop sets of variables which clearly focus on inputs, outputs, outcomes and impacts before going on to develop a set of variables that can be used to contextualise their analysis (such as skills, infrastructure, access and attitudes). While Verdegem *et al.*'s work is still evolving and they acknowledge that more work is needed to develop a longitudinal approach, their research gives valuable insights into the nature of the frameworks that are needed to monitor the development of e-Government and, more importantly, to learn from these developments.

Abstract: As ICT provides a lot of possibilities, high expectancies exist towards electronic public service provision. All governments are increasingly establishing their e-strategies. However, e-Government still faces many challenges as it continues to develop. The current status of electronic services delivery opens up a lot of questions, both for practitioners and researchers. Therefore, further progress in e-Government needs a profound knowledge base. e-Government policy has focused for several years on bringing public services online and on benchmarking their availability and sophistication. Simultaneously, e-Government measurement and monitoring activities are often based on the so-called supply-side benchmarking. Although this is important knowledge, it is under criticism because it lacks a user-centric viewpoint of e-Government development. This article presents and discusses a bottom-up and data-driven approach about how research can help to manage user-centric e-Government strategies. Based on statistical testing (techniques of structural equation modelling, or SEM) of large-scale sample data from the Belgian government, the authors have investigated which relations do exist between contextual variables and the availability and/or satisfaction of electronic public services. In doing so, this paper presents an illustration of a data-driven approach to e-Government monitoring and explains how this can support and enrich the management and evaluation of e-Government policy.

Keywords: e-Government, methodology, management, benchmarking, evaluation, satisfaction, structural equation modelling (SEM)

1. Introduction

The rise of information and communication technologies (ICT) began in the mid-1990s. The public sector could not ignore the new developments and was forced to implement innovations and explore new possibilities, just as the private sector (Heeks, 2003). In the middle of this 'e-evolution' e-Government became the buzzword and was believed to be the driving force behind the modernization of public administration (Bekkers & Homburg, 2007). After more than a decade, all Western countries have developed e-Government policies that enable the service offers through different channels. Although the Internet still is the main channel for electronic service provision, some governments are experimenting with a so-called multichannel delivery (OECD, 2005). In addition, the sophistication of electronic public services is continuously increasing: electronic full case handling and advanced identification methods become more common in e-Government.

Despite the promising expectations, e-Government still faces many challenges as it continues to develop (Jaeger & Thompson, 2003; Traunmüller & Wimmer, 2004; Verdegem, 2009). One of the main pitfalls of e-Government is its relatively low uptake: in most Western countries the usage of e-services has not increased over the last years (Eurostat, 2009). Therefore, the current status of electronic service delivery opens up a lot of questions, both for practitioners and for researchers (Carter & Bélanger, 2004; Dimitrova & Chen, 2006; Hung, Chang, & Yu, 2006; van Dijk, Peters, & Ebbers, 2008). In this regard, e-Government development and monitoring needs a profound knowledge base: knowledge is needed about user needs, ICT literacy levels, satisfaction of e-services, impact of online public services, etc.

In this chapter a data-driven research approach is discussed that can help in (the evaluation of) e-Government policies. Efforts are needed to bring together knowledge concerning both technical developments and evolutions in user needs. In addition, several scholars have emphasized the need for investigating the demand side of e-Government instead of a purely supply-oriented approach (van Dijk et al, 2008; Kunstelj, Jukic, & Vintar, 2007; Verdegem & Verleye, 2009). This approach entails the centralization of different sources of information that have an influence on e-Government progress. Simultaneously, it needs to be decided what should be measured in e-Government development, and how to measure it.

First of all, we argue in this chapter why e-Government measurement is increasingly put in the foreground. We explain why there seems to be a shift from efficiency to effectiveness in the evaluation of public e-services delivery. Starting from a conceptual viewpoint, we move to the daily-based activities in e-Government measurement in Belgium. Furthermore, we discuss research results in the development of a Belgian e-Government monitor and how a data-driven approach is helpful in this effort. Last but not least, some lessons learned as well as recommendations for future measurements are presented.

2. e-Government Policies and e-Government Measurement: A Need for Rethinking?

2.1. The Shift from Efficiency to Effectiveness

There are many definitions of e-Government and the term itself is not universally used. The differences are not simply semantic and may reflect priorities in government strategies (Heeks & Bailur, 2007; Relyea, 2002; Yildiz, 2007). Moreover, definitions and terms adopted by individual countries have shifted as priorities have changed and as progress was made towards particular objectives (Verdegem & Hauttekeete, 2010). This is as it should be: the area is a dynamic one and policies as well as definitions need to remain relevant. The Organisation for Economic Co-operation and Development (OECD) defines 'e-Government' as:

"The use of information and communication technologies, and particularly the Internet, as a tool to achieve better government" (OECD, 2003, p. 23).

It can be stated that this is a more 'traditional' definition of e-Government in which the focus is mainly on the government itself.

In line with the definition above, e-Government policies in Europe have focused for several years on bringing electronic public services online and benchmarking their availability and sophistication (Codagnone, 2008). This is important knowledge, however it is not free of criticism that claims too much attention is given to the supply-side of e-Government (Kunstelj et al, 2007; Reddick, 2005; van Dijk et al, 2008). Given the relatively low uptake of e-Government – one of the main arguments to rethink electronic service delivery – several authors made a plea for more user-centric development of e-Government (Bertot & Jaeger, 2006; 2008; Verdegem & Verleye, 2009).

Closely related with the shift from a government orientation to a citizen orientation is the paradigm shift from efficiency to effectiveness (Verdegem & Hauttekeete, 2010). The latter refers to goals of government policy in general and e-Government in particular. Millard (2008) distinguishes three types of goals concerning public policy: i) efficiency, which can be seen as the search for savings, and consequently mainly deals with value for government; ii) effectiveness, which deals more with the search for quality services with, as a result, an emphasis on value for the users (both citizens and businesses); iii) governance which, more generally, is concerned with the search for good governance in which value for society is the keyword.

The paradigm shift, i.e. equal attention for both efficiency and effectiveness, has partly originated from the rethinking of e-services policy as well as strategies concerning the evaluation of e-Government (measurement activities). Not only the supply-oriented approaches of e-Government have come under criticism, critiques also exist towards the so-called supply side benchmarking (Bannister, 2007; Heeks, 2006; Janssen, Rotthier, & Snijkers, 2004; Peters, Janssen, & van Engers, 2005). Codagnone & Undheim (2008) summarized the main lines of criticism as follows: the overall relevance and validity of purely supply-side approaches and the reliability, comparability and transparency of the methodologies used are strongly questioned. In addition, the maturity model of stages (Andersen & Henriksen, 2006; Layne & Lee, 2001) as well as the 20 basic online public services (e.g. benchmarking studies performed by consultancy firms such as Accenture or Capgemini) seem to be no longer sufficient for accurately evaluating e-Government progress.

2.2. e-Government Monitoring: Measurement for Knowledge

Policymakers increasingly use electronic channels to deliver a wide range of information, interaction and transaction services at a growing level of sophistication. Consequently, the measurement of progress of e-Government development became a hot topic in e-services policy (Heeks, 2006; Janssen et al, 2004; Kunstelj & Vintar, 2004; Peters et al, 2005). It can be stated that these evaluation activities serve a double goal: first of all, in the light of rethinking e-Government policies and moving towards a more user-centric approach, more than the current provision of services should be evaluated. A thorough understanding of the demand side is also important (Kunstelj et al, 2007; van Dijk et al, 2008; Verdegem & Verleye, 2009). This relates to the question of effectiveness of e-Government strategies. Secondly, governments are also under pressure to offer more and better services while spending less at the same time. In this light, e-

Government is seen as a catalyst for a productivity-driven way of working (Jaeger, 2003; Millard, 2008).

It must be clear that electronic service delivery as well as the underlying business processes and information flows are quite complex whereby it is difficult for governments to determine adequate measures for evaluating efficiency and effectiveness of the financial outlays (Kunstelj & Vintar, 2004; Peters et al, 2005). Measurement for knowledge is thus an important but difficult challenge. For this reason, it must be based on a holistic framework utilizing different information sources. The framework should be comprehensive on the one hand, but flexible to adapt to new trends and evolutions on the other (Centeno, van Bavel, & Burgelman, 2005). Another point of note is that e-Government measurement strategies should be integrated in daily activities. Once-only screenings of spending of government on IT or assessment of user needs and expectations hinder the development of long term e-Government strategies (Bertot & Jaeger, 2006; Jaeger & Bertot, 2010; Kunstelj & Vintar, 2004). Therefore, robust methodologies and measurement frameworks are needed.

The question remains as to what is to be measured and how to develop a holistic framework? Figure 1 depicts the classical conceptual framework for the measurement of efficiency and effectiveness of public sector policies and services (based on: Codagnone & Undheim, 2008).

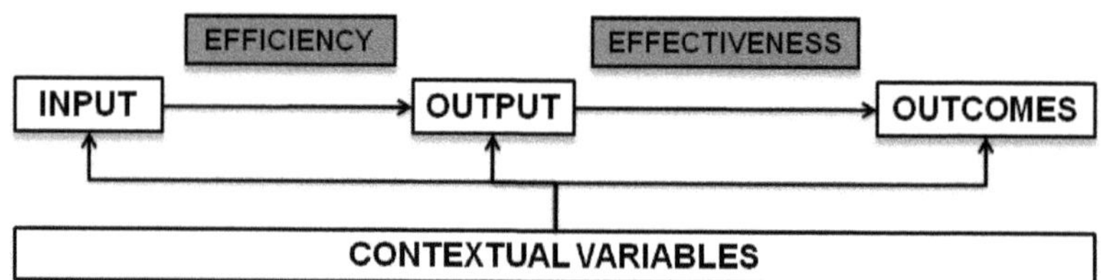

Figure 1: Basic Framework – Efficiency versus Effectiveness

This framework distinguishes three elements in the public service value chain: input, output and outcomes (Heeks, 2006). According to Codagnone & Undheim (2008) inputs are all the monetary and non-monetary costs that go into the production of an output and in the achievement of outcomes. Outputs can be seen as the final product of processes and activities that are less influenced by external variables and more under the control of the producing unit. This way, efficiency can be seen as an input/output ratio. In addition, outcomes can be seen as the result of the input & output activities, or, in other words, outcomes can be measured by the degree to which input and output are capable of achieving the intended results for different groups of stakeholders (citizens, businesses as well as governments).

The 'input-output-outcomes' relation does not exist within a vacuum. Other variables may have an influence on input, output and outcomes as well as on efficiency and effectiveness. In general these variables can be aspects of (amongst others) regulation, public sector functioning, economic and social factors, cultural attitudes, politics (Codagnone & Undheim, 2008). Especially with regard to e-Government, these variables also may be related with (e-)readiness and other external variables (Heeks, 2006; Millard, 2008; van Deursen & van Dijk, 2009).

3. Evaluating e-Government Development in Belgium

3.1. Context and Field Experience

E-Government in Belgium is an important driver for public modernization. However, as in its neighbouring countries, a lot of work remains to be done. In the OECD Peer Review Report of Belgium (OECD, 2008) it is stated that:

> "*Belgian governments could consider acquiring a systematic basis on knowledge of user needs and channel this knowledge into the design and development of targeted e-Government services, with the purpose of making these services more attractive to users and more adapted to their true needs* (p. 19)."

This is a clear call for more user-oriented strategies. Other points worthy of attention are the intergovernmental cooperation management strategies of integrated e-Government (regarding the complex state structure) as well as reducing the digital divide (stimulating ICT access and use is necessary to make up arrears in comparison with other OECD countries), and are thus important challenges for Belgian e-Government policy (OECD, 2008).

The OECD Peer Review report highlights e-Government measuring and monitoring activities as an important plan for action in Belgium. Some first initiatives were begun in the last few years. The Federal Government has monitored user needs (Fed-e-View/Citizen) as well as the computerization of administrative departments (Fed-e-View/Administration) since 2004 (OECD, 2008). Another Fed-e-View study (focusing on e-Government for businesses) is planned for the near future. The Fed-e-View studies are good initiatives, however a systematic framework for monitoring and evaluating e-Government is currently lacking. Hence, the need for setting up an e-Government monitor. Although this monitor can build on the experience of the Fed-e-View studies a holistic framework still needs to be developed.

More particularly, this framework should provide a complete overview of all aspects that relate to e-Government progress. Therefore, the measurement initiatives regarding citizens' needs and expectations should be combined with a continuous assessment of back-office development, as well as other aspects related to the provision of electronic public services. In a nutshell, the measurement of e-Government should pay attention to information containing the different aspects of the e-Government value chain.

3.2. What to Measure?

One of the most important questions regarding the measurement and evaluation of e-Government is the strategic decision of what to measure or, in other words, which domains can be distinguished? And how can adequate measurement indicators (as the basis of concrete data collection) be formulated? Based on prior research in this field (Codagnone & Undheim, 2008; Heeks, 2006; Kunstelj & Vintar, 2004; Millard, 2008) a general framework has been developed. Figure 2 provides an overview of this framework. The five key domains are: contextual variables, input, output, outcomes and impact.

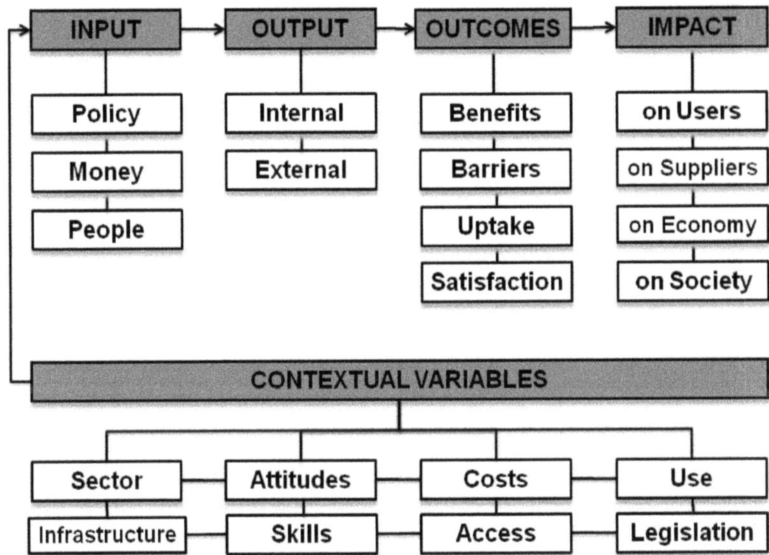

Figure 2: General Framework for Measuring e-Government in Belgium

The figure illustrates how each domain can be subdivided in underlying blocks of indicators that will consist of different (key) indicators. In our research project a total of 830 e-Government measurement and evaluation indicators are formulated, corresponding to approximately 160 key indicators. The indicators originate from different sources such as Eurostat, eUser, SIBIS, eGEP, etc. as well as the national statistics department (ADSEI – FOD Economie).

'*Contextual variables*' consist of different categories of indicators that have an indirect influence on e-Government progress. It contains information about the ICT sector (e.g. '*employment and turnover, investment in ICT research*', etc.), infrastructure variables (e.g. '*availability of Internet access points*', '*geographical coverage of Internet or GSM/DTV by access platform*', etc.), attitudes of users towards ICT (e.g. '*intentions to purchase ICT infrastructure*', '*reasons for not having access to Internet*', '*reasons for not using a computer*', etc.), skills of users (e.g. '*levels of computer and Internet skills*'), costs (e.g. '*price of cheapest Internet access by access platform*'), levels of access to ICT of both citizens and businesses (e.g. '*level of Internet access at home by access device*', '*level of Internet access in enterprises by type of connection'*, *'availability of ICT equipped workstations in public administrations'*, etc.), use of ICT (e.g. *'computer use by individuals'*, *'Internet use in enterprises'*, *'use of ICT devices in public administrations'*, etc.) and legislative matters (e.g. *'the legal framework to regulate ICT'*). In sum, these contextual variables mainly correspond with e-readiness and related issues.

The block *'input'* deals with investments of government (monetary and non-monetary) with regard to e-Government provision. Under the category 'policy' key indicators are listed such as *'the acceptance and implementation of strategic e-Government elements'* or *'strategic policies regarding ICT'*. The categories 'money' and 'people' are self-explanatory.

'Output' corresponds to two groups of indicators: 'internal' and 'external'. The first group assembles key indicators such as *'the implementation of joined up service delivery'* or *'the use of monitoring tools or the use of technical e-Government components'*. Under the second group we have listed variables such as *'accessibility of government websites'*, *'availability of electronic public services by channel'*, *'online availability of basic public services for businesses by type of service'*, etc.

The blocks *'outcomes'* versus *'impact'* are less self-evident. In particular, this poses the question of which indicators should fall under outcomes and which under impact. We decided to view outcomes as the collective term for both issues preceding e-Government acceptance (benefits and barriers), the uptake of electronic public service itself and the direct results of e-Government usage (satisfaction). Examples of indicators measuring benefits are *'the ease of use of online public services'*, *'the perceived benefits for enterprises of using online public services'*, etc. 'Barriers' is the opposite category of benefits, containing indicators such as *'the perceived barriers for citizens to uptake e-Government'* or *'the perceived cost of e-Government for enterprises'*, etc. The uptake of e-Government can be measured using variables such as *'channels used by citizens for interaction with public authorities'* or *'the use of basic online public services for enterprises by type of service'*, etc. Satisfaction is also a sub domain of outcomes and assembles key indicators such as *'citizens' evaluation of government websites'* or *'satisfaction of enterprises using the Internet for interaction with public authorities'*, etc. Other projects such as eGEP (Codagnone &

Boccardelli, 2006) or authors (Heeks, 2006) view user satisfaction as a part of the impact of e-Government. This contrasts with our (preliminary) perception of 'outcomes' versus 'impact'.

In this framework *'impact'* is perceived as the (direct or indirect) results of e-Government uptake. Therefore, four categories can be distinguished: impact on users, impact on suppliers, impact on the economy and impact on the society. Unlike other domains, a lot of work needs to be done in order to develop reliable variables for measuring impact of e-Government.

3.3. How to Decide What to Measure?

Regarding the development of a measurement framework, at least two issues need to be clarified: first, the frameworks consist of different types of variables. Some are quantitative while others are more qualitative in nature. We also have to be aware of the distinction between different types of indicators: key indicators, indicators, sub indicators and composite indicators. Secondly, it is important to decide what to include in the monitor and what to exclude. Particularly, various indicators concerning e-Government exist: our research database consists of more than 800 indicators. Therefore, in order to keep the monitor manageable, it is important to explore strategies that prioritize indicators. Different approaches and techniques could help on this.

A first approach is a top-down method, meaning that (key) indicators could be selected individually by experts. Via Delphi analysis (Linstone & Turoff, 1975) for instance, it becomes possible to move toward consensus about which indicators (and underlying data) can or should be measured. A second approach is a bottom-up method. This way of working is data-driven as statistical techniques can be used to detect which (key) indicators have the most impact while they simultaneously cover the overall model. In the next section we reflect on research activities as part of a quantitative approach in e-Government measurement.

4. Illustration of the Data-Driven Research Approach

4.1. Methodology

The second method that is elaborated in this chapter consisted of a bottom-up approach. Structural equation modelling (SEM) was applied to the data in order to determine whether a set of sub indicators existed that measured the same underlying construct, being the indicator they are supposed to measure. The models that are developed within this analysis (using the Amos software, from SPSS) (Arbuckle, 2005) also give an indication of which sub indicator performs best in measuring this construct.

The applied statistical technique, SEM, allows for estimation of the goodness of fit of a hypothetical model given the data at hand. Estimating measurement models to validate conceptual (theoretical) models has a long tradition in marketing and consumer research (Bagozzi, 1980; Chin, 1998). SEM offers a sub-model (measurement model) to test assumptions regarding the strength of the relationships between indicators (items in the questionnaire) and latent variables (the concepts), with simultaneous estimation of the correlations/co-variation between the concepts.

Two series of sample data were used in the application of the bottom-up approach. The first set of data originated from longitudinal panel research consisting of three data waves, carried out among Internet users and non-users. This set of data was collected by a commercial Internet research company, commissioned by the Federal Public Service for Information and Communication Technology (Fedict, Belgian federal government). The second set of data was collected by the national statistics department of Belgium (ADSEI, part of the Federal Public Service for Economy, SMEs, Self-employed and Energy).

4.2. Results

During the analysis we collected sub-indicators in the data corresponding to several indicators within the conceptual model (see Figure 2). Where possible, a SEM model was built to test the assumption that the sub-indicators did a good job of measuring the same underlying indicator. In Figure 3 an example is shown of one of the models that were developed. In this case, several questions measuring the same construct were analyzed.

This SEM model is based on four variables (squares). These four variables are supposed to be sub-indicators for the indicator *'Citizens' evaluation of government websites'*. The question that was used to measure this was:

"how satisfied are you with the website of your ...":

- City (City);
- Province (Prov);

- Regional government (Regio);
- Federal government (Federal).

For each of these websites the respondents were asked to give their evaluation on a scale ranging from 1 to 10, in which 1 corresponded with 'not satisfied at all' and 10 with 'very satisfied'.

The ellipse in the model is the latent variable (which means that it is not directly measured in the questionnaire) that is supposed to be measured by the four manifest variables (which means that they are directly measured in the questionnaire).

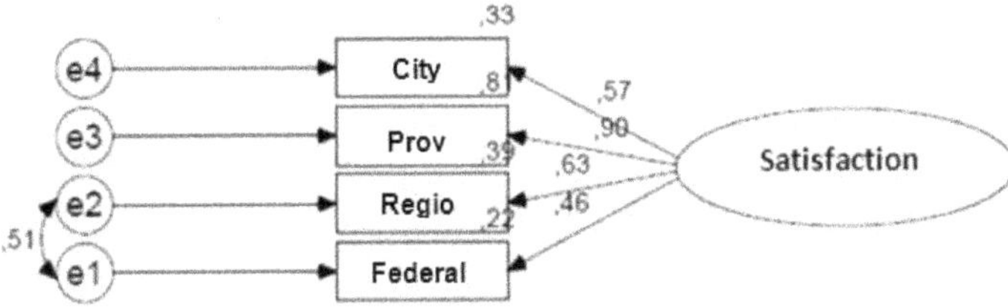

Standarised estimates
Chi-square=3.297
df= p-value=.069
nfi=.998
rfi=.984
tli=.989
cfi=.999
rmsea=.023

Figure 3: Example of a Structural Equation Model

The four small circles represent the measurement errors for each of the variables. The effect of the construct 'Satisfaction' on its four indicators is represented by single arrows. The numbers on these arrows are the standardized regression coefficients. These coefficients have a value between 1 and -1. The higher their absolute value, the more important the corresponding variable is as a source of information about the underlying concept ('Satisfaction'). The number in the right upper corner of the manifest variables gives us the amount of variance explained by the latent variable. The double arrow between error e1 and e2 represents a correlation between these measurement errors. An error correlation can only be added if a meaningful explanation can be found for it. The hypothesis in the example of Figure 3 is that citizens do not see any difference between the Federal and Regional governmental levels, as they are both perceived as part of the national (central) government.

Besides the detailed parameters on the model there are also a number of goodness-of-fit parameters that give a global evaluation of the model to be assessed. For any model, the Chi-square (Chi^2) should not be significant, the fit indices NFI (Normal Fit Index), RFI (Relative Fit Index), IFI (Incremental Fit Index), TLI (Tucker-Lewis Index) and CFI (Comparative Fit Index) should have a value of at least 0.90 and the RMSEA (Root Mean Square Error of Approximation) should be lower than 0.05.

The model presented in Figure 3 confirms that the four manifest variables measure the concept of satisfaction with government websites in a reliable way. The same methodology was applied for a range of indicators and corresponding data (when available) as was illustrated in the conceptual model of Figure 2, including 'contextual variables', 'input', 'output' and 'outcomes'. For the category 'impact' no existing indicators and data were yet available.

5. Discussion and Recommendations

The main finding of our analysis is that the data we were provided in order with to build the structural equation models gave us validated indicators that are highly representative for the population. Also, a database with almost 10,000 respondents makes it possible to get statistically significant results.

However, some important reflections should be discussed. First of all, the questionnaire was not designed to fill in the indicators in the conceptual model presented. It was designed to measure items on an individual level, not on an aggregated level, as is normal when building models like ours. An example of this is that a lot of the questions were to be answered in a binary way (either 'yes' or 'no'). Statistical methods like SEM require ratio-scaled variables for good results. This means that questions should have answer categories that go more into detail than yes/no possibilities. Rather, they need answering scales of five-points or even higher. Of course, this is not possible for every question but for a long list of items concerning motivation, attitudes, etc. these scales are a better way to go.

Another problem with working with databases originating from other research/data collection projects is that they can contain a lot of information that is not relevant to one's own research. So a selection has to be made on which data could be used and which could not. In addition, the lack of possibilities to aggregate the data from sub-indicators to indicator models (as shown in the example) make it hard to fill in the indicators in the conceptual framework.

The ultimate solution to these problems is the development of a questionnaire that is rooted in the conceptual framework. This approach makes it possible to formulate adequate sub-indicators while keeping the indicators they are supposed to measure in mind. Developing the questions yourself will give the possibility to formulate them in way that allows the application of advanced statistical techniques such as modelling (e.g. SEM). This way of working allows the development of valid indicator models.

Once these models are developed the analyses do not have to stop. They allow the testing of assumed relationships between different indicators within the domains of the conceptual framework. Using SEM, numerous hypotheses can be formulated and tested statistically, such as how perceived benefits and barriers of e-Government use are related to the uptake of e-Government services? What is the role of a person's Internet or computer skills in this context? Does gender or other socio-demographic variables have a moderating role in these relationships? All of these insights can be obtained using structural equation modelling (SEM) as the proposed method.

On a more general level, it must be emphasized that a well-elaborated framework for monitoring e-Government development is absolutely necessary. This framework needs to be comprehensive but also flexible in order to adapt to new trends. Based on our research experience, however, we argue that measuring the impact of e-Government only becomes possible when good data collection goes in hand with a well-considered conceptual framework. This way, robust methodologies will support monitoring in the long term.

6. Conclusion

In this chapter it is demonstrated why e-Government measurement is increasingly important. After a long period of (purely) supply-oriented measurement approaches, a strong plea is made for a more comprehensive way in analyzing e-Government development. The research here presented is part of a larger research project that is carried out in order to develop an e-Government monitor, commissioned by the Belgian government.

During the research a conceptual model was developed covering the full e-Government value chain. This conceptual model corresponds with a database containing 160 key indicators and more than 800 indicators. For some of the indicators data is already collected while for other indicators no information is currently measured. In order to keep the e-Government measurement activities (and the e-Government monitor) manageable, an approach is needed to select indicators and data that are more important as compared with others. During the research project both a qualitative (top-down) and a quantitative (bottom-up) approach was applied. In this chapter the methodology of a data-driven approach is illustrated.

Based on structural equation modelling it was possible to validate indicators based on several sub-indicators using statistics. This statistical validation technique of the models (groups of indicators) also allows the identification of which sub-indicator is more suitable in measuring the proposed variable. This data-driven approach is one method for developing a measurement framework that needs to be comprehensive and flexible regarding new developments. The first aspect refers to the goal of covering the overall e-Government value chain, while the latter refers to new types of services and channels that will become available in the future.

The statistical testing must be seen as an approach offering valuable knowledge for policymakers. Firstly, an evaluation can be made whether the indicators employed in the questionnaire do a good job in measuring the proposed variables. In other words, SEM (or other validation techniques) is helpful in testing validity of the measurement instruments. Secondly, as there exist many indicators that can be used for the assessment of e-Government progress, an approach is needed to decide what to measure. A bottom-up and data-driven approach is at least as important as a top-down approach. Thirdly, when evaluating the current measurement activities based on existing data, several recommendations can be formulated in profit of e-Government practitioners. Specifically, feedback can be provided on methodology (data collection, answer categories, sample size, etc.) and related aspects. This knowledge is necessary when developing a comprehensive framework for measuring e-Government development. A robust instrument is needed for setting up assessments over the time: only when we are capable of using validated frameworks for measurements in the long term will we be able to build reliable knowledge on e-Government impact.

Acknowledgments

The results of this chapter are based on a research project funded by the Belgian Science Policy (Agora Programme) and conducted in close collaboration with Fedict, Federal Public Service for Information and Communication Technology (Belgian federal government).

References

Andersen, K. V., & Henriksen, H. Z. (2006). E-Government maturity models: Extension of the Layne and Lee model. *Government Information Quarterly*, 23(2), 236-248.

Arbuckle, J.L. (2005). *AMOS 6.0 User's guide*. Chicago, IL: SPSS.

Bagozzi, R.P. (1980). *Causal models in marketing*. New York: Wiley.

Bannister, F. (2007). The curse of the benchmark: An assessment of the validity and value of e-Government comparisons. *International Review of Administrative Sciences*, 73(2), 171-188.

Bekkers, V. & Homburg, V. (2007). The myths of e-Government: Looking beyond the assumptions of a new and better government. *The Information Society*, 23(5), 373-382.

Carter, L., & Bélanger, F. (2004). The influence of perceived characteristics of innovating on e-Government adoption. *The Electronic Journal of E-Government*, 2(1), 11-20.

Centeno, C., Van Bavel, R. & Burgelman, J.C. (2005). A prospective view of e-Government in the European Union. *The Electronic Journal of E-Government*, 3(2), 59-66.

Chin, W.W. (1998). Issues and opinion on Structural Equation Modeling. *MIS Quarterly*, 22(1), 1-11.

Codagnone, C. (2008). Editorial: Efficiency and effectiveness. *European Journal of ePractice*. No. 4, August 2008, 2-3. Retrieved 14/01/2010, from: http://www.epracticejournal.eu/volume/4.

Codagnone, C. & Boccardelli, P. (2006). *Measurement framework final version*. Delivered within the eGEP Project for the European Commission, DG Information Society, Unit H2. Retrieved 14/01/2010, from: http://82.187.13.175/eGEP/Static/Contents/final/D.2.4_Measurement_Framework_final_version.pdf.

Codagnone, C. & Undheim, T.A. (2008). Benchmarking e-Government: Tools, theory and practice. *European Journal of ePractice* , No. 4, August 2008, 4-18. Retrieved 14/01/2010, from: http://www.epracticejournal.eu/document/4970.

Dimitrova, D. V., & Chen, Y.-C. (2006). Profiling the adopters of e-Government information and services: The influence of psychological characteristics, civic mindedness, and information channels. *Social Science Computer Review*, 24(2), 172-188.

Eurostat (2009b). *E-Government usage by individuals by gender - Percentage of individuals aged 16 to 74 using the Internet for interaction with public authorities*. Retrieved 14/01/2010, from: http://epp.eurostat.ec.europa.eu/tgm/table.do?tab=table&init=1&plugin=1&language=en&pcode=tsiir130.

Heeks, R. (2003). *Reinventing government in the information age. International practise in IT-enabled public sector reform*. London: Routledge.

Heeks, R. (2006). *Understanding and measuring e-Government: International benchmarking studies*. Paper presented at the UNDESA Workshop, e-Participation and e-Government: Understanding the present and creating the future, Budapest, Hungary, 27-28 July 2006.

Heeks, R. & Bailur, S. (2007). Analyzing e-Government research: Perspectives, philosophies, theories, methods and practice. *Government Information Quarterly*, 24(2), 243-265.

Hung, S.-Y., Chang, C.-M., & Yu, T.-J. (2006). Determinants of user acceptance of the e-Government services: The case of online tax filing and payment system. *Government Information Quarterly*, 23(1), 97-122.

Jaeger, P. T. (2003). The endless wire: E-Government as global phenomenon. *Government Information Quarterly*, 20(4), 323-331.

Jaeger, P.T. & Thompson, K.M. (2003). E-Government around the world: Lessons, challenges, and future directions. *Government Information Quarterly*, 20(4), 389-394.

Jaeger, P.T. & Bertot, J.C. (2010). Designing, implementing, and evaluating user-centered and citizen-centered e-Government. In: C.G. Reddick (Eds.) *Citizens and e-Government: Evaluation policy and management* (pp. 1-19). Hershey, New York: Information Science Reference (IGI Global).

Janssen, D., Rotthier, S. & Snijkers, K. (2004). If you measure it they will score: An assessment of international e-Government benchmarking. *Information Polity*, 9(3-4), 121-130.

Kunstelj, M., Jukic, T. & Vintar, M. (2007). Analysing the demand side of e-Government: What can we learn from Slovenian users? *Lecture Notes in Computer Science*, 4556, 305-317.

Layne, K., & Lee, J. (2001). Developing fully functional e-Government: A four stage model. *Government Information Quarterly*, 18(2), 122-136.

Linstone, H.A. & Turoff, M. (1975). *The Delphi method, techniques and applications*. Reading, M.A.: Addison-Wesley

Millard, J. (2008). E-Government measurement for policy makers. *European Journal of ePractice*, No. 4, August 2008, 19-32. Retrieved 14/01/2010, from: http://www.epracticejournal.eu/document/4971.

OECD (2003). *The e-Government imperative*. Paris: OECD E-Government Studies.

OECD (2005). *E-Government for better government*. Paris: OECD Publications Service.

OECD (2008). *Belgium: OECD Country Report*. Paris: OECD E-Government Studies.

Peters, R., Janssen, M. & van Engers, T. (2005). *Measuring e-Government impact: Existing practices and shortcomings*. In Proceedings of the 6th International Conference on Electronic Commerce, session: E-Government services and policy track (Copenhagen, August 22-26, 2005), New York, ACM Press, 480-489.

Relyea, H.C. (2002). E-Gov: Introduction and overview. *Government Information Quarterly*, 19(1), 9-35.

Traunmüller, R. & Wimmer, M. (2004). E-Government: The challenges ahead. *Lecture Notes in Computer Science*, 3183, 1-6.

van Deursen, A. & van Dijk, J. (2009). Improving digital skills for the use of online public information and services. *Government Information Quarterly*, 26(2), 333-340.

van Dijk, J., Peters, O. & Ebbers, W. (2008). Explaining the acceptance and use of government Internet services: A multivariate analysis of 2006 survey data in the Netherlands. *Government Information Quarterly*, 25(3), 379-399.

Verdegem, P. (2009). *The digital divide and/in e-Government: Challenges for policymakers in the information society. Unpublished Ph.D. dissertation*. Ghent University – Department of Communication Sciences.

Verdegem, P. & Verleye, G. (2009). User-centered e-Government in practice: A comprehensive model for measuring user satisfaction. *Government Information Quarterly*, 26(3), 487-497.

Verdegem, P. & Hauttekeete, L. (2010). A user-centric approach in e-Government policies: The path to effectiveness? In: C.G. Reddick (Eds.) *Citizens and e-Government: Evaluation policy and management* (pp. 20-36). Hershey, New York: Information Science Reference (IGI Global).

Yildiz, M. (2007). E-Government research: Reviewing the literature, limitations, and ways forward. *Government Information Quarterly*, 24(3), 646-665.

Business Process Improvement in Organizational Design of e-Government Services

Ömer Faruk Aydinli[1], Sjaak Brinkkemper[2] and Pascal Ravesteyn[3]
[1]Logica, Public Sector, Arnhem, The Netherlands
[2]Institute of Information and Computer Sciences, University of Utrecht, The Netherlands
[3]Research Centre for Process Innovation, University of Applied Sciences Utrecht, The Netherlands
omer.aydinli@logica.com
S.Brinkkemper@cs.uu.nl
pascal.ravesteijn@hu.nl
Originally published in EJEG (2009) Volume 7, issue 2.

Editorial Commentary

Aydinli et al describe an interesting business process and organisational redesign project undertaken in a major government department in the Netherlands. The department supports and promotes the delivery of electronic communications within the wider governmental environment. The authors use a range of tools and techniques (such as modelling the enterprise's information architecture, business process remodelling to identify and focus on the organisation's core business processes and knowledge management to facilitate learning and continuous improvement) to bring about the process redesign and organisational restructuring needed to enhance service delivery and organisational performance. Importantly, the methodologies used were selected to ensure that the organisation's business processes and activities were aligned with its business strategy and to ensure that the measurement and monitoring systems were in place to support organisational learning.

Aydinli et al demonstrate clearly the advantage of using suites of methods to assist senior managers in the process of defining business strategy, identifying key business processes, defining and making explicit the information architectures that have previously been implicit and putting in place the measurement and monitoring systems that will facilitate continuous improvement. The authors argue that the suite of tools and techniques they have integrated can be used effectively to analyse and understand operational business problems and to identify where and how business processes can be improved. The authors admit the exploratory nature of their project and raise the issue of whether their approach is scaleable from the organisation where they conducted their initial study to larger, more complex organisations. Only further research will answer that particular question.

Abstract: This paper describes a business process and organizational re-design and implementation project for an e-Government service organization. In this project the initial process execution time of a Virtual Private Network (VPN) connection request has been reduced from some 60 days to two days. This has been achieved by the use of a new business process reengineering (BPR) implementation approach that was developed by the Utrecht University. The implementation approach is based on a combination of Enterprise Information Architecture (EIA), Business Process Modelling (BPM), Knowledge Management and Management Control methodologies and techniques. The method has been applied to improve the performance of a Dutch e-Government service department (DeGSD). DeGSD is an e-Government service department that supports and promotes electronic communication. It can be described as an electronic mail office for consumers that provides the ICT Infrastructure to communicate with the government. The goal is to reduce administrative activities for both the government and consumers. Supporting technology and part of the process is outsourced. In our approach we used EIA as a starting point because it describes all relations and information exchange with all stakeholders. This is different compared to more traditional approaches which tend to have a main focus on the internal processes (when it comes to automation) whereas our approach aligns the processes and systems across different participants, such as suppliers and customers, in the supply chain. Also included in the implementation approach are management control design mechanisms to ensure that the organizations strategy is in sync with its processes and activities that are performed by the employees. Management control is crucial in enabling the continuous measuring and improving of the organizational performance. Although the proposed BPR implementation approach worked in the project at DeGSD, further validation is necessary. Therefore we suggest that more case studies are performed at both government and profit organizations.

Keywords: business process improvement, organizational (re-)design, business process reengineering, enterprise information architecture, knowledge management, e-Government services

1. Process design for e-Government service departments

During the past decade we have seen that more and more governments in the world are providing their services via information and communication technology (ICT). Governments wish to improve the services they provide to citizens and companies by using the options offered by ICT. In this paper we use the following definition for Electronic government (e-Government) services:

"Government activities that take place by digital processes over a computer network, usually the Internet, between the government and members of the public and parties in the private sector, in particular governmental organizations. These activities generally involve the electronic exchange of information to acquire or provide products or services, to place or receive orders, to provide or obtain information, or to complete financial transactions" (MoMS 2004).

e-Government services reduce operating costs and provide direct communications between citizens, companies and governmental organizations. To provide these ICT services new governmental departments are being set up. They are responsible for the communication between governmental organizations and both citizens and companies in a secure way. These departments have a portal function. They are providing digital signatures to citizens for authentication and they set up VPN connections between companies and governmental systems to enable exchanging information in a secure way.

DeGSD is such an e-Government service department that supports and promotes electronic communication. It can be described as an electronic mail office for consumers that provide the ICT infrastructure to communicate with the government. The goal is to reduce administrative activities for both the government and consumers.

The department has been set up in 2005. In the first year several pilot projects were set up for service delivery. During these projects the organization discovered that connecting to other companies turned out to be very problematic. This was caused by a lack of process governance, bad communication with the customer and non-controlled knowledge transfer from the initial system developers to the operational staff. Therefore it was decided to redesign the process. This decision was based on recent research in the government domain (Martin and Montagna 2006), which suggests that before implementing an e-Government strategy the back office processes should first be changed with the help of BPR.

Ever since the start of the business process reengineering movement (Davenport and Short 1990; Hammer and Champy 2001) the success has been debated (Zairi 1997; Teng, Jeong and Grover 1998). Many implementation methods or principles have been proposed (Harrington 1995; Armistead 1996; Burlton 2001; Chang 2006) in which the essence stays the same (Kettinger, Teng and Guha 1997). All proposed methodologies have an envision phase in which management should acknowledge the need for change. This is followed by the initiation of a project that starts with diagnosing or analyzing the existing processes after which suggestions for redesign are made. Finally the changed processes should be implemented and evaluated against a set of performance measurements. So to help solve the problems facing the e-Government service department DeGSD in the implementation phase of their e-strategy a new approach was developed consisting of the following six phases:

- Map the EIA the department using Enterprise Architecture Modelling (EAM)
- Choose a strategy discipline
- Define the primary processes of the department by using business process modelling (Primary processes have to be in line with the chosen strategy discipline)
- Optimize processes
- Choose a knowledge management strategy and implement a tool and procedures that are in line with the chosen strategy
- Define and implement controlling mechanisms for the all departments that are involved

The remainder of the article is as follows: in section 2 a detailed description of the project phases is given, then in section 3 the improvement project executed at DeGSD is elaborated upon after which conclusions will be drawn and discussed in section 4.

2. Organizational designing of e-Government services

The developed approach as described earlier consists of six phases that are described further in the following subsections.

2.1. EIA

Decisions made by managers have an important effect on the communication processes between citizens and the government. Wrong decisions can have a big impact on the functioning of the government. Regulations and security issues are also very important.

To provide proper information to politicians and managers who are responsible for the e-Government services, enterprise information architecture is a useful tool, because the main benefit of enterprise information architecture lies in its holistic approach of all aspects of the enterprise. (Koning, Bos and Brinkkemper 2008) This includes the ICT infrastructure and procedures, the business related issues, like business process or business excellence and the internal and external information exchanges. EIA deals with the documentation, communication, legal aspects and decision making of the complete information infrastructure of an enterprise.

With regard to this subject, the information which is the most critical for managers to decide includes 1) Mission, vision and strategy 2) Enterprise context 3) Enterprise functions 4) Information and communication systems and 5) IT infrastructure (Koning, Bos and Brinkkemper 2008). EAM is a method for creating enterprise information architectures. The process of creating an information architecture by using the EAM modeling technique consists of the following steps: (Koning, Bos and Brinkkemper 2008)

- Create a supply chain diagram (SCD)
- Create an enterprise function diagram (EFD)
- Create application and scenario overlays
- Create a system infrastructure diagram

2.2. Strategy discipline

A strategy discipline defines the main focus of an enterprise and therefore influences design decisions when developing a business process. In this project the company chose the value discipline model of Treacy and Wiersma (1995) as strategic discipline, but other disciplines can be chosen as well. This depends on the environment and situational factors of the enterprise. The value discipline model can make the direction of the organization clear to employees so that they can act in line with the wishes of the organization. Treacy and Wiersma describe three generic value disciplines. Any organization can choose one of these value disciplines and consistently act upon it. The primary processes of an organization have to be in line with the chosen value discipline. The three value disciplines according to Treacy and Wiersma (1995) are:

- Operational excellence: Company excels in superb operations and executions. The focus is often on providing products and services with a reasonable quality at a low price. There is a task-oriented vision towards staff. The main focus is on efficiency, streamlined operations, supply chain management and high volume. There is a limited variation in product sets.
- Product Leadership: Company excels in innovation and brand marketing. The focus is on development, innovation, design, time to market and high margins.
- Customer Intimacy: Company excels in customer attention and customer service. It tailors its products and services to individual customers. There is a large variation in products and services. The main focus is on customer relationship management.

2.3. Defining primary processes

BPM is the discipline of defining and outlining business practices, processes, information flows, data stores and systems. (Sparx 2007) BPM is an important part of understanding and (re-)structuring the activities and information flows within an organization. The emphasis of BPM is on how the work is done within an organization. It is an important tool in understanding the activities an organization undertakes and the kind of information it needs to successfully engage in those activities (Sparx 2007). There are numerous business process modeling techniques developed in the last decade. Some examples of these techniques are Petri Nets, Event-driven Process Chains, Workflow Nets, Unified Modeling Language (UML) and

Business Process Modeling Notation (Weske 2007). These techniques are based on different views on processes. Some aim at modeling processes from an IT perspective (such as UML), while others are based on a business perspective. In the project we used elements from both UML and Testbed (Telematica Institute) to satisfy both the IT and business stakeholders involved in this project. One of the main goals of modeling the business processes is to create transparency in how the work is currently done (as-is situation) within an organization. This is also the basis for the process analysis in the optimization phase.

Based on the analysis the e-Government service department can define a set of standard processes that describes how to perform the departments' services in the future (to-be situation). These standard processes are used to establish consistency across the organization. The chosen value discipline is an important factor when (re-)designing the primary processes. For example, if an organization chooses product leadership instead of the operational excellence discipline there will probably be more quality control mechanisms required in the primary processes.

2.4. Optimize processes

Optimization is the use of specific techniques to determine the most cost effective and efficient solution to a problem or a process. Process optimization is the practice of making changes or adjustments to a process to get better results. (Ranjit 2001) Although process optimization is part of BPM and has therefore received much attention in industrial engineering and management literature, there is not much known on how to use these concepts in the public sector. Gulledge and Sommer (2002) have done research on how to implement BPM in the public sector and state that among the most important activities are documenting the existing processes, managing the process (measuring and optimizing performance) and improving the process to optimize the product/service quality. This is also in accordance with the 'streamlining the process' and 'continuous improvement' phases of the Process Breakthrough Methodology that is developed by Harrington (1995). In these phases processes are continuously optimized by redesigning them, for this purpose it is important to benchmark processes, perform risk analysis and measure improvements in terms of costs and time.

The main goal of process optimization is to resolve complex challenges and improve product, service, process and business performance and this is supported by Bhatt and Troutt (2005), who have found that business process improvement initiatives directly affect customer responsiveness and product/service innovation.

e-Government services that choose the operational excellence value discipline have to optimize their processes to serve customers in an efficient and cost effective way.

In order to achieve the major goals of business process improvement, managers need to fully understand the cost, time, and quality of activities performed by employees throughout an entire organization. A method for understanding the costs structure of processes is Activity Based Costing (ABC). After defining the primary processes, the most costly parts can be identified by the ABC method. Then these parts can be improved by eliminating redundant or irrelevant activities or automation.

2.5. Knowledge management

Michael JD Sutton (2003) defined a list of reasons why an organization should implement knowledge management to gain advantage. Stan Garfield (2006) described a set of goals and benefits in order to create added value with knowledge management. Some examples of these benefits are:

- Avoid redundant effort by using knowledge management systems.
- Make it easy for employees to find the necessary information and resources to do their jobs.
- Communicate important information widely and quickly in the organization.
- Capture key information on all work performed so that everyone will know what others have done and who to contact for further details.
- Provide and create methods, tools, templates, examples and data to streamline business and services.

In sections 2.1 and 2.3 we described the business processes where knowledge creation takes place. By identifying these business processes and understanding them, we can describe information architectures, business process models and working procedures. It also enables us to describe the roles and functions of the employees including the knowledge and experience needed to execute these. This knowledge and experience has to be shared and (re-)applied within the organization to provide services in an efficient and controlled way. Furthermore the knowledge and experience has to be evaluated periodically and adapted if necessary. Knowledge management is a continuous process (Weggeman 1997) that needs to be managed. This can be done via a knowledge management strategy (KMS). There are two types of KMS described by Jashapara (2004). First there is codification, which is based on technology and use databases to codify and store knowledge. It is heavily based on codifying explicit knowledge. Second is personalization, which is less about technology and more about people. It is heavily based on tacit knowledge.

For small organizations often one KMS can be selected. Before an organization chooses a KMS the properties of the organization have to be identified. Hansen, Nohria and Tierney (1999) provide a list of questions to help guide an organization in establishing a KMS. By answering these questions the various properties of the organization will be established. Thus enabling the organization to formulate or choose a better KMS based upon these properties. The questions are:

1) Do we offer standardized or customized products/services? E-Government services are standardized. They are not customized for a special group.
2) Do we have mature or innovative product/services? E-Government services are mature.
3) Do our employees rely on explicit or tacit knowledge to solve problems? In most situations employees of an e-Government service organization use explicit knowledge to solve problems or provide services. This kind of knowledge can also be codified.

Because of the properties of the service that is provided by the e-Government services, a codification strategy seems right. Therefore the e-Government services have to develop or buy an electronic document system that codifies, stores, disseminates, and allows reuse of knowledge. (Hansen et.al. 1999). They of course also have to develop and implement associating working procedures.

2.6. Controlling mechanisms

In organizations management control is one of the most critical functions; it involves managers taking steps to help ensure that the employees do their work according to the best interests of the organization. "Management controls are necessary to guard against the possibilities that people will do something the organization does not want them to do or fail to do something they should do" (Merchant and van der Stede 2003). Besides this the management control issue has also become more important because of various scandals like Enron, WorldCom and Ahold. These scandals triggered governments and institutions to create laws and rules concerning corporate governance.

The laws and rules that have been designed and implemented requires organizations to improve the alignment between governance, risk management and compliance (Brown and Nasuti 2005; Drew 2007; Elgar 2006).

This aspect is very important for e-Government service departments. Mistakes made by employees during execution of processes or activities can have large impact on the reliable functioning of the government. Therefore e-Government service departments have to minimize the chances that mistakes can occur. There are three types of control described by Merchant and van der Stede (2003). The first is result control; this involves rewarding individuals for generating good results, while bad results are penalized. Result control influences the actions of employees because they motivate employees to be concerned about the consequences of the activities they perform. "The organization does not dictate to employees what actions they should take; instead employees are empowered to take those actions of which they believe that it will produce the desired result" (Merchant and van der Stede 2003).

Results should be measured precisely and objectively in order to be able to control and improve activities and actions of employees. A second type of control is action control. This "control ensures that employees perform (or do not perform) certain actions known to be beneficial (or harmful) to the organization. It is important to define what actions are acceptable or unacceptable, to communicate those definitions to employees and to observe or otherwise track what happens and reward good actions and punish those that deviate from the standard set" (Merchant and van der Stede 2003). The last control is personnel control which builds on employee's natural expectancy to be controlled and motivated in an organizational environment. Three major methods of implementing personnel controls are: selection and placement of employees, training and job design.

3. Project execution at DeGSD

In the first year after the set-up of DeGSD, several pilot projects for electronic service delivery were initiated. The development of technical facilities was outsourced to specialized ICT companies. The main function of the DeGSD department was managing the outsourcing and implementation processes and after implementation providing the service to the public. A year later when some pilot projects were finished and the government decided to make them operational some organizational problems occurred:

- The operational environment and scale differed significantly from the pilot projects.
- The technical ICT product can be innovative and well engineered, but if the organizational structure is poorly designed (no working procedures, staff not well trained, etc.), then the resulting service to the end-user will be very problematic.
- and because of these operational problems, citizens and companies were reluctant to use the new electronic services.

The aim of the improvement project was to analyze and understand these operational issues and to propose and implement possible solutions, based on the new BPR method as discussed in the section 2. One of the pilot projects was the set-up of VPN connections between companies, governmental institutes and DeGSD. The way in which VPN connections are setup is illustrated in Figure 1.

The first message is sent by the requesting company via a VPN connection to the server of DeGSD and then DeGSD forwards it to the addressed governmental institute. By sending messages to the DeGSD server, the company will be authenticated automatically. If it is an unknown company or the company has no permission to communicate with the governmental organization, the message will not be forwarded. There are special requirements for the format type of the message. The mail-server software of the company has to generate and support this format.

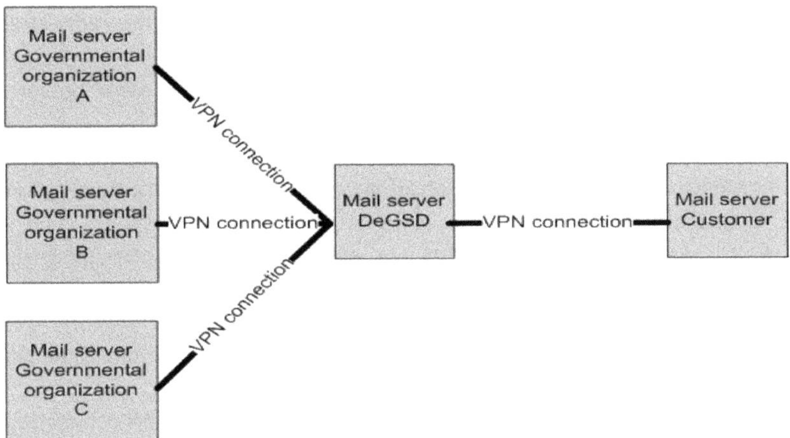

Figure 1: Communication model DeGSD

The steps in the connection process are as follows:

- A company (customer) sends a requests for connection to DeGSD.
- DeGSD requests to their outsourcing partner (KPN an incumbent Telco) to set up a VPN connection between the server of DeGSD and the server of the customer. To do this KPN contacts the customer and sets up a VPN connection.
- DeGSD and the customer will test the connection.
- The governmental organization and the customer will test the message mark-up and format.
- The customer runs the first production (e.g. information exchange).

The outsourcing and implementation process of this VPN connection project was successfully finished. But when management decided to go live, too many requests for connection came from companies and governmental institutes and DeGSD discovered that the organization was not designed well enough to handle these numbers of requests in an efficient way. The major problems were:

- The process on how to set up a VPN connection with DeGSD was not described in detail. The technical criteria were vaguely formulated. The helpdesk received many questions and problems when companies where trying to set up VPN connections.

- The functional administrators who were responsible for the connection process where not well trained.
- It was not clear to employees who was responsible for what (governance problem).
- The registration process for functional administrators was very inefficient. The time spent in registration was sometimes more than in connecting companies.
- ICT specialists and consultants who were hired in the outsourcing and development phase left the organization. The knowledge transfer from them to functional administrators was not managed well.
- It was not clear to employees and managers what the direction and strategy of the organization was.
- It sometimes took 2 months for companies to set up a VPN connection, which obviously caused a lot of frustration.
- The cooperation with DeGSD and governmental organizations was not optimal. There was disappointment because of the connection problems.
- There was a need for formal procedures between DeGSD and the governmental organizations.

To solve the different problems it was decided to redesign the business process. The first phase in the developed BPR approach was to develop an EIA for the organization. The goal was to:

- Identify all parties the organization has relations with.
- Identify the type of information exchange between external and internal parties.
- Identify who is responsible for which processes.
- Identify all applications and tools used in the organization.

The SCD of the organization identifies all parties with whom the organization has a relation and it visualizes the kind of information exchange between the different parties (see Figure 2).

Then an EFD was developed to identify the responsibilities pertaining to the various parts of the connection process. The hierarchical ordering of EFD shows managers the departments and activities under their supervision. By applying an application overlay it is possible to identify all applications and tools used in an organization. Based on the application overlay it was detected that some applications and tools had the same function, so management decided to remove redundant applications.

The EIA was used to visualize how the organization was functioning and to address the responsibility problem in the organization.

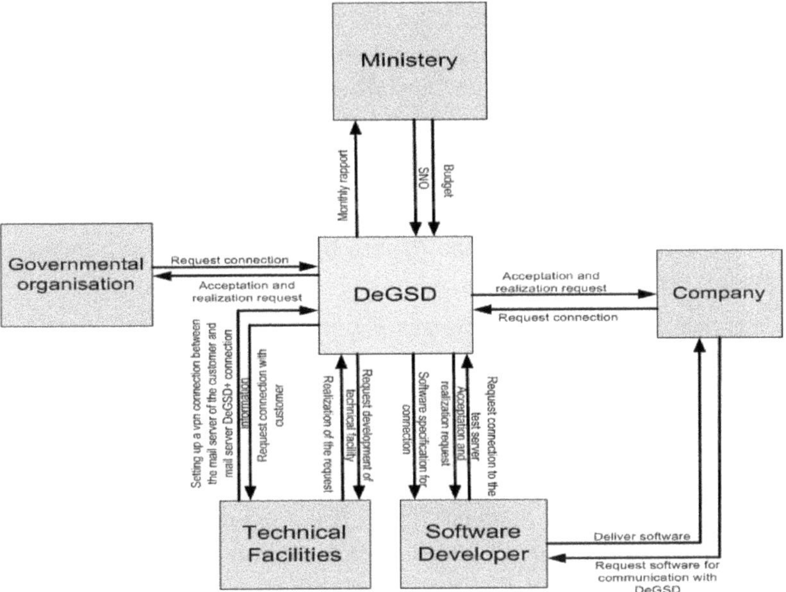

Figure 2: Supply chain diagram DeGSD

The next phase was choosing a strategy discipline to get a clear sense of direction within the organization. As stated before DeGSD used the value disciplines model of Treacy and Wiersma. The best value discipline in this model for e-Government service departments is operational excellence. The service that e-Government organizations provide is not tailored but standardized and the main focus is on efficiency, also the volume of provided services is high.

The EIA and the decision for operational excellence were explained to employees by means of presentations to make clear in which direction the organization would go and how the organization was going to function. By having a clear strategy and involving employees there was already a slight improvement in performance, mostly because employees came with suggestions on how to improve processes to achieve the operational excellence strategy. Although EIA and the chosen value discipline already improved the performance of the processes, the connection time was still 6 weeks and it was still not clear for companies how the connection process worked. There was a need for a detailed process description. In phase 3 of the BPR approach the connection process and what is needed to setup a VPN connection was described and visualized in detail by using business process modelling techniques. When a new request for a VPN connection was received, the functional administrators sent the requesting company first the diagrams in which the connection process was explained. Questions about the connection process from companies promptly decreased. In figure 3 the initial situation (before optimization) of the connection process is depicted.

Once the as-is connection processes were described it was clear that it had to be optimized. There were steps in the process that were needed in the pilot phase to test the applications but which were no longer needed in the operational phase. Other processes were still done manually although they could be automated. Management decided to automate and optimize the most costly parts of the processes based on the information that was visualized by the developed model. The costs per phase were determined by using the ABC method. It turned out that the two test phases were the most expensive part of the connection process. A test-robot was developed to enable customers testing the connection process and message format in an automated way. Also new outsourcing agreements were made with KPN to setup VPN connections in a faster way. After the optimization the connection time was decreased to two days. Figure 4 shows the new process that consists of less phases, sub processes and activities.

The knowledge that was created by developing the EIA, process models and descriptions had to be shared and applied throughout the organization. In phase 5 of the BPR approach management chose for the codification knowledge management strategy. Based on this decision the process models and descriptions were stored in a logical way. All employees have access to this information while authorized employees can also make modifications and changes.

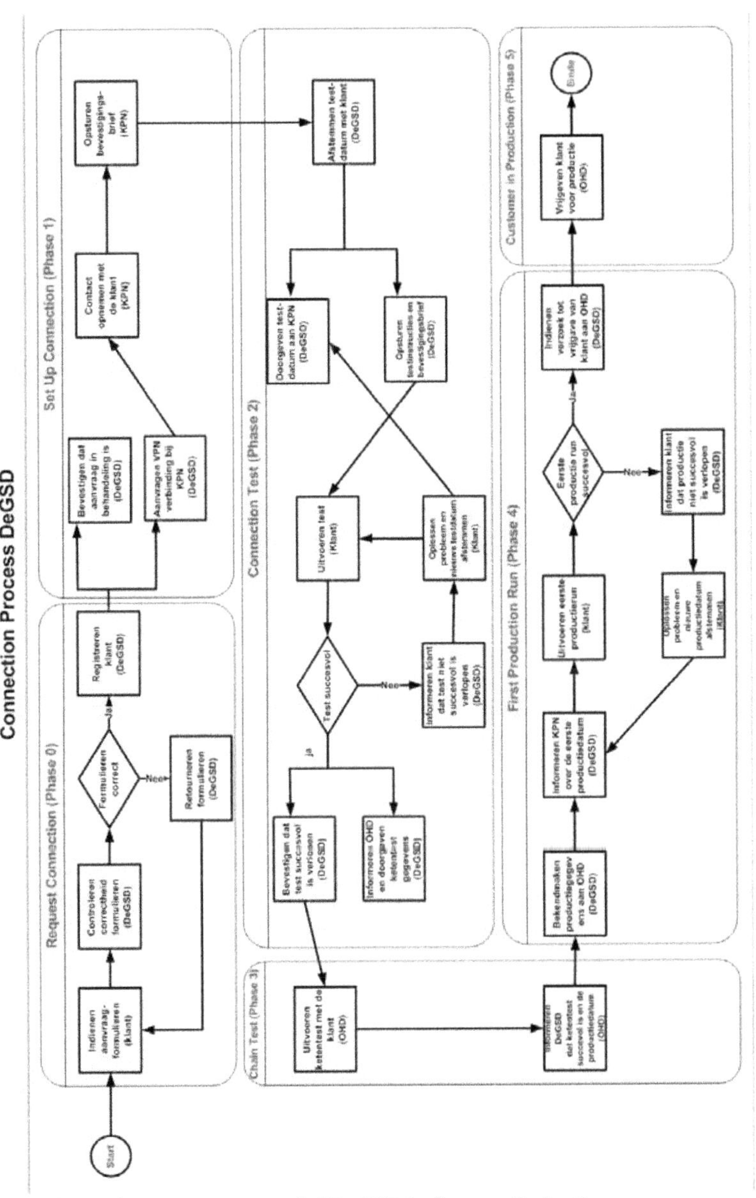

Figure 3: Business process model DeGSD before optimization

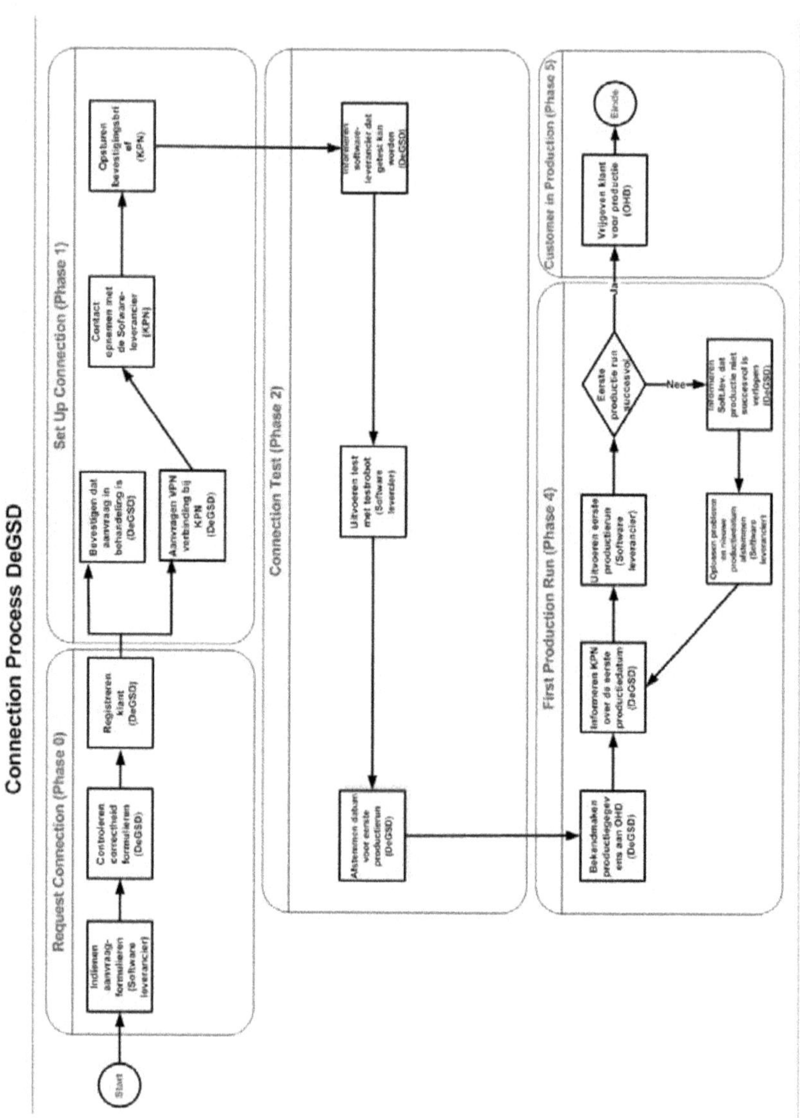

Figure 4: Business process model DeGSD after optimization

The final phase in the BPR approach is to create a management control system for the organization. For every sub department within the e-

Government services a control mechanism or a combination of control mechanisms should be implemented. It is very important to choose the control mechanism that is in line with the nature of the function. Wrong control mechanisms can jeopardize the performance of the organization.

For example, applying result control to help desk personal is risky because they have to perform their job with ITIL standards. They don't have the freedom to take those actions they believe will be best to produce the desired result. The actions they have to take are formally described in work instructions. There are standard procedures to establish consistency across the organization. Otherwise customers will be served in different ways for the same request. Action control is more in line with the nature of this function. It was decided not to choose one control strategy for the whole organization. Every department will be controlled with the control strategy that is in line with the nature of the functions that are provided by the department. For the help-desk the action control strategy was chosen while the functional administration is controlled by a combination of result and action control mechanisms. For the project management department the result control mechanism was implemented.

4. Conclusions

Modern governments have some innovative challenges. They have to keep in pace with the growing demands of their customers for more efficient service delivery. This can be realized by offering ways of interacting with the government via ICT. However in most government organizations this will mean that the back-office processes need to be redesigned.

The business improvement project at DeGSD has demonstrated that the developed BPR approach consisting of EIA, BPM, Management Control and Knowledge Management techniques can be used in a very successful way to analyze and understand operational business problems in an ICT environment.

In our approach we used EIA as a starting point because it describes all relations and information exchange with all stakeholders. This is different compared to more traditional approaches which (when it comes to automation) tend to have a main focus on the internal processes whereas our approach aligns the processes and systems across different participants in the supply chain. Besides, our approach also includes management control mechanisms to ensure that the organizations strategy is in sync with its processes and activities performed by the employee's. Management control is crucial in enabling the continuous measuring and improving of the organizational performance and to realize governance. In the DeGSD case, the process execution time to set up a VPN connection with companies has been reduced from some 60 days to 2 days.

5. Discussion and future research

This research can be labelled as explorative and the BPR approach is applied to improve the primary processes of a single organization. Therefore, we should be careful to generalize the results and findings of this investigation. Although the proposed BPR implementation approach worked in the DeGSD case further validation is necessary. Therefore we suggest that more case studies should be done. Future experiences from the application of this approach in different case studies in different parts of the public sector will be included into the BPR method. Also the developed method might be used to improve business processes in organizations in the commercial sector.

Furthermore the organization in which the method is applied is relatively small so the scalability of the developed BPR method should be researched. Another interesting research project is to determine whether all phases in the approach are equally important, in the described project no distinction in importance between the project phases was made or found, however this could be different in other situations.

References

Armistead, C. (1996) "Principles of business process management", *Managing Service Quality*, Vol 6, No. 6, pp 48-52.

Bhatt, G. D. and Troutt, M. D. (2005) Business Process Management Journal, 11, 532-558.

Brown, W. and Nasuti, F. (2005) Sarbanes–Oxley and Enterprise Security: IT Governance — What It Takes to Get the Job Done, *EDPACS, 33*(2), 1 – 20.

Burlton, R.T. (2001) *Business process management: Profiting from process*, Sams publishing, Indianapolis.

Chang, J.F. (2006) *Business process management systems: Strategy and implementation*, Auerbach Publications, Boca Raton, FL.

Davenport, T.H. and Short, J.E. (1990) "The new industrial engineering: Information technology and business process redesign", *The Sloan Management Review*, Vol 31, No. 4, pp. 11-27.

Drew, M. (2007). Information risk management and compliance — expect the unexpected, *BT Technology Journal*, *25*(1), 19 – 29.

Elgar, E. (2006). Handbook on International Corporate Governance: Country Analyses, Celtenham.

Gulledge, T. and Sommer, R. (2002) Business Process Management Journal, 8, 364-376.

Hammer, M. and Champy, J. (2001) *Reengineering the corporation: A manifesto for business revolution*, updated and revised, Harper Business, New York.

Hansen, M.T., Nohria, N. and Tierney, T. (1999) *What's your strategy for Knowledge Management*, Harvard Business Review.

Harrington, J.J. (1995) *Total improvement management - the next generation in performance improvement*, McGraw-Hill, New York.

Jashapara, A. (2004) *Knowledge management: An integrated approach*, First edition, Essex, Prentice Hall.

Merchant, K.A., van der Stede, W.A. (2003) *Management Control Systems: Performance Measurement Evaluation and Incentives*, First edition, Prentice Hall.

Kettinger, J.W., Teng, J.T.C. and Guha, S. (1997) "Business process change: A study of methodologies, techniques, and tools", *MIS Quarterly*, Vol 21, No. 1, pp. 55-80.

Koning, H., Bos, R., Brinkkemper, S., (2008) "A Lightweight Method for the Modelling of Enterprise Architectures – Introduction and Usage Feedback". Proceedings of the 3th Workshop on Trends in Enterprise Architecture Research, Sydney, Australia, December 1, 2008.

Martin, R.L. and Montagna, J.M. (2006) *Business process reengineering role in electronic government*, In World Conference on Computers 2006, Springer, Santiago de Chile.

Michael JD Sutton, (2003), Knowledge Taxonomies: *"Measuring Knowledge: Why Use Knowledge Management Metrics and What Can We Actually Measure."* pp: 405-692, McGill University

Ministry of Management Services (MoMS) (2004) "Annual Service Plan report, British Columbia", [Online], http://www.bcbudget.gov.bc.ca/Annual_Reports/2004_2005/mser/mser.pdf

Ranjit K.R. (2001) *Design of Experiments Using the Taguchi Approach: 16 Steps to Product and Process Improvement*, John Wiley & Sons.

Sparx S. (2007) "Tools for Business Process Modeling using the BPMN", [Online], http://www.archaeol.freeuk.com/EHPostionStatement.htm

Stan Garfield, HP, (2006), *Priorities for setting up a KM program*, [Online], Available:http://www.destinationkm.com/articles/default.asp?ArticleID=1138 [27 June 2006]

Telematica Institute, http://www.telin.nl/index.cfm?ID=678&context=681&language=nl. Accessed on December 8, 2008.

Teng, J.T.C., Jeong, S.R. and Grover, V. (1998) "Profiling successful reengineering projects", *Communication of the ACM*, Vol 41, No. 6.

Treacy, M., Wiersema, (1995) *The Discipline of Market Leaders: Choose Your Customers, Narrow Your Focus, Dominate Your Market*, Addison-Wesley.

Weggeman, M.C.D.P. (1997) *Kennismanagement: inleiding en besturing van kennisintensieve organisaties*. Schiedam: Scriptum. pp. 222.

Weske, M. (2007) *Business Process Management: Concepts, Languages, Architectures*. Springer-Verlag, Berlin..

Zairi, M. (1997) "Business process management: A boundaryless approach to modern competitiveness", *Business Process Management Journal*, Vol 3, No. 1, pp.64-80.

Migration Strategies for Multi-Channel Service Provisioning in Public Agencies

Anne Fleur van Veenstra and Marijn Janssen
Delft University of Technology, The Netherlands
a.f.e.vanveenstra@tudelft.nl
m.f.w.h.a.janssen@tudelft.nl
Originally published in 2010 Volume 8 issue 2

Editorial Commentary

Government engagement with e-Government is increasingly being driven by cost-reduction and improving efficiency and effectiveness. To achieve these ends, Veenstra and Janssen argue that government agencies need to be increasingly proactive in implementing multi-channel service provisioning (MCSP - is geared to providing individual services by means of a number of channels). The rationale of MCSP is that individual citizens or businesses can use their preferred channel to interact with government based on their preferences, needs, abilities and circumstances. Additionally, service users can choose to change their channel if their preferences, needs, skills or circumstances change. Increasingly, as new channels are created, it is in the interest of governments to encourage, incentivise or coerce users into using those channels which enable government departments to save most money though user familiarity and preferences are clearly important here. The authors point out, however, that many organisations are struggling to implement MCSP and many are in need of guidance on how to construct and implement effective migration strategies for MCSP.

The authors conducted four cases studies to gain insights into how effective MCSP can be developed given that these strategies require organisational change, the dismantling of silos within organisations, changes to business and work processes, the deployment of new technologies and culture change within the provider organisation. Van Veenstra and Jonsson, even though they acknowledge that their research is still developing, identify the key issues that organisations need to work through and lay bare some of the critical decisions that organisations need to take if they are to develop effective migration strategies.

Abstract: Many public agencies aim to realize better service delivery for citizens and businesses by implementing multi-channel service provisioning (MCSP). MCSP coordinates service delivery channels to enable citizens and businesses to choose their preferred channel for their contact with the government. As the introduction of MCSP requires substantial organizational and technical change, organizations are in search of the right migration strategies. This study explores migration strategies for MCSP deployed in practice. We found that migration strategies for MCSP can be divided into two types: design and change management strategies. By looking at four case studies and evaluating the findings during an expert workshop, we found that organizations prefer a gradual migration process, as both step-wise migration and the celebration of quick-wins were often mentioned strategies. Furthermore, the strategy to implement MCSP starting in the front office was observed more often than starting in the back office, as the client needs were usually taken as a starting point for the migration. And finally we found that the public agencies under study consider having the right change management strategy in place more important than deploying the right design strategy.

Keywords: multi-channel service provisioning (MCSP), integrated service delivery, multi-channel management, migration strategies, change strategies, e-Government

1. Introduction

e-Government is concerned with creating better service delivery to citizens and businesses (Curtin and al. 2004). Citizens and businesses are demanding faster delivery of public services and much better information (Ongaro 2004). One of the elements that can improve public service delivery is implementation of multi-channel service provisioning (Parisopoulos et al. 2009). Multi-channel service provisioning (MCSP) is the use of multiple service delivery channels as part of one public service delivery process. The rationale of MCSP is that citizens or business can use their preferred channel to interact with the government, or change their preferred channel depending on their needs and circumstances while interacting with the government. While the service desk may be preferred for complex services, the internet may be preferred for tracking and tracing. MCSP contributes to the creation of integrated service delivery, as service delivery across multiple channels is integrated (Kernaghan 2005). From the point of view of the organization new electronic channels can be used to lower costs of service delivery (Ebbers et al. 2008). Service channels are often viewed as complementary to each other. Yet new channels may substitute the old – often expensive – channels to lower costs. The main complexity is that these new channels need to be synchronized with the traditional and other new channels such as the telephone, twitter and the service desk.

Implementing e-Government is considered a challenging process as it requires substantial organizational and technical change (e.g. Bannister 2001; Beynon-Davies and Williams 2003). For years it has been acknowledged that silos should be dismantled (Bannister 2001); with MCSP it is necessary that these silos are coordinated and synchronized. Given the complexities involved, many organizations struggle to implement MCSP and are in search of the right migration strategy. Determining the right migration strategy likely depends on the situation within an organization and on its environment, but not much is known about which strategies are effective in specific circumstances (Van Veenstra et al 2009). This study investigates which migration strategies are deployed in practice and explores which migration strategies for MCSP are effective in the specific circumstances of an organization and its environment. First, migration strategies were identified in an expert workshop. We found that migration strategies for MCSP can be divided into two categories: design strategies that describe the migration process from the perspective of the order of implementation and change management strategies that describe the migration from a perspective of managing the changes in an organization. For each of the two categories we identified four different strategies.

Then, to find out which of these strategies are deployed in practice and in which specific organizational context, four cases studies in the Netherlands were examined: two executive agencies and a large and a mid-sized municipality. The organizations are in different stages of MCSP implementation. The findings from the case studies were evaluated during an expert meeting consisting of government officials that are involved in the implementation of MCSP. After investigating the migration strategies used in practice, a comparison is made between these two categories to investigate whether organizational characteristics influence the migration strategies used. This paper first presents an overview of the migration strategies identified. Then, the four case studies are described followed by the findings from the cases and the evaluation of the expert meeting. Finally, we present conclusions and recommendations.

2. Migration strategies

Many public organizations are in search of a migration strategy for MCSP. During an expert meeting with practitioners implementing MCSP we found that migration strategies can be broadly divided into two types: strategies that are concerned with the design (or the 'product' of implementation) and strategies that guide the implementation process (or the process of change). *Design strategies* are those strategies that determine the order of the migration to MCSP. These are called design strategies as they are usually defined – or designed – at the start of the implementation process, e.g. by designing enterprise architecture (Armour et al. 1999; Janssen and Van Veenstra 2005). They are usually based on the vision for multi-channel service delivery in an organization.

Change management strategies are those strategies that guide the implementation project. They are not concerned with choices of how to design MCSP but with the process of migration. In contrast with the design strategies that set out progress beforehand, they mainly deal with the challenges that come up during the migration process. They are meant for managers that have to bring about organizational change. During the migration process the influence of managers and stakeholders is considered important, as a solution is dependent on their support (De Bruijn and Ten Heuvelhof 2000; Chisholm 1989; Fernandez and Rainey 2006; Powell 1991) and the migration strategy has to be flexible enough to mitigate any problems that come up during the process (Van der Voort et al. 2009).

During a workshop with practitioners involved in implementing MCSP in the public sector we identified eight common decisions that need to be taken when implementing MCSP. Although these decisions are presented separately, they may influence each other. The first decisions refer to the design strategies (1-4), whereas the latter refer to decisions concerning the change management strategies (5-8) for migration to MCSP:

1. Starting by changing the front office or the back office?

2. Starting by changing the technology infrastructure or the organization?

3. Changing the channels one by one or all at the same time?
4. First implementing quick-wins or radically redesigning the whole organization?
5. Big-bang migration or step-by-step change?
6. Managing migration as a 'project' or as a 'process'?
7. Implementing change top-down or bottom-up?
8. Making middle management or the project team responsible for the migration?

In order to research the occurrence of these strategies in practice, we use 'ideal types'; the strategies are defined by presenting the extremes. The strategies are identified in such a way that they describe the migration from scratch; as migration takes place in an organization without MCSP. In such a situation all service delivery channels are developed and maintained separately. After migration MCSP is fully implemented: service channels are coordinated and communication strategies are in place. In order to get from the first situation to the second situation, the two extremes of the strategy can be followed during the migration process. Although we do not expect to find any of these 'ideal types' in practice, but rather a combination of both extremes, ideal types have a heuristic use to explain a specific situation. The migration strategies are elaborated in the next section.

2.1. Design strategies

'Starting by changing the front office or the back office?'

The one extreme of the first design strategy is to start with changing the front office and the other extreme is to start by changing the back office. In case the decision is made to start by changing the front end, the migration often starts by making changes that are quickly beneficial for customers, such as identifying how the service delivery can be set up in a more client-oriented manner. After these decisions and reorganizations have been made, the content of the channels is harmonized and finally changes are made in the back office to ensure that the different channels in the front office use the same information provided by the back office systems. The disadvantage of this strategy is that it may take long before the changes in the back end have followed the changes in the front end. The risk associated with starting with changing the front end is, thus, that the back end cannot 'keep up' with a MCSP front end, leading to a suboptimal performance of service delivery.

The second option is to start at the back office and harmonize processes, information and systems first, to ensure that after these changes have been made the front office can be easily migrated using the new back office systems to improve service delivery. This strategy focuses on creating the technological and organizational foundations before moving forward. Although this path is more likely to result in a coherent design of MCSP, this path is also found to be very costly. Large investments in information systems will have to be made before any improvement of service delivery can be noticed by the customer. This strategy may not be aligned with the objectives of elected politicians to show visible results quickly, or at least within their term of office. The main risk of this strategy is, thus, that high investments in a 'heavy' back office will not lead to improvements for customers in the short-term, causing the migration to be labeled a failure before benefits have been realized.

'Starting by changing the technology infrastructure or the organization?'

This strategy is concerned with starting to migrate to MCSP by implementing new technological infrastructure for MCSP or by re-organizing the organization. For migration to MCSP, both need to be changed as both work processes and information technology need to be adjusted to the new situation. The technological infrastructure provides the foundations and facilities for creating MCSP or e-Government (Janssen et al. 2009). The organization needs to harmonize its activities to be able to serve clients in the same way though every service delivery channel, while the software applications may need to be changed to support this harmonization. Both changes can be the starting point of the migration process.

When the choice is made to start with changing the organization and its work practices first, activities such as training employees are the starting point of the migration process. The organization will be changed from a functional to a customer-oriented organization structure. Also re-organizing the business processes and work practices are part of this adjustment process. The main pitfall is, however, that the information systems that are subsequently implemented do not follow the changes in the organization, thereby undoing part of the organizational changes. This means, that while the organization is ready for the new situation, service delivery may be still reliant on old information and systems, causing employees to fall back on their old habits.

Starting by implementing new information technology could mean that an application integration infrastructure is introduced. An organization can be divided in a front office and a back office (Richardson 1994). A technical infrastructure that can be used as an information broker for sharing information between front office and back office is called mid office. The advantage of a mid office implementation is that harmonization between front office and back office is taken care of. The pitfall of starting with the technical implementation is that it may be costly to implement new technology first without training employees to use the IT, which may result in a slow process with high costs, in which clients do not notice any of the changes. In this case, the main risk is that the potential of information technology is not realized or that it takes very long before it is realized.

'Changing the channels one by one or all at the same time?'

The choice between the strategies of changing all channels at the same time or rather one by one is represented by the third migration strategy. Changes can be made according to topic, by changing this topic in all channels at the same time, or they can be made by changing all topics at the same time within one channel. The main advantage of starting with the former, is that harmonization of the content is likely to happen smoothly. There is, however, a low tolerance for mistakes, as service delivery cannot be shut down altogether. In case channels are migrated by attuning them to the other channels one by one, risk of this happening is lower, because at least one channel will be available for clients at any time. The reliability of the service provisioning is, thus, higher. Synchronization of channels, will, however, be more difficult in this case. The main risk associated with a migration process changing channels one by one is that it may resulting a situation in which there are discrepancies between service channels, which is undesirable for MCSP.

'First implementing quick-wins or radically redesigning the whole organization?'

The fourth design strategy represents the choice between first identifying and implementing quick-wins as visible intermediary results or starting out with a radical redesign of the organization as well as the new information technology. The latter strategy requires designing a whole new situation and getting a precise overview of everything that needs to be altered, such as work processes, technology and organizational changes. Its greatest asset as well as its greatest risk is that it is all-encompassing. The complexity attached to this situation may lead to large failures, whereas making smaller changes may result in a less coherent redesign but it is also less risk-prone. When a choice is made to first identify and implement quick-wins, the first results are visible quickly. This my help in convincing people who resist changing the organization for MCSP. Overall, there is a risk associated with this strategy that the redesign will be less coherent, which may result in a longer lead time, as additional changes need to be made constantly to be able to fully migrate to MCSP.

2.2. Change management strategies

'Big-bang migration or step-by-step implementation?'

A first change management strategy is represented by the choice between big-bang implementation of all necessary changes or a change process that takes place step by step (Van der Voort et al. 2009). Whereas a big-bang migration aims to quickly implement all necessary changes, step-by-step change results in a longer-term gradual implementation process. The former strategy, however, requires much more control than the latter, as the changes are more likely to influence each other and delays need to be overcome quickly. The risk of failure, however, is also larger because of the interrelations between changes. Furthermore, there is a risk involved that employees of are resistant to a big-bang implementation of organizational changes. Step-by-step implementation aims at a migration in a gradual manner that can be managed easily. An associated risk is, however, that discrepancies in the design emerge as the process evolves over a longer period of time.

'Managing migration as a 'project' or as a 'process'?'

A second choice that needs to be made while implementing MCSP is whether to manage the migration as a 'project' or as a 'process' (De Bruijn et al. 1998). The former means that the migration process is tightly managed by steering towards clearly defined results, whereas during the process of migration in the way of the latter strategy happens in a more organic manner. In this case there is more room for building commitment by the various stakeholders during the project. Whereas lack of consensus for the new situation is a major risk of the former strategy, the latter strategy has a slow implementation process as a risk as well as the risk of incoherency emerging as a result of focusing on building consensus instead of steering towards clear results (De Bruijn et al. 1998).

'Implementing change top-down or bottom-up?'

The third change strategy represents the choice between top-down and bottom-up migration. Whereas top-down migration requires a strict planning by the management, bottom-up migration originates at the bottom of the organization, within the operational layer. Top-down enforcement has similarities with radical redesign as well as with a project implementation style as both need careful management setting clear guidelines and deadlines. Bottom-up migration on the other hand, needs careful coordination as it is likely to lead to quick-wins for customers and for operations, but it may also lead to a slow implementation process that halts half-way without truly changing the whole organization. It also requires involvement of the employees on the operational level, who need to drive the change. Although this presents a risk, it also provides an opportunity to involve them in the change process. The main risk of top-down migration is resistance to change that is enforced on the operational level and a lack of support for MCSP.

'Making middle management or the project team responsible for the migration?'

The final change management strategy concerns the responsibility for the migration process. A choice can be made to make the middle management responsible or a specialized project team can be set up. In case the project team is responsible, the team has more freedom to be innovative as they operate at a greater distance from everyday operations. Its risk is, however, that the organization may not accept a solution designed by a project team that is seen as an 'outsider'. When the middle management is responsible for the migration, the process is more likely to become easily accepted as part of day-to-day operations. The risk is, however, that the current way of doing business is the dominant factor in determining the migration process. This could mean that innovations do not find their way in the organization, implementing MCSP in a suboptimal way.

3. Case studies

In order to find out which of the eight migration strategies that were identified in the previous section are used in practice, we carried out four case studies in government organizations implementing MCSP in the Netherlands. The organizations were selected as they were in different stadia of development and we explored which migration strategies they employed as well as the reason for choosing a specific migration strategy. Furthermore, we investigated situational factors that were considered influential in determining the choice for a specific migration strategy for MCSP. Two cases are large executive agencies and the other two cases are local government organizations, one large municipality and one medium-sized. We used a combination of studying policy documents and semi-structured interviews for gathering information. Six people were interviewed in total, including four project leaders responsible for implementing MCSP as well as an architect and a manager of the service delivery department. The interviews were held in June and July 2009. Each interview lasted around one hour.

3.1. Mid-sized municipality

The first municipality under study is a local government with a little over 200.000 inhabitants. A few years ago the municipality set out to improve its service delivery after a very critical article appeared in a local newspaper. Implementation of MCSP was one among a number of initiatives to improve service delivery to citizens. The department driving these improvements of service delivery was the citizens' services department, as this department was the front runner in the area of service delivery within the municipal organization.

For implementation of MCSP an organization-wide action plan was set up by a project team within the citizens' services department and all other municipal departments were persuaded to get on board. The migration, thereby, effectively started in the front office of the organization and was initiated in a bottom-up manner. Simultaneously, MCSP was also enforced top-down as the management team of the municipality announced that it would oblige departments to migrate to MCSP. Until this enforcement was effected, a strategy was pursued aiming to achieve efforts bottom-up within those departments willing to change their way of working. Another top-down strategy deployed by the project team was to make MCSP a political issue ensuring that a sense of urgency is created in the organization. For political reasons, the potential efficiency gains of MCSP were stressed within the implementation program.

The migration took place stepwise by first engaging those departments that are willing to collaborate and change their work practices. Furthermore, the migration took place channel by channel by making 'smart combinations' and finding quick-wins in the existing information systems. The main reason for this was that it was believed to be important to celebrate the achievements during the project. These achievements were then used to create commitment among managers, who were ultimately made responsible for the migration to MCSP within their department. In time, a more top-down enforcement became effective for those departments in the organization not willing to change on a voluntary basis. Until then, fragmentation of the organization was considered a major obstacle as budgets are tied up with departments. It remained difficult, therefore, to develop a plan for the organization as a whole.

3.2. Large municipality

In 2005 this municipality started a program to improve its service delivery across the organization. Shortly afterwards, the program merged with the municipality's citizen's service department. The first phase of the program, between 2005 and 2008, aimed to develop the different service delivery channels, separately. Since 2008, joining up of services using life events and implementation of MCSP were aimed for. For the implementation of MCSP, an action plan was set up to develop the internet channel further and to make this channel leading in all service delivery. An important reason for this was the financial situation of the municipality that made setting up service delivery in a more cost-efficient way even more important than before. As the front office initiated the necessary changes, back office and mid office began to lag behind and their information supply and content management needed to be made up-to-date to enable further improvements in service delivery. Although it was considered important that the back office was sufficiently developed to support MCSP, it was decided that the program could not wait for this. Therefore, development of the channels and coordinating the channels continued at the same time.

The first steps of migrating to MCSP were made by identifying quick-wins, for example by making the migration of the top-10 of the most used products (e.g. parking license issuance and complaint filing) a priority. In this way, the first benefits would be visible to citizens soon. The employees working in the service delivering front office were involved in the changes that were made, as they possess a lot of knowledge on how to improve their daily operations. Purely enforcing things top-down was not believed to achieve the right things, while stakeholder involvement was considered very important for showing the organization how MCSP can be used to improve operations. The topic by topic migration was, thus, undertaken by employing a process management strategy, engaging stakeholders from the different sub-departments for every step that was taken. The organization was convinced that this was the only way to commit all its different departments to such a large-scale changes.

Implementing MSCP in this large municipality was even more complex than in a smaller municipality because of the large, highly autonomous departments within the organization. Additionally, the administration of this municipality consists of a number of elected area councils for specific neighbourhoods in addition to a city council for the whole municipality. Service delivery to citizens is undertaken by these offices instead of centrally. As a result, a number of different websites and offices existed throughout the city with a relative high degree of autonomy. To get all departments and organizations on board was a difficult process, especially as many local politicians had different targets for the service delivery in their area. To mitigate some of the fragmentation, the implementation program deliberately sought top management support. Another factor considered very important was to include management and steering information in the information systems. Otherwise, management would not be able to understand the implications of implementation.

3.3. Inland Revenue Service

The Inland Revenue Service (IRS) already had well-developed channels, but its channels were hardly coordinated. Instead, all channels were supported by separate information systems and different departments were responsible for the various service channels, which made it difficult to harmonize the service delivery of channels. Still, the first steps towards MCSP were taken as the organization saw the need for coordinating its service delivery channels. MCSP migration would be driven by client demands, as this was considered to be the only way to achieve the necessary consistency of service delivery. Segmentation of clients was used as a way to distinguish channels as different client groups have different needs and wishes for their contact with the organization.

Before migration started, to support the front end, the information used in the back office for the different service channels needed to be harmonized. The first steps towards this harmonization were made by sharing the data used by the telephone (the leading channel) with the internet channel and the service desks. But before any coordination could take place, the back office supporting the channels with essential data needed to be updated first. If the necessary data were not available for the different channels in a synchronized manner, MCSP could not be achieved. Therefore, work process change was considered as the only possible starting point for the migration. Furthermore, the organization started out by migrating the processes that have the largest scale as this would have most impact on the organization.

The interviewees indicated that the most important strategies for migration to MCSP were related to the organizational change that needed to be made to ensure that the whole organization works with a consistent image of the client in mind. This change took place step by step as making large-scale changes at once was not feasible in such a large organization. Also, to manage change, middle management remained responsible for the migration as they were ultimately responsible for the service delivery of the organization. The front office changes preceded the changes in the back office as this allowed all process changes to be undertaken in a client-centred manner.

3.4. Student loan organization

Service delivery of the student loan organization used to be organized very badly. So badly, that total redesign of the organization was considered necessary; low ratings of its services required radical change. Coordinating the service channels was considered necessary to solve the problems of the telephone channel that was unable to handle all service requests. Therefore, one front office department was set up to support MCSP. Its main objective was to relieve the phone channel and attract more people to the website. This front office department harmonized the client image in order for all channels to treat the clients in the same manner using the same information. Service delivery, thereby, became a second primary process (in addition to handling student loans) instead of a secondary process. By now, the organization has successfully attracted many clients to its website.

This migration took place incrementally over the course of five years, and currently, the organization successfully employs MCSP as one of the first organizations in the Netherlands. However, as the front office was the starting point of implementing MCSP, the back office started to represent a major problem for multi-channel service delivery, as it could not keep up with the re-organized front office. Back office systems, thus, were subsequently migrated to support the new situation. To achieve the migration top management support has been paramount. The drive for efficiency ran into resistance at other departments that felt threatened by the developments. Therefore, it was necessary to have a formalized mandate for MCSP to be implemented, supported by the management levels. This mandate functioned as a 'stick' forcing departments to change according to the requirements of the service delivery department for MCSP.

4. Findings

After the strategies for implementing MCSP deployed in the case studies were identified, they were evaluated in an expert workshop held in December 2009. Around twenty-five officials from government agencies implementing or planning to implement MCSP took part in this workshop.

4.1. Findings from the case studies

The findings from the case studies per strategy are summarized in Table 1. This table shows that a variety of strategies is employed. Still, some recurring patterns can be observed. The design strategies that had a clear tendency towards one of the extremes were the first (front office or back office) and the fourth (quick-wins or radical redesign). To be able to improve the service delivery to clients quickly, changing the front office first was considered to be the best option in all cases.

Table 1: Migration strategies deployed in case studies

	Mid-sized municipality	**Large municipality**	**Inland Revenue Service**	**Student loan organization**
Front office - Back office	Front office	Front office; but also call for changing back office at the same time	Front office; no money for large re-organization projects	Front office; re-organization starts with the client in mind
Changing IT – Organization	IT for specific projects that need to be implemented fast; organizational change at the same time	Both; IT still needs to be implemented, but organizational change is considered important	Organizational change	Both
Channel by channel – All at the same time	Channel by channel	All at the same time	Channel by channel	All at the same time
Quick-wins – Radical redesign	Quick-wins	Quick-wins	Quick-wins	Radical redesign; because of urgency
Big-bang – Step-by-step	Both; different strategies for different channels	Step-by-step	Step-by-step	Step-by-step
Project – Process	Process; emphasis on getting departments involved	Process; emphasis on getting departments involved	Process; parts as a project	*Unknown*
Top-down – Bottom-up	Both at the same time	Top-down	Top-down (consistent leadership) and bottom-up (execution)	Top-down; but also bottom-up examples
Management – Project team responsible	Both; project team in place, management responsible	Middle management	Middle management	Both; responsibility with management, project team for implementation

Also the need to create 'a consistent image of the client' throughout the organization was mentioned as a reason to change the front office first. Our interviewees remarked that perhaps in case the back office has considerable legacy it may need to be updated first to be able to achieve a sufficient degree of information quality that is necessary before the front office can be updated. The second design strategy that was widely considered more suitable for migration to MCSP was a migration process implementing quick-wins first before moving on to organization-wide redesign. The celebration of quick-wins to create support among 'non-believers' was found to be very important, while sense of urgency was mentioned as the one incentive for the choice to radically redesign the organization first. The two strategies that were not clearly indicated to entail a best option were said to depend on the specific circumstances. For instance, the choice for changing all channels at the same time or one-by-one was said to depend on the degree to which the channels already use the same information.

The preferred change trajectory was incremental to ensure a high level of involvement and participation. The tendency to migrate gradually became apparent as this was considered better manageable than taking a 'big-bang' approach. This can be explained by the Dutch organizational culture which is characterized by negotiation and seeking consensus. Similarly, three of the four case studies favoured managing the migration as a 'process' giving greater attention to creating support for the change process. Still, some portions of projects were managed as a 'project', as this was found to be more efficient. Furthermore, these three cases emphasized the need for process management and for gaining support of all (important) stakeholders. MCSP is considered to be a change that needs to have a broad support within the organization and process management is believed to be more suitable for such a large-scale migration process. Top-down implementation was more often mentioned than bottom-up because vision and leadership were considered very important in the migration process. Still, some cases did carry out parts of the migration bottom-up to involve the operational level in an early stage. And finally, responsibility tends to be in the hands of the middle management more often, although a project team is responsible for implementation in some cases. The reason for this was that the case studies favoured management support over innovation.

4.2. Evaluation of findings in expert workshop

After the strategies employed by the case studies were identified, we evaluated the findings in a second expert meeting.

We set up a survey in which we asked the participants, firstly, which type of strategies they consider to be more important for achieving successful migration: design strategies or change management strategies.

We asked them to rank the importance of design strategies in relation to change strategies on a seven-point scale ranging from (1) only the former strategy important to (4) both strategies equally important to (7) only the latter strategy important. Secondly, we asked the respondents which strategies they employ in their own organizations by asking them to score the extent to which each of the two axes of the eight migration strategies are deployed within their organizations on a comparable seven-point scale. We deliberately evaluated the findings from the case studies by asking the participants to express a preference for a type of strategy or to indicate which of the two extremes most resembled the situation in their organization. Although some of the participants indicated that they found it hard to make this decision as they maintained that both extremes go hand in hand, some patterns can be recognized giving insight in the preferences for certain migration strategies in practice. Thirteen people filled out this survey and its findings are summarized in Tables 2 and 3. The numbers in the tables refer to the amount of experts that chose the specific answer.

The findings of the expert workshop confirm the findings from the case studies. Nevertheless, some small differences can be observed. First of all, the workshop confirms the relative importance of having a change management strategy in place, which was observed in the case studies. Secondly, also the tendency to start with changing the front office was confirmed. A third observation is that while the implementation of IT was seen to be leading in some cases (even though all case studies considered organizational change to be very important), during the evaluation in the expert workshop a clear tendency to change the organization first can be observed. The interviewees from the case studies indicated that there are some situations in which it is useful to change the IT first. For example, this can be the case when the complexity of the technology to be implemented is low or in case there is it will take too long to wait for everyone in the organization to be ready for implementation. As was the case in the cases, also in the evaluation workshop the choice between changing all channels at the same time and changing the channels one-by-one is spread out more evenly.

Table 2: Evaluation of migration strategies in expert workshop

Relative importance of change management and design strategies							
	Only former strategy important	Former much more important	Former strategy more important	Both strategies equally important	Latter strategy more important	Latter much more important	Only latter strategy important
Change management – Design strategies		4	3	6			

Table 3: Evaluation of migration strategies in expert workshop

Migration strategies deployed in practice							
	Only former strategy employed	Former much more employed	Former strategy more employed	Both strategies equally employed	Latter strategy more employed	Latter much more employed	Only latter strategy employed
Front office – Back office		1	7	4	1		
Changing IT – Organization			1	4	4	4	
Channel by channel – All at same time	1	3	3	2	1	1	2
Quick-wins – Radical design		3	8	2			

Migration strategies deployed in practice							
	Only former strategy employed	Former much more employed	Former strategy more employed	Both strategies equally employed	Latter strategy more employed	Latter much more employed	Only latter strategy employed
Big-bang – Step-by-step			1	1	2	7	2
*'Project' – Process'**			1	3	2	5	2
Top-down – Bottom-up		1	3	4	1	4	
Management – Project team responsible	1	5	3	3			
* One respondent indicated not to know the answer to this question.							

The findings of the expert workshop confirm the findings from the case studies. Nevertheless, some small differences can be observed. First of all, the workshop confirms the relative importance of having a change management strategy in place, which was observed in the case studies. Secondly, also the tendency to start with changing the front office was confirmed. A third observation is that while the implementation of IT was seen to be leading in some cases (even though all case studies considered organizational change to be very important), during the evaluation in the expert workshop a clear tendency to change the organization first can be observed. The interviewees from the case studies indicated that there are some situations in which it is useful to change the IT first. For example, this can be the case when the complexity of the technology to be implemented is low or in case there is it will take too long to wait for everyone in the organization to be ready for implementation. As was the case in the cases, also in the evaluation workshop the choice between changing all channels at the same time and changing the channels one-by-one is spread out more evenly.

During the expert workshop celebrating quick-wins was considered more important but not much more important as was observed in the case studies, thereby implying that having a vision for the redesign is also valued highly. For the change management strategies, the importance of step-by-step change and managing the migration as a process are confirmed. And top-down implementation was more often mentioned than bottom-up because vision and leadership were considered very important in the migration process, while during the expert workshop a tendency towards bottom-up implementation can be observed. Finally, the importance of making the middle management responsible for the migration process is clearly confirmed by the expert workshop.

5. Discussion

In both the case studies and the expert workshop the importance of having a clear change management strategy in place was stressed, indicating that having the right design strategy is considered less important. All interviewees and respondents during the expert workshops indicated that undertaking such a complex organizational change requires most attention in guiding the changes within the organization. The exact order of changes was considered to be of secondary importance, although, naturally, having a plan for migration in a certain order was valued highly too. While this research makes use of ideal types representing two 'extremes' for analytical purposes, both the interviewees in the case studies and the experts in the workshop indicated that in reality often a mix between the two extremes can be found. Still, among the design strategies as well as the change strategies some strategies were considered more effective than others and patterns were identified.

Which factors influence effective migration likely depends on the organizational characteristics as well as on the organizational environment. Between the two categories of case studies examined, some fundamental differences could be observed potentially influencing the migration strategies deployed. Therefore, we investigated the major differences between the two types of organizations, which are summarized in Table 5.

Some of the major differences between the two types of organizations are the client base, the number and variety of products and the number of applications of a certain product and the political involvement. While the client base of an executive agency that deals with a specific government service is often more homogeneous, such as in the case of the student loan organization that deals with students, municipalities as well as the IRS have to deal with all inhabitants.

Table 5: Differences in organizational characteristics between municipalities and executive agencies

	Municipalities	**Executive agencies**
Client base	Heterogeneous	Usually more homogeneous (does not apply to the IRS client base)
Number and variety of products and services	Many heterogeneous	Less and more homogeneous
Number of product applications	A few per product	Many per product
Political involvement	City council is heavily involved	Larger distance to central government, except when things go wrong

They may, thus, encounter much greater differences in clients' needs and wishes than most executive agencies. The same is the case for the number and the variety of products on offer. While municipalities deal with a great number of different services and products, executive agencies can usually focus on less and more homogeneous services and products. The number of applications for a certain service, however, is usually much larger for executive agencies (the IRS and the student loan organization process millions of applications of a specific product every year) than for municipalities, who may, in certain cases, only process a few applications of a product per year. A final major difference between the two types of organizations is the political involvement. While every municipality has an elected local government involved in its operations, executive agencies fall usually under the responsibility of a Ministry. Only when things go wrong Parliament may decide to interfere in its business, but usually they have more discretionary space for action.

Which choice for a migration strategy is most successful likely depends on the situation within the organization that undertakes migration as well as on its environment. Situational factors that were found to be of influence in the case studies on the choice for a specific strategy include: coherence among the channels, complexity of the new situation, lead time, client-centeredness, acceptance within the organization, innovation, support for the change process and speed of first success. While looking at the situational factors and the difference between the different types of organization, factors of influence on the choice for a specific strategy include the scale of the processes and the number of applications for a single product, the degree of autonomy of the different departments having to cooperate realizing MCSP and the level of political involvement. Further research should look into how these factors influence the effectiveness of the migration strategies more closely. The impact and relative importance of these situational factors and organizational characteristics should also be looked at more closely by deriving critical success factors (CSF's) for migration to MCSP.

6. Conclusion

Migration to MCSP is a complex undertaking, requiring changes to occur in the organization, work processes and the technology as well as in the culture of the organization. Public organizations are in search of the right migration strategy for their specific circumstances. This paper explores which migration strategies are deployed by government organizations in the Netherlands and the circumstantial factors influential in choosing a specific change strategy. Eight decisions are identified influencing the strategy and subsequently divided into two types: design strategies and change management strategies. By looking at four case studies we have indications that practitioners consider having a change management strategy in place guiding migration more important than choosing a design strategy determining the order of migration. The findings from the case studies were confirmed by an expert panel evaluating the findings, although some minor differences were observed, mainly depending on differing situational factors.

Although our findings should be generalized with care, we observed that public agencies foremost manage migration to MCSP as a re-organization process. This is reflected in the higher occurrence of the migration strategy managing the migration as a 'process' carefully making decisions, than as an implementation 'project' with clear implementation deadlines. Furthermore, we found that organizations prefer a gradual migration process, as both a step-wise migration and the celebration of quick-wins are often mentioned strategies. Many organizations also consider the client to be the leading factor in reorganizing the organization, by choosing an order for implementing MCSP starting in the front office more often than in the back office. A final observation is that responsibility for the migration process is more often in the hands of the middle management than the responsibility of a separate project team. Further research should look into deeper the matter of which strategies are most suitable under which circumstances and determine critical success factors.

References

Armour, F.J., Kaisler, S.H. and Liu, S.Y. (1999) "A big-picture look at Enterprise Architecture," *IEEE IT Professional*, Vol. 1, No. 1, pp. 35-42.

Bannister, F. (2001) "Dismantling the silos: extracting new value from IT investments in public administration," *Information Systems Journal*, Vol. 11, No. 1, pp. 65-84.

Beynon-Davies, P. and Williams, M.D. (2003) "Evaluating electronic local government in the UK," *Journal of Information Technology*, Vol. 18, No. 2, pp. 137-149.

Bruijn, J. A. de, ten Heuvelhof, E.F. and in ’t Veld. R.J. (1998) *Procesmanagement. Over procesontwerp en besluitvorming*, Academic service, Schoonhoven.

Bruijn, J.A. de and ten Heuvelhof, E.F. (2000) *Networks and Decision Making*, Lemma, Utrecht.

Chisholm, D. (1989) *Coordination without Hierarchy. Informal structures in multi-organizational systems*, University of California Press, Berkeley.

Curtin, G.C. and Sommer, M.H. et al. (2004) *The world of e-Government*, Haworth Press, Binghampton.

Ebbers, W.A., Pieterson W.J. and Noordman, H.N. (2008) "Electronic government: Rethinking channel management strategies," *Government Information Quarterly*, Vol. 25, No. 2, pp. 181-201.

Fernandez, S. and Rainey H.G. (2006) "Managing Successful Organizational Change in the Public Sector," *Public Administration Review*, Vol. 66, No. 2, pp. 168-176.

Janssen, M. and van Veenstra, A.F. (2005) "Stages of Growth in E-Government: An Architectural Approach," *Electronic Journal of e-Government*, Vol. 3, No. 4, pp. 193-200.

Janssen, M., Chun S.A. and Gil-Garcia, J.R. (2009) "Building the Next Generation of Digital Government Infrastructures," *Government Information Quarterly*, Vol. 26, No. 2, pp. 233-237.

Kernaghan, K. (2005) "Moving towards the virtual state: integrating services and service channels for citizen-centred delivery," *International Review of Administrative Sciences*, Vol. 71, No. 1, pp. 119-131.

Ongaro, E. (2004) "Process management in the public sector: The experience of one-stop shops in Italy," *International Journal of Public Sector Management*, Vol. 17, No. 1, pp. 81-107.

Parisopoulos, K., Tambouris E. and Tarabanis, K. (2009) "Transformational Government in Europe: A Survey of National Policies," In: *Lecture Notes in Artificial Intelligence 5736*, Lytras, M.D. et al. (Eds.), Springer, Berlin Heidelberg.

Powell, W.W. (Ed.) (1991) *Neither Market nor Hierarchy: Network Forms of Organization*, Sage Publications, London.

Richardson, R. (1994) "Back-officing front office functions - organizational and locational implications of new telemediated services," in: *Management of Information and Communication Technologies, Emerging Patterns of Control*, ASLIB, London, pp. 309-335.

Veenstra, A.F. van, Janssen, M. and Klievink, B. (2009) "Strategies for Orchestrating and Managing Supply Chains in Public Service Networks," *Electronic Journal of e-Government*, Vol. 7, No. 4, pp. 425-432.

Voort, H. van der, de Bruijn, H. and Janssen, M. (2009) "Shared Service Centers in the public sector: Benefits, risks and transformation strategies," in: *Handbook of Research on ICT-Enabled Transformational Government: A Global Perspective*, Weerakkody, V., Janssen, M. and Dwivedi, Y.K. (Eds.), Information Science Reference, Hershey, NY.

Government as Part of the Revolution: Using Social Media to Achieve Public Goals

David Landsbergen
Ohio State University, Columbus, Ohio, USA
Landsbergen.1@osu.edu
Originally published in EJEG (2010) Volume 8, Issue 2.

Editorial Commentary

In the last five years there has been a massive increase in the use of social media: Landsbergen points out that social media are being hailed as "paradigm shifting" and their effect is likely to be as significant as the printing press as a means of disseminating and sharing information and knowledge. Hyperbole aside, Landsbergen argues that social media provide national and local government with an opportunity to reconsider "how it does things" and to change policy and procedures "in a way that improves government". His research is an exploratory in that he focuses on developing answers to the question of how social media can help government do things differently and perhaps penetrate the consciousness of population groups that have previously been marginal to government.

Landsbergen emphasises the communications potential of social media in that they are interactive and multimedia, they can exploit or facilitate the development of human networks and they are non-hierarchic. Perhaps the most important lesson that government has to learn here is that social networks are not broadcasting tools but two-way communications tools: this is important in that government has traditionally displayed a broadcasting mindset given its long history of using newspapers, press releases and static web pages. Of critical importance is that social media have the potential to blur boundaries between government and the governed and between government and the multitude of public and private bodies with which it interacts. Given this blurring, Landsbergen emphasises that developing trust is essential in enabling networks to operate effectively. He argues that government bodies will need to develop the skills of administrators so that they become more responsive to citizens while maintaining public trust in the probity and responsiveness of government. Government use of social media is not without risk but Landsbergen identifies various strategies by which these risks can be mitigated. Social media do, indeed, provide government with a "window of opportunity" but government still has many lessons to learn here.

Abstract: Social media is growing rapidly because it supports some important social needs. Government will need to understand how social media support these social needs if government is to use social media well. Social media supports the increased reliance on human networks, the need for rapid interactive communications, the need to blur what is private and public, and the need for engaging multimedia. Whether government can use social media will depend upon how well government can see, understand, and attend to these needs. Can government move from hierarchical, controlled communications to where it is just an (important) node within a network? Social media is about fast, interactive communications. How will bureaucracies adapt to the increased pressures for timely responses? Social media, therefore, presents novel and challenging strategic, policy, and managerial issues for many US governments. This paper reports on an environmental scan of the important issues facing US governments and the creative ways in which they are adapting to the challenges. This is supplemented by an in-depth participant-observation study of the use of social media by several departments within the City of Columbus, State of Ohio, USA. Proponents of social media, like those of the early days of the Internet, are wildly enthusiastic about how much social media can do to improve government. Claims are made that this technology is paradigm-shifting, like the printing press, which put knowledge into the hands of the ordinary person. Given the many policy and managerial issues yet to be resolved, it is clear that there is no technology imperative that will necessarily drive government to become more democratic. Early web government pages could have been made more interactive, yet they primarily took on the task of broadcasting a one way instead of a two way flow of information. There is no reason to believe that Twitter would not follow the same path. It could easily become an application whose only benefit is in more quickly broadcasting information to a mobile phone. A better way to think about social media is that it merely provides a small window of opportunity, which for a short period of time, allows government to comprehensively re-examine how it does things, and thereby, provides the opportunity to change policies and procedures in a way that improves government. Governments typically ask how can we adapt social media to the way in which we do business? A very different question is how can social media provide us a way to do things in way that we have not done before? The question that is asked will determine whether a revolution will actually place.

Keywords: social media, Gov 2.0, e-governance, e-Government, social capital

1. Should we take the chance?

A recent *Cleveland Plain-Dealer* newspaper article reported on the use of Twitter by US state governments.

"When a tanker truck exploded July 15, closing a section of Interstate 75 near Detroit, hundreds of motorists were notified of the crash and detours via tweets from the Michigan Department of Transportation...

"The beauty of tweeting is that it just lends itself to emergency communications," said department spokeswoman Barbara Hicks...

Michigan is among about a dozen states that provide transportation information on social-networking sites by posting updates on Twitter, videos on YouTube and project details on Facebook...

Ohio isn't one of those states...

'We want to make sure that if we decide to use some of the social-networking sites we do it properly,' Varner [Ohio Department of Transportation spokesman [ODOT]] said." (Adapted from (Nieves, 2009))

Citizens were given space to comment on the article. One Ohio citizen came to the defence of Scott Varner. Most of the citizens excoriated ODOT's inability to keep up with the newest technologies.

While there is a risk in implementing these new communications poorly, there is also a risk in not doing it, or even doing it too slowly. Part of ODOT's hesitancy may come from not fully understanding what social media is, who is using it, and from that, being able to derive a good strategy, policy, and best practices.

2. What is social media? Why is it important to government?

2.1. Social media

Social media is really a communications tool rather than an IT application. It is a tool that supports communications within social networks.

The tremendous growth in social media is occurring because it is a set of tools that service several social communications needs. Social media is a tool that: 1) allows individuals to more easily use human networks; 2) expects interactive rather than broadcast communications; 3) is powerful because it uses not only text, but video and audio as well ("multimedia") and 4) relies on measures and objectives to facilitate communication.

Social media is growing because of the increasing importance of networks. There is an ongoing debate within policy circles about the relative efficacy of markets or bureaucracies (government or private sector) in getting things done. But there is a third institution – networks. Networks span across and within, public, private, and non-profit sector organizations. In many cases, they can more quickly and accurately provide answers to questions like: "Whom do you know that can get something done for me?" "Who can I ask to get the correct information I need?"

Social media is also powerful because it supports two-way, interactive rather than one-way, broadcast communications. People want easy access to the information they need and the relationships they want to develop. In a world dominated by broadcasting, whether it is television, the daily newspaper, or static web pages, institutions dictate what information is communicated.

Interactive communications, the use of multimedia, becoming "part of" a network instead of assuming command and control imply very different ways for how government does its work. At this juncture, governments are deciding whether they want to cultivate, support, and become an integral part of these networks, or just remain on the periphery.

This view is very new and probably challenging to the current way of getting things done and how government engages in building a longer-term strategy. It is also challenging to how the government conducts its day-to-day operations and the long-term goal of improving its relationship with its citizens.

One of the most important trends in governance, and perhaps society as a whole, has been the blurring of the public and private sectors (Bozeman, 1987). Whether it is contracting out, collaborative government, the many hybrid organizations now being created, or the increasing interdependency of private organizations and public organizations, it is becoming increasing difficult to rely on notions of hierarchical command and control governance. The same blurring of what is public and private also permeates social media. Because social media blurs the public and the private (shows our humanity) and because it is interactive rather than broadcasting, it can help re-establish trust in government administrators.

Multimedia is a powerful component of most social media technologies, either because they employ or point to, visual and sound information as well as text. Humans are visual creatures and social media can tell a story or make the case for an argument in a far more compelling manner.

Objectives and measures are important to every public policy and management initiative. In the social media culture, they are of central importance. There are two important aspects of social media that need to be understood when it comes to objectives and measures. The first aspect is that if an organization or individual uses social media just to "be cool" or "with it", those efforts will quickly become diffused and scattered and a waste of time and resources. Focused objectives are necessary to use social media well. The second important aspect is that metrics are a central part of this culture. People count all things: messages, postings, and communications, across all kinds of groups. These measures of network influence focus on how important the message is and how important the communicator is. The ability to collect this data is enabled by the open source nature of the technology.

Popularity, membership in networks, and being seen and heard in these networks directly influences how effective governments will be in effectively using the technology. Popularity, in part, derives from the quality of the material and its potential interest to the intended audience. But popularity (and effectiveness) also are dependent upon how well the media is intrinsically understood by government, how creative its users are in thinking about the media can be used, and how well the particular features of the communications media are used on a daily basis. Governments can decide to "dabble" in social media, but the measures that are part of social media will quickly reveal if government is doing it well and if anybody is really listening.

It is important to see that these characteristics reinforce each other. The need for quick and reliable information is supported by the move to networks. The reduction in formality, the highly interactive and rapid nature of the technology, and the blurring of what is public and private, reduces communications barriers among the varied users within a network. The use of multimedia entices users into the networks and engages them. Measures help users gauge the quality of the message. Networks allow users to find other users who can "vouch" for the insure that the relevance, quality, and trustworthiness of the information.

Clearly, there are many government objectives and communications needs that are being adequately serviced by other communications media. What might be some examples of important government issues that could be addressed by using social media?

2.2. Why is it important to government?

Trust and social capital

Trust, or "social capital", is essential to how networks operate. Trust has also been an essential in explaining what constitutes good public administration (Wilson, 1887). In networks, individuals use trust in evaluating how good information is and they use social capital in evaluating a person's reputation and whether they can be trusted. In public administration, trust involves maintaining the delicate balance between having administrators be appropriately responsive to the people, and also having citizens trust administrators' experience and expertise so that citizens are not involved in every government decision. Administrators must also trust in democracy's sovereign – the citizen. In an age where networks are rising in importance, it is important to understand how trust is used in both bureaucracies and in networks to maximize government's efforts in achieving public goals.

Recent work on "social capital" offers promise in understanding how social media networks operate. "Social capital" includes the reputation that one has among their peers (Putnam, 1993) or the: 1) obligations and expectations that we have of one another; 2) the important information channels that sustain networks and informal organizations; and 3) the social norms that bind our actions and create an expectation that others will behave in predictable ways (Coleman, 1988). Research in this area examines how trust is created, nurtured, and measured.

If government wants to increase trust, it is important to understand that it is easier for citizens to vest their trust, not in the abstract institution "government" (Giddens, 1990), but in the people who work in government. Social media, unlike state web pages, offers citizens access to people. It offers a way to create tighter, social networks that support trust in government. The less that government is seen as a "faceless" website, and more as individuals who have a name, have a reputation, and can give a commitment about what can and will be done, the easier it will be to see government as something (someone) working on their behalf.

Social media strongly supports network communications and enables governments to communicate better within the multiple networks outside of government and the informal organization (networks) within government. Leveraging these networks offers enhanced opportunities to achieve public goals.

Making more effective use of dwindling resources

Government also faces tremendous challenges in finding the resources it needs to advance the public interest. It is clear that government cannot do it alone but, instead, must find creative and innovative ways to leverage resources outside of its control. Effectively using, and participating in, networks of individuals, organizations, and institutions, offers great promise in finding and mobilizing these resources towards achieving public goals.

Effectively using, and participating in, networks of individuals, organizations, and institutions, offers great promise in finding and mobilizing these resources to work for the public good ("co-production" (Ostrom, 1996) or "collaborative government" (Bingham et al., 2005)). Coordination of networks and managing partnerships and networks will become an increasingly important skill (Agranoff, 2007).

Increasing trust and making more effective use of dwindling resources are just two ways in which social media might be useful to government. Empirical research is needed to determine whether governments use social media in these ways and what implementation barriers they face.

3. Methods

At present there is very little empirical research on the use of social media by government. When the City of Columbus, Ohio, USA, decided to engage in an experiment with social media, the author was asked to provide advice and guidance on the study. In particular, the author was asked to make suggestions about: 1) how social media could be better utilized; 2) to conduct a scan of how other governments were using social media; and 3) to write up specific recommendations on how Columbus might want to change its various ITC policies.

This request provided an opportunity to conduct an embedded singe-case study to develop insights about how government could use social media and what some of difficulties in using social media might be. The goal was to develop a "thick description" of the important issues and their interplay that could generate propositions for further study. The participant observant research yielded a report (Landsbergen, 2009) identifying the opportunities and risks in using social media, best practices as revealed through an environmental scan of what Columbus and other US governments were doing, and specific language supporting the recommended policy changes. Further discussion of some of the issues uncovered and the recommendations on how to deal with these issues can be found in Sections 4 and 5, below.

3.1. Let all flowers bloom

Columbus is the state capital of Ohio, a Midwestern state in the United States. It is the sixteenth largest city in the US and has a population of approximately 755,000, ahead of Cleveland, Ohio (population 438,000) and Cincinnati (population 331,285) (2008 US Census).

Interestingly, the City's decision to experiment was instigated by the need to respond to a potential crisis situation - the Health Department's success in using Twitter and Facebook to broadcast information about the H1N1 virus. In addition, earlier initiatives by a rival branch of government – the elected City Council - in using Twitter and Facebook, created competitive pressures the executive branch departments to innovate.

With the explosion of interest in social media, The Department of Technology (DOT) wanted to make sure that any "rogue experiments" in social media were covered by the City's policies on communications, information technology, security, and public records. In addition, the DOT, to its credit, decided that every department could benefit from the collective experience of those departments already using social media. The shared experience could also help in developing a shared vision for how central resources could make better use of the new technology. City departments were asked to send representatives to an *ad hoc* group (hereinafter, "Social Media Group"). Representatives included staff already working with social media, as well as communications professionals, IT security professionals, and human resources managers. Approximately twenty core members participated on a regular basis and up to thirty-five members who participated at least once. The Department of Technology sponsored the meetings and provided technical and logistical support.

3.2. Participatory action research to generate insights and recommendations

The study utilized a participatory action research approach on a single case study with an embedded design (Kemmis and McTaggart, 2000, Yin, 2003). The City of Columbus was the unit of analysis of the case study. Embedded within that case study, was an examination of how the different city departments utilized social media. (See Table 1, *infra*.) The goal of participatory action research is to become a member of a group and thereby gain trust and greater access to the thoughts and opinions of the group. The action orientation comes in taking the thick description resulting from the case study and then pushing the group towards action outcomes, including recommended policies and management practices.

The research began with the author being introduced to the Social Media Group and given an opportunity to explain his role of both facilitating the discussions of the group and providing outside ideas from what other cities and states were doing with social media. After this initial introduction, the researchers attended the weekly meetings, and mostly listened, in order to learn the culture, identify key informants, and gain trust.

The weekly meetings lasted approximately two hours with the first hour devoted to exchanging ideas and technical knowledge. The second half of the hour consisted of a presentation from someone in the larger community on some aspect of social media, including such topics as the importance of marketing or branding. In addition to the weekly meetings, a Facebook was set up to facilitate asynchronous discussion. Informal interviews were conducted with all of the core members at least once during the regular meetings. The conversations surfaced the various concerns of the group and were captured and posted on the Facebook page for comment.

Table 1: Use of social media by the City of Columbus

Columbus Unit	Link to relevant pilot project
City Council	*Twitter*: http://twitter.com/ColumbusCouncil *Facebook*: http://www.facebook.com/pages/Columbus-OH/Columbus-City-Council/75764527681?ref=ts *Podcasts*: http://www.columbuscitycouncil.org/media.aspx?id=5104&menu_id=520
Dept. of Health	*Twitter*: http://twitter.com/columbushealth *Facebook*: http://www.facebook.com/ColumbusPublicHealth
Dept. of Development	*Facebook*: http://www.facebook.com/pages/Columbus-OH/Columbus-Planning/115991001536
Dept. of Public Service	*Twitter*: http://twitter.com/pavingthewayoh
Columbus Police	*Twitter*: http://twitter.com/columbuspolice *Facebook*: http://www.facebook.com/pages/Columbus-OH/Columbus-Division-of-Police/92955766761?ref=ts

Observational notes of the meetings were taken by both the author and his graduate student and immediately compared after the meeting. Triangulation was employed to validate the observations and the action recommendations using the participant-observer notes, the various Facebook posts, Twitter messages, and interviews.

Systematic, structured interviews were conducted of almost all of the core members. Interview questions were drawn from prior research about the drivers and inhibitors of public sector ITC. Over time, however, the interviews yielded additional questions that were unique to social media. Interviews typically lasted about an hour and included such general questions as the genesis for using social media; 2) what successes they had enjoyed; 3) what challenges they faced; and 4) how their work related to the unit of analysis, the City of Columbus. The observations and recommendations were posted on the group's Facebook page for feedback.

The group was also provided with information from the environmental scan of what other governmental units were doing with social media (See Table 2, *infra*) so that the group could make more informed decisions about what the significant issues and potential solutions were. A final report was made to the City that was based upon both the environmental scan and the findings and recommendations of the social media group.

4. Results

4.1. Environmental scan – how are other governments using social media?

While several Columbus units individually began experimenting with social media, the best way to understand what social media can possibly do, is through actually seeing many examples of how other cities and government agencies are using these media in new and powerful ways. A broad environmental scan complemented the in-depth case study of Columbus.

The environmental scan involved a comprehensive search for any interesting use of social media by national federal, state, and local governments of English-speaking nations. There were several goals. The most immediate goal was to identify policies and best practices that could help identify issues and policies for the two social media of immediate concern, Twitter and Facebook. Moving beyond the short-term goal of finding wording and concepts that could build a good policy and set of practices, was the longer-term goal of identifying other ways in which other types of social media could be employed. Phone interviews and email exchanges were used to obtain details about interesting and unique implementation schemes. These various uses of social media were collected into one framework. Table 2, identifies the many ways in which social media can improve government and governance. (See Table 2, *infra*). For a more thorough discussion of this framework, interesting and representative examples, and some of the attendant implementation issues, see (Landsbergen, 2010). Five basic mechanisms were identified:

- Competitive elites (political and bureaucratic) respond to requests for information and service from voters. Some of the linkages include obtaining information, working through groups to articulate their interests, politically influencing those elites, and then holding those elites accountable. This is an ideal model. Supporting the claim that social media can improve government would require examining all of these, and other, linkages.
- Social media can increase rule compliance by involving citizens in the formation of rules leading to higher legitimacy and therefore higher compliance. It can also enlist citizens in the policing of legal norms.
- Civic Virtue increases because social media supports human networked communications and the cultivation of social capital. Here, the claim is not that decision-makers will be more responsive to peoples' needs, but rather that the preferences of those demands will become more public in nature (Boix and Posner, 1998).
- Bureaucratic efficiency and effectiveness increased for silo-driven government and by facilitating the networks that characterize informal organizations.
- Social media increases social and digital inclusion and thereby political inclusion. It also supports the identification of new leaders and leading organizations.

Table 2: Mechanisms by which social media can realize Gov. 2.0

Mechanism	Variety
1. Ideal model: Rational voters and competitive elites	
	Respond to requests for information
	Public / Private partnerships to respond to requests for information
	Respond to requests for service
	Public / Private partnerships to respond to requests for service
	Helps citizens educate each other
	Helps citizens synthesize, refine, and articulate needs
	Hold government accountable
2. Rule compliance: Creating, implementing and enforcing governmental policies & regulations	

Mechanism	Variety
	Participation in the policy process
	Implementing laws and rules
	Enforcement of thefts
3. Civic virtue : Will social media, because of its public nature, create more civic virtue?	
	Political elites push for, and highlight, the innovative use of social media
4. Bureaucratic efficiency: Improved communications within bureaucracies, among bureaucracies, and between bureaucracies and their stakeholders (G2C and G2B).	
	Cheaper and more effective communications
	Faster communications
	Produce an *esprit de corps* within government
5. Empowering individuals and developing new leaders	
	Digital Inclusion – Demographics of social media
	Social Inclusion - Empowering stakeholders who would not other-wise be heard
	Political Inclusion – Translating digital and social inclusion into greater political inclusion
	Enabling the faster exchange of good ideas and practices
	Making it easier for persons of similar interests to find and work with one another

4.2. Case study analysis

The case study and environmental scan yielded interesting and unexpected sets of issues. The group debated these issues and made many recommendations, including changes to the various policies, in a final report to the City (Please see Section 3. Methods). Due to space limitations, a subset of issues and recommendations are discussed for their potential interest to an international audience.

Lack of organizational resources

Twitter and Facebook are technologies that support both one-way and two-way communications. The easy, and perhaps first use of this medium is similar to a static web page in which the same information is simply broadcasted to the public. The added value in using Twitter or Facebook is that interested parties would receive faster updates of information.

But most people see the real benefit of social media in its support of two-way, interactive communication. The social media culture is such that, unless there is a clear reason to do otherwise, users get tired of being sent a steady stream of information that they could always see. Unfortunately, there is a danger that most governments are now becoming "stuck" in this familiar mode.

But a genuine concern was raised as to how some departments could afford the time to support still another media outlet to populate with information? Of even greater concern was whether an expectation that communications officers now be required to respond to direct requests for information? Where there are not enough people to get the job done now, what would happen if now the organization had to spend time on social media everyday? Interviews with other jurisdictions, however, revealed that the resources demands were not as high as expected.

As to the use of an additional media to manage, good managerial practice is to use multiple media for the same message and technical solutions make that task easier. Interviews with other governments indicated that, where there was a focused project, there was not a significant increase in the demand for resources. Even more interesting is San Francisco's SF311 service, by which any citizen can send a short Tweet requesting a city service like fixing a pothole or cleaning up a refuse problem. San Francisco acknowledged that there was a danger that this could create an unrealistic expectation about government's ability to respond, but San Francisco also believed that it was still useful information. It could help the city understand demand and could be used to inform a collective discussion about the City's resource and spending priorities. Although the city had no numbers to substantiate the claim, they did not believe that there was a significant increase in the demand on resources.

Privacy

The issue of the blurring of public and private thoroughly suffuses social media implementation. On the positive side, the blurring of public and private might enable bureaucracies to present a human face to citizens. A more complicated set of issues surrounds the private lives of public employees. For example, does a government agency have the right to make demands on how public employees spend their time outside of the work environment? Because of the pervasiveness and ubiquity of social media, many codes of conduct now require employees to present themselves even in their private lives "in a professional light" that would not caste a negative light on the government. Insisting on this policy, and more importantly, how violations are sought out, raise significant privacy questions. Privacy could also include protecting the privacy or anonymity of citizens using Twitter or Facebook to contact a government entity.

Public records and records management law

Are the communications in Facebook and Twitter a public record? No clear case law has emerged on this yet, but according to Ohio statutory law, public records do not depend on the type of media but its content:

"An electronic record, …. , created … under the jurisdiction of any public office … which serves to document the organization, functions, … or other activities of the office." (Ohio Revised Code 149.011)

Once a record is deemed a public record, managers also need to attend to the records management concerns surrounding the: 1) retention, 2) retrieval, 3) disclosure, and 4) disposal of public records.

Given the possible ephemeral nature of electronic records, one very real concern was how to manage these records so that they could be made available should there be a public records request. New tools are appearing, but in the interim, RSS feeds could be used as the basis for sending the Twitter messages, so that the RSS feeds could be archived and managed. As to the Facebook pages, a similar problem occurs with web-based material. Two basic kinds of strategies have been developed: object-based or event-based capture of information. The choice of strategy depends on the nature of the material, how dynamic that material is, and the particular managerial responsibilities for oversight of that information.

An even more interesting development for the US is the "open data" movement. In these early experiments, the US federal government and cities like San Francisco, Washington DC, and London are supplying data using open standards to "civic entrepreneurs" who are then creating very useful phone "apps" or web pages. Especially exciting is asking the public to come up with ideas ("crowd-sourcing") about what combination of datasets might be useful. For example, combining information on schools and libraries might allow an entrepreneur to create a service identifying opportunities for after-school care.

Security

One of the important findings is that it is important to view social media as a communications tool rather than another computer-based technology. The immediate implication is that management of social media should really involve communications managers more than computer professionals. To do otherwise, may severely inhibit understanding its potential and limit its utility. But when two-way communications exists, there is a possibility of inserting malware into the government environment. Security, therefore, is one area in which the IT department should take a lead role in the communications team. Security concerns were repeatedly cited by IT professionals as to why there should be no use of social media or very strict policies governing its use. So far, however, it appears that the same precautions and instructions governing the use of email (in downloading and executing alien files or succumbing to a phishing expedition), would apply to social media as well.

Wise use of taxpayer time / perception of use of taxpayer time

While Columbus is a large Midwestern city, it still has populations that do not always value the "latest technology". Consequently, a very heated discussion arose over whether there should be some kinds of restrictions imposed upon the use of social media by city employees. The concern was that: 1) persons should not be pursuing personal social media while they are on the job; 2) that social media can be addictive for some people; and 3) that the city cannot risk a public situation where someone is on the payroll and word gets out that that city employee is on the job but doing personal business. Table 3 describes this proposal.

Table 3: Ownership and content matrix for public and personal social media activity

Computer / Content	Professional	Personal
City-Owned	Internet accounts to carry out the work of the city must be established on a city-owned computer in order to insure that appropriate security protections are in place. [1]	Short Term: Individual use of city-owned computer for personal Internet use, except for email, is prohibited. Long-Term: It will become necessary very soon to allow users access to other Internet services. [2]
Personally-Owned	With the online culture moving towards a 24/7 lifestyle, it may become necessary to revisit the rule that all City-related work be performed on a City-supplied computer. Consider modification of Laptop Policy.	Train and remind employees that even in personal communications that they still have responsibilities. [3]

[1] When you discuss City of Columbus or City of Columbus-related matters, coordinate with the Department's communications officer.

[2] In the short term, prohibit individual use of city-owned computer for personal Internet use, except for email, until the City acquires a reputation that it uses other media well and establishes a culture and base of users who know how to use that internet service. Revisit this policy within six months. Long Term Use: in order to recruit talented employees it will become necessary to allow them to use these services for both their own personal and professional needs.

[3] If you publish content to any website outside of the City's official online presence (this may include City websites as well as City's official presence on third party sites) and if the content:

i. has something to do with subjects associated with the City of Columbus, consider a disclaimer such as this: "The following opinions and statements are my own and do not necessarily represent the City of Columbus's positions, strategies or opinions." Never use or reference your formal position when writing in a non-official capacity. Consult your communications officer when in doubt.

ii. is not related to subjects associated with the City of Columbus, you must still be aware of your association with City of Columbus in online social networks. If you identify yourself as a City of Columbus employee or have a public facing position for which association with the City of Columbus is known to the general public, ensure your profile and related content (even if it is of a personal and not an official nature) is consistent with how you wish to present yourself as a professional, appropriate with the public trust associated with your position, and conforms to existing standards, such as *Central Work Rules, Sensitive Information, Ethics Policy, Privacy Policy, and Public Records Policy*.

Employees should be advised that "published content is persistent in the public domain and that anything you do or say on the Internet could be seen by anyone or everyone." They should assume that all communications are in the public domain, available for publishing or discussion in all forms of media.

Encouraging social media

The questions posed, and the recommendations made, predominantly concern limiting or directing how social media should be used. There is a concern that this bias towards control may limit innovation by already risk-averse government agencies. There also needs to be consideration of how to encourage the use of social media by providing support where it is needed. Some of those items include:

- Training
- Understanding how to use the media strategically? "How do I begin?"
- Streamlining processes to obtain permission to use of social media within a government department

One positive alternative is New Zealand's "Guide to Online Participation" that uses principles and aspirations to encourage civil servants to actively find ways to increase online participation rather than guiding action by enumerating all the actions that are prohibited (State Services Commission, 2007).

Other concerns about policy and procedure

The Social Media group debated, researched, and made recommendations on other varied issues, some of which are familiar to the ITC literature while others are quite novel.

- The social media culture is different. How do we insure that new users are aware and practice appropriate "netiquette" and cultural practices? For example, how should organizations make Twitter personable rather than the dull, gray voice of an institution, while at the same time, making sure that the voice is accountable, and if that person leaves, that it will continue? Or, how do we make government understand and accept the importance of metrics in social media that essentially measures the "popularity" of their message?
- How to deal with web accessibility and disability standards?
- How to communicate with those people who are on the wrong side of the "digital divide"?
- The importance of communicating a policy on how to use and refer individuals to non-government information and links.
- How do make sure that social media is not hijacked by malicious users who really are not interested in a conversation? Should government expose itself to persons who are not interested in sincere communications and would use opportunities for two-way communications to "drag the conversation down"? One example often cited is the "Wall Feature" in Facebook to post negative comments about Columbus and / or post derogatory or impolite comments. How can government use the technology to limit the damage done by a malicious user, but not in a way that inhibits free speech?
- Finding the right balance between centralized policy and local departmental needs.
- Another concern surrounded the "branding" and "marketing" of the Department and its use of social media as it relates to the overall "brand" or "marketing" that the City of Columbus wants to project? A final concern is the use of recognizable names and naming conventions that make it easy for our citizens to locate the various social media outlets. If all departments have the same name, or naming convention, it is one step closer to establishing an overall brand. This overall need, however, might militate against the names that many departments have already adopted for themselves.

The recommendations made to the City of Columbus on each of these points usually involved a holistic approach that included a combination of changes in policy, complemented by management and technology best practices, and finally, good training.

Clearly, there is a large set of issues. Some of these are not new, but are really "old wine in new bottles." More importantly, the long list of issues also clearly underlines that, much to the chagrin of those who believe that social media portends changes as the printing press, that there are many implementation issues that need to be addressed before social media can be used as a mechanism to achieve the goals of Gov. 2.0 (See Table 2, *supra*).

5. Findings and recommendations

5.1. How to understand the implications of social media for government

Each of the individual issues discussed above are significant and it will take time to work out effective legal, policy and managerial solutions. However, really understanding how to deal with these issues and what social media means for government involves understanding that social media is more of a communications tool than an information technology tool. Once this is understood and that this type of communications - fast, interactive, personal - is quickly becoming the type of communications that citizens desire, government will need new ways of looking at how they communicate and work with their citizens. Social media is about cultivating networks and using them well. This means that governments should now think about how social media can support its relationships within their larger social network of individuals, groups, organizations, and institutions.

The report included an explanation of social media for public managers, an explanation of how Columbus was using social media and the risks and opportunities, as well as the results of the external scan including the results of interviews on the risks and opportunities therein and the general concerns and issues raised by the social media group.

Having identified the opportunities as well as the risks, the report made positive recommendations including suggested change to current communications policy (and other policies) as well as a suggested policy for one specific social media (blogs) and Twitter with specific recommendations on HOW to Use it. The central importance of having clear objectives and measures and how to deal with the risks also motivated the development of suggested Risk Mitigation Strategy and Objectives and Measures (both using Twitter as an example). Finally, social media is about communications and a detailed strategy for managing the communications channels was provided. This section discussed what the City should talk about, how the City should talk about it, and who should do the talking (Williams, 2009).

Risks

Risk in the public sector, and especially when it comes to public sector IT, is a high barrier to innovation. To directly deal with this issue, a risk management strategy was adopted. The risks considered include those emanating from adopting this technology as well as not adopting it or implementing it poorly. Table 4 provides an example of some of the risks considered using the Twitter social media as an example.

The best way to encourage and also mitigate risks in departments is through a team approach. During the time that social media remains a new technology, the team should minimally consist of the communications officer (head of team), a Department of Technology representative, and the line or staff responsible for programs.

Table 4: Risk mitigation (using Twitter as an example)

Risk	Mitigation Action
Criticism arising from an inability to meet the demands of users to join conversations/answer enquiries, due to resource and clearance issues	Reduce by managing expectations with clear, published Twitter policy; use holding replies where answer will need research; (only if swamped) respond to 'themes' not individual replies; respond to common requests through Web pages
Criticism arising from perceptions that our use of Twitter is out of keeping with the ethos of the platform (such as too formal, self-promoting or 'dry')	Reduce by sourcing varied content. Accept that there will be some criticism regardless. Listening before talking to learn culture of those users.
Criticism of jumping on the bandwagon/waste of public money/lack of	Reduce by evaluating against objectives above and adhering to content principles

Risk	Mitigation Action
return on investment/pointless content	below
In line with government policy (City of Columbus Executive Orders and Policy, State of Ohio law on open records, records management, and Constitutional protections);	Clear notice on published Twitter policy to public on Twitter page and any entry points on how information will be collected, used and retained; Establish 'light' but effective procedural controls and guidelines for Twitter users; require clearance of all tweets through nominated people in digital media team; Training; Easy to use tools that will capture and store information in order to comply with law
Inappropriate content being published in error, such as: Protectively marked, commercially or politically sensitive information	Establish 'light' but effective procedural controls and guidelines for Twitter users; require clearance of all tweets through media team.
Technical security of the Twitter account and potential for hacking and vandalism of content	Change Twitter password frequently using strong passwords; only two members of digital media team to have access to pw; use cotweet.com to devolve access securely; avoid using unknown 3rd party tools that require the account password
Lack of availability due to Twitter being over capacity	Accept (affects all Twitter users, occurs rarely and is brief). Take backup using tweetake.com and upload every month
Changes to the Twitter platform (to add or change features, or to charge users for accessing the service) Squatters/spoofers on Twitter	Review business case for continuing to use the service when any such changes are made. Reduce by registering alternative names. Accept residual risk and monitor for this occurring. Report spoof accounts to Twitter for suspension. (look into the potential for city sites to branded as, "Verified Accounts" through twitter).
Separate government from politics	Create separate Twitter accounts for those in public office or politically appointed.

Adapted from Neilo Williams (2009) '*Template Twitter Strategy for Government Departments*' http://www.scribd.com/doc/17313280/Template-Twitter-Strategy-for-Government-Departments

Strategy

Once government sees the possibilities for change, as did Scott Varner in Ohio, they may also see risk and avoid taking any action. Managers should also realize, however, that there is also a risk in ignoring social media or waiting until the risks are known and minimal before acting. Waiting too long to climb onto the learning curve may mean incurring significant costs in always catching up.

To maximize the opportunity to learn and mitigate risks, experiments should focus on small, well-defined projects. (One example could be announcing a public event in which a department uses social media as well as traditional media to "create buzz" and catch the attention of the target audience.) This recommendation to focus on small, well-defined projects aligns with best practices suggested for both the private and non-profit sectors.

An important element of crafting a well-defined strategy includes specifying the important objectives and measures. See Table 5, below, for an example of the kinds of objectives and accompanying measures as might be used with Twitter.

Table 5: Objectives and measures (using Twitter as an example)

Objective	**Measure**
Targeted communication – facilitating building communities around specific topics such as: neighbourhood green initiatives, economic development and competition, innovation, education, volunteers	Number of followers; relevance and type of followers per topic
Extend reach of existing messages online (e.g. news, speeches, web updates, YouTube videos) by building relationships with relevant audiences including intermediaries, stakeholders, and key influencers such as journalists and bloggers	Number of followers; relevance and type of followers; number of web traffic referrals from Twitter to our website content
Provide an informal, 'human' voice of the organization to promote engagement with our messages	Feedback from followers (unsolicited and solicited
Provide thought leadership and credibility, increasing our visibility as the experts in	Feedback from followers (unsolicited and solicited); number of re-tweets

Objective	Measure
our remit within the online space	(Twitter users repeating our updates); clickthroughs
Demonstrate commitment to and understanding of digital channels with exemplary use of this emerging channel	Feedback from followers (unsolicited and solicited); +ve, -ve and neutral mentions elsewhere on blogosphere
Provide an additional, low-barrier method for audiences to interact with the Department to provide feedback, seek help and suggest ideas	Volume and quality of @reply and DM contact from followers; impact of this feedback on the Dept
Provide ways for audiences to subscribe to updates (RSS, email)	N/a. Achieved by using a presence on Twitter
Monitor mentions on Twitter of Columbus, elected leaders and policy initiatives, engaging with our critics and key influencers to resolve problems, correct factual inaccuracies, and satisfied customers thanking them and amplifying positive comments	*Qualitative* assessment of individual cases of turning negatives to positives and positives into brand advocates
Provide live coverage of events (such as policy launches, summits or promotions) for those who cannot attend	*Number of* events covered per year; positive feedback on that coverage

6. Is social media a force for change?

Social media has been compared to the printing press in its potential for radically changing communications and access to information. But not too long ago, similar claims were made for how the World Wide Web (Web 1.0) would flatten organizations, increase government transparency, and democratize society. Empirical research has shown that a better way to see technology is that it creates a "window of opportunity" to reexamine how things are done, and in the process, to configure processes that are more democratic. This empirical research, the history of the Web, and the long list of implementation issues listed herein provide evidence that social media will not automatically improve government and governance.

Clearly, this paper has outlined just some of the issues that governments must address if they are to use social media well. Twitter and Facebook can engage citizens in two-way communications or just be another way to broadcast a government initiative without encouraging honest feedback.

Governments typically ask “how can we adapt social media to the way in which we do business?” A very different question is “how can social media provide us a way to do things in way that we have not done before?”

This realization should put a tremendous onus on every decision maker to ask: what are our values and principles and how can we use this technology to further those principles? Will government be a part of the revolution?

References

Agranoff, R. (2007) Managing within networks: Adding value to public organizations, Washington, D.C.: Georgetown University Press.

Bingham, L., O'Leary, R. and Nabatchi, T. (2005) 'Legal frameworks for the new governance: Processes for citizen participation in the work of government', National Civic Review, vol. 94, pp. 54-61.

Boix, C. and Posner, D. (1998) 'Social capital: Explaining its origins and effects on government performance', British Journal of Political Science, vol. 28, pp. 686-693.

Bozeman, B. (1987) All organizations are public: Bridging public and private organizational theories, San Francisco, California: Jossey-Bass.

Coleman, J. (1988) 'Social capital in the creation of human capital', American Journal of Sociology, vol. 94, pp. 95-120.

Giddens, A. (1990) The consequences of modernity, Stanford, California: Stanford University Press.

Kemmis, S. and McTaggart, R. (2000) 'Participatory action research', in Denzin, N. and Lincoln, Y. (eds.) 2nd edition, Thousand Oaks, California: Sage Publications.

Landsbergen, D. (2009) 'Social media prototype evaluation: Policy, strategy, and best practices for the City of Columbus', Columbus, Ohio: John Glenn School of Public Affairs, The Ohio State University.

Landsbergen, D. (2010) Government as part of the revolution: Using social media to open government. Manuscript submitted for publication to Government Information Quarterly. Columbus, Ohio State University.

Nieves, F. (2009) ODOT wary of Twitter, Facebook, other social-media sites as other states jump in. The Cleveland Plain Dealer, 29 July, 2009, http://blog.cleveland.com/metro/2009/07/odot_wary_of_twitter_facebook.html.

Ostrom, E. (1996) 'Crossing the great divide: Coproduction, synergy, and development', World Development, vol. 24, pp. 1073-87.

Putnam, R. (1993) Making democracy work: Civic traditions in modern Italy, Princeton, N.J.: Princeton University Press.

State Services Commission, New Zealand. (2007) Guide to Online Participation, [Online], Available:http://wiki.participation.e.govt.nz/index.php?title=ParticipatioNZ:About&oldid=10048.

Williams, N. (2009) Template Twitter Strategy for Government Departments http://www.scribd.com/doc/17313280/Template-Twitter-Strategy-for-Government-Departments

Wilson, W. (1887) 'The study of administration', Political Science Quarterly, vol. 2, pp. 197-222.

Yin, R. (2003) Case study research: Design and methods, Thousand Oaks, California: Sage Publications.

Citizens2Citizens: Mapping Participatory Practices on the Internet

Albert Meijer, Nils Burger and Wolfgang Ebbers
Utrecht School of Governance, The Netherlands
A.J.Meijer@uu.nl
Originally published in EJEG (2009) Volume 7, Issue 1.

Editorial Commentary

The new technologies that have emerged over the last ten years have had a massive impact on the economic, social and political practices that are embedded within society. Understanding the relationship between emerging technology and the changing shape, structure and operation of social interaction is critical if we are to develop more effective and more inclusive e-Government. So too, is understanding what shapes citizen desire and ability to engage with political processes. Meijer et. al. develop the notion, using structuration theory, that technology and how it is used are shaped by existing social practices but that technology has a major role to play in transforming social and political processes. Consequently, developing an understanding of how technology shapes and is simultaneously shaped by social practices is important if we are to successfully develop e-Government. It is undeniable that the new communications technologies that have become socially accepted over the last few years (especially Web 2.0 technologies) have created new opportunities for citizens to interact with each other, to develop their common interests and to mobilise either for or against national or local political issues. The new opportunities for citizen mobilisation have often come into conflict with the formal and informal rules and procedures that have determined how government interacts with its citizenry. The rules have evolved in an era when the world was more hierarchic and structured around top-down communication to citizens than peer-to-peer communication with citizens. Perhaps we need a new set of rules?

The authors develop an interesting typology of the forms of policy participation that has recently emerged having been facilitated by the emergence of Web 2.0 technologies. These include: citizens co-operating to pressure for government to implement policies accurately; citizens supporting each other to contest public policy; citizens collectively exposing non-compliance with government policy; and; and citizens working with each other to undermine the implementation of public policy. The authors develop an interesting and useful categorisation of public participation focusing on what they term policy participation (e.g. citizens undermine the implementation of unpopular government policies); political participation (e.g. citizens discuss political issues within their own social networks) and social participation (e.g. citizens develop bonds built out of social networks focused around specific issues). The authors argue that we need to rethink many aspects of public participation as new models of citizen participation are being constructed, "to fit then new routines of the information society".

Abstract: Many important forms of public participation take place in interactions between citizens. Studying these interactions is crucial for understanding e-governance, defined as steering in the public domain. The new forms of public participation can be labelled *Citizens2Citizens* interactions (C2C). Citizens use the Internet to facilitate policy participation (meant to support or undermine government policies), political participation (directed at influencing political decision-making and agenda-setting) and social participation (to increase social capital). Attention to these forms of digital participation coincides with the rise of a new set of Web applications which are grouped under the label 'Web 2.0'. This chapter is an attempt to conceptualize and categorize the wide variety of types and forms of C2C to provide a basis for further development of this new research field. We do not claim that our exploration will lead to a final and complete description of C2C; we merely aim to present an overview of the diversity of forms of C2C initiatives that are taking place in the digital world. The argument we are putting forward is that new technologies offer new avenues for participating and that these new practices will constitute both a replication of and an addition to existing offline practices of public participation. Our explorative research of C2C initiatives results in a map of political, policy and social participation. This map of C2C initiatives can provide insights into a variety of Internet practices and help subsequent researchers in their selection of initiatives for in-depth studies. Additionally, our research results in an exploration of the implications such initiatives can have for participation in the public sector.

Keywords: political participation, policy participation, social participation, e-governance

1. Introduction

Government agencies find it difficult to attract citizens to their websites and participate in discussions on political issues whereas political content swarms well-known websites such as Youtube and Facebook. Citizens seem to be interested in the public sphere but discuss issues in digital places that they are familiar with rather than visit government websites (Calenda & Meijer, 2009). Many analyses of e-participation disregard these interactions since they do not directly result in signals to government. E-participation is often limited to a study of how governments use website to elicit signals and feedback from citizens.

Public participation is generally regarded as a matter of contact between government and citizens but many important forms of public participation take place in interactions between citizens. A traditional perspective on public administration may ignore these practices since there is no direct relation with government. From a governance perspective it will immediately become clear that a focus on these practices is crucial for understanding steering in the public sector. Rhodes (1997, pg. 15) emphasizes that governance refers to self-organizing networks in the pursuit of common goals with significant autonomy from the state. Citizen interactions in new digital spaces often concern common goals and the perceived common goods and therefore merit the interest of scholars interested in understanding e-governance.

These forms of public participation can be labelled Citizens2Citizens interactions (C2C). C2C interactions on the Internet are used to facilitate various forms of participation which are all efforts to realize common goals, either through bringing forward demands to the political and administrative system or by creating forms of mutual support. In this paper we distinguish between policy participation (meant to strengthen government policies), political participation (directed at influencing political decision-making) and social participation (to increase social capital).

Attention for C2C coincides with the rise of a new set of Web applications which are grouped under the label 'Web 2.0'. Defined in a technological way Web 2.0 refers to the emergence of new technologies such as RSS and blogging (O'Reilly, 2005; Rapoza, 2006). Defined in a sociological way the changing role of the user takes centre stage, particularly in the growing importance of user-generated content and social networking (Pascu et. al., 2007) which are key features of Web 2.0 that are extremely useful for supporting interactions between citizens. The sharing and exchanging of video images, pictures, opinions, informative texts, personal preferences, et. has become commonplace. Such online behaviour has implications for the public sphere. The 'new Internet' is no longer a collection of information websites but rather a network of platforms that support diverse interactions between users. C2C is just one type of interaction that is taking place through Web 2.0 applications, but for political scientists probably one of the most interesting ones.

Studying new forms of participation is important for political scientists who want to understand governance in the information age. The characteristics of the medium influence the interactions between citizens and, consequently, may induce new relations between citizens and governments. To be more precise, in this paper we depart from the government-centred position that is characteristic for most investigations into e-participation and we focus on new patterns of interactions between (networks of) citizens to understand these forms of e-governance.

This paper is an attempt to conceptualize and categorize the wide variety of types and forms of C2C. We do not claim that our exploration will lead to a final and complete description of C2C; we merely aim to present a first overview of the diversity of forms of C2C initiatives that are taking place in the digital world. The argument put forward is that new technologies offer new venues for participating and that these new practices will constitute both a replication of and an addition to existing offline practices of public participation. The research question leading our research is: how can we map and categorise the variety of citizen to citizen initiatives on the Internet and what are the possible implications of these initiatives for different sorts of participation?

The aim of this paper is twofold. First of all we present an international explorative research into the varied domain of C2C in the form of a web analysis. The explorative research should be regarded as a 'mapping exercise'; the variation in forms of C2C is investigated to show how new technologies lead to a replication of, but also an addition to, existing offline practices. A map of C2C initiatives can provide insights in the variety of Internet practices and help subsequent researchers in their selection of initiatives for in-depth studies. Our map is mainly biased toward websites in the Netherlands but we have also included English and American websites. Nevertheless, we hope that this map can be helpful in focusing the attention of e-participation researchers on interaction forms that they would have missed if they had departed from a narrow definition of public participation. Our second aim is to explore the implications that the initiatives we have studied can have for the three different forms of participation we identified. These implications are relevant and interesting for the academic community but also for government practitioners interested in public participation.

2. Three Types of Participation

Public participation is a key concept in political science and is generally defined as involvement in political, administrative and social processes. The central concept is that citizens transform themselves from bystanders to actively-involved people aiming to realize what they perceive as the public good. The active involvement may take the form of putting demands on the political and administrative system but also includes developing systems of mutual support to reach common goals. Reasons for developing forms of public participation vary from recognition of basic human rights concerning democracy and procedural justice to a practical recognition that public participation may result in more support for government policies (Rowe and Frewer, 2000). A closer look at public participation shows that three types of participation can be distinguished: political participation, policy participation and social participation.

Within these three forms of public participation, political scientists traditionally focus on *political participation* and describe this in terms of power and influence on political decision-making (Arnstein, 1969; Smith, 1983). Political participation is defined as the actions of citizens that aim to influence the selection and behaviour of political decision-makers. Smith (1983) stresses that participation is about designing a group of procedures to consult, involve and inform the public to allow those affected by a decision to have an input into that decision. Coleman, Morrison and Svennenig (2007) use the word *efficacy* to refer to 'a citizen's capacity to intervene in political affairs'. Following this conceptualization, political participation does not only refer to influencing decision-making processes but also includes political agenda setting. Political participation often focuses on influencing formal political arenas, but also includes self control (e.g. squatting) and protest against other actors (e.g. protest against killing whales).

Citizens participate in political agenda setting and decision-making to influence these processes in a certain direction. Lobbying, writing letters to representatives, writing newspaper articles and organizing protests are some well-known forms of political participation. Political participation is often organized in the form of referenda, public hearings, citizens' panels, focus groups, etc. (Rowe and Frewer, 2000). Barber (1984) argues that a high degree of political participation strengthens democracy since citizens are more involved in political processes. Voting is seen as a 'weak' form of democracy which does not require much effort whereas political participation is a characteristic of 'strong' democracies. A growing political trust and the construction of a political identity are important by products of political participation. Political participation is therefore regarded as a means to strengthen citizenship.

Traditional perspectives on public participation focus on the first phases of policy processes (agenda setting and decision-making) whereas modern perspectives also focus on the later phase (implementation). Participation in the implementation phase of policy processes can be referred to as public participation in policy implementation (Desai, 1989) or *policy participation*. This form of public participation has escaped the attention of many political scientists but it has been studied by policy scientists and scholars investigating administration (Desai, 1989; Edwards, 2003; Meijer, Homburg and Bekkers, 2007). Different forms of policy participation have been mentioned in the scientific literature. Desai (1989) describes how citizens are involved in the implementation of environmental policies concerning surface mining control. Edwards (2003, pg. 41) highlights the active role that citizens play in public service delivery and shows that the actual implementation of tax and income policies is the result of interactions between government and citizens. Civic competence is a core element of these forms of policy participation, something which can be illustrated with the example of citizens helping one another when filling in tax forms.

Newer forms of policy participation focus on the role of citizens in regulation. Meijer, Homburg and Bekkers (2007) mention the opportunities that have been created to signal bad smells, unsafe labour conditions or poor hygiene in restaurants. Citizens can become the 'eyes' of regulators and this enhances the effectiveness of policies. Common goals such as safe food, a safe environment and safe working conditions can be realized by involving citizens in implementing regulatory policies. Policy participation may not always serve the interest of government: citizens can also help each other to avoid certain forms of regulation. Well known in the Netherlands are the notices of police speed controls on the radio. Citizens mention these speed controls to the radio stations and thus help each other to avoid tickets for speeding.

Public participation does not only refer to relations between citizens and government but includes interactions between citizens as well. These forms of participation can be grouped under the heading of '*social participation*'. Central to this concept is the idea that citizens vary in the extent to which they are involved in society and hence they vary in their systems for mutual support. Social participation has been studied mainly in the field of sociology. Axelrod (1956), for example, describes the relation between urbanization and social participation. Important for our thinking about social participation has been Putnam's 'Bowling Alone' (2000). Putnam describes how social capital is created through interaction between groups in society and these interactions can take the form of 'bonding' when persons from the same group interact with each other and 'bridging' when the interactions cross the boundaries between different groups in society.
Governments in Europe and North America pay a great deal of attention to social capital since this is seen as an important way to prevent disintegration of societies (and, additionally, social capital also contributes to material wealth). Traditional connections in societies are wearing out and Putnam paints a grim picture of people who do not spend time with friends

and family but rather go 'bowling alone'. Others have argued that new societal groups such as environmental and social groups still play a crucial role and Putnam's book is misleading (Wellman, 1999).

Public participation is often regarded as something 'good' which is important for 'strong democracies'. However, public participation can also hamper government policies and lead to all kinds of anti-social behaviour on the Internet. Public participation certainly has, to use Putnam's phrase, a 'dark side' (Putnam, 2000: 350) to it. Political participation by extremist groups can result in undermining democratic regimes, policy participation by people intending to violate policies can result in a decrease in compliance with government rules and social participation in the form of exclusive bonding can strengthen stereotyping of groups in society. Public participation has to be studied and understood within a specific context and evaluated from a normative frame for a sophisticated view on its effects on political and social systems.

The three types of public participation have been summarized in Table 1:

Table 1: Three Forms of Public Participation

	Political participation	Policy participation	Social participation
Goals	Influencing agenda-setting and decision-making	Influencing policy implementation	Creating mutual support
Public good	Debated in political system	Debated in administrative system	Realized in social networks
Relevance for e-governance	Influencing the political system	Influencing the administrative system	Influencing the public sphere
Research community	Political science	Policy sciences	Sociology

Three types of participation have been described but the distinction between these types cannot always be made easily. Well known are Habermas' (1991) coffee houses in London and Vienna where citizens would discuss personal but also public issues. These coffee houses combined political and social participation. Policy participation can, then and now, not always be distinguished from political participation since influencing policy processes also has an influence on political decisions. Even though we acknowledge that distinguishing the types of participation in practice is not always easy, we suggest that this distinction can be used as an analytical tool to map the diversity of forms of participation on the Internet. As will be seen later, the initiatives analyzed here do not always fit neatly into these theoretically deduced forms of participation, but the three forms of participation have proven to be a useful heuristic device in categorizing and understanding the differences between the initiatives.

3. Structuration and e-participation

Researchers in political science have always shown a strong interest in public participation and nowadays exhibit a growing interest in the developing field of e-participation (Macintosh and Whyte, 2006). To conceptualize e-participation, one needs a theoretical perspective on the relation between technology and new social and political practices. How can we understand the relation between the Internet and public participation? We suggest that technology is neither an instrument nor a determinant of social practices: the confrontation of technology and social practices can be understood by using a structuration framework (Giddens, 1984; Orlikowski, 1992; DeSanctis and Poole, 1994). Central to the structuration framework is the idea that technology is shaped by social practices but, at the same time, technology also transforms these practices. This argument is summarized in Figure 1 (adapted from Orlikowski, 1992).

We will explain the various relations in the model:

Relation A. Citizens have certain patterns of interaction with other citizens and various media are used for these interactions. The Internet will be used as an additional medium for their interactions.

Relation B. The Internet offers citizens new opportunities for interacting with each other. They can, for example, more easily interact with citizens that share their interest. In that sense, the Internet influences how citizens interact.

Relation C. Formal and informal rules regarding public participation influence how citizens interact. Legal rules regarding political participation, for example, and informal rules for social participation, as another example, structure how citizens interact.

Relation D. Formal and informal rules only exist when they are being reproduced through citizen interactions. Rules that are not being followed in any citizen interactions lose their meaning.

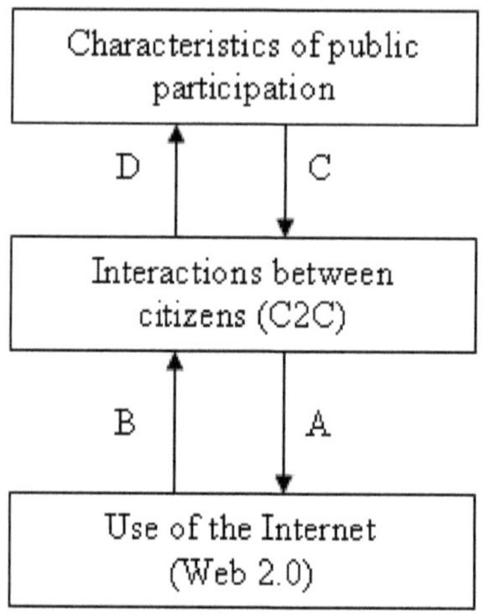

Figure 1: Interrelation Between Use of the Internet and Public Participation (adapted from Orlikowski, 1992)

In addition to this model we argue that the Internet has certain characteristics. DeSanctis and Poole (1994: 126) refer to the structural features such as the algorithm and hardware characteristics and spirit of technologies which can be regarded as the 'script' underlying the technology. The characteristics of communication media are a central tenet of the so-called 'new medium studies' (Deibert, 1997; Hutchby, 2001, 2003). These studies highlight the way media structure communication by facilitating certain forms of interactions while hindering other forms. The concept of 'affordance' plays a key role in these studies. Sellen and Harper (2003) write, "An affordance refers to the fact that the physical properties of an object make possible different functions for the person perceiving or using that object."

The following affordances of the Internet at large have been highlighted in various research studies: transparency, many-to-many communication, virtuality, calculability, etc. (Bekkers, 1994; Frissen, 1999). New medium studies, however, highlight that these affordances do not determine outcomes. The outcome should be conceptualized as the results of affordance, the context of use and individual choices. This makes this theoretical approach compatible with structuration theory, although new medium studies do not emphasize that the context also changes in the use of technology.

The model shows that the outcome of the interaction on the Internet emerges from the various relations and loops into the model and cannot be predicted. In this paper we study the forms of e-participation that emerge from these interactions. For analytic purposes, we will characterize these outcomes as either replications of current practices (when social structures are not challenged by the new medium) or transformations of these practices (when the structure of political participation is transformed through the new medium). The new forms of public participation on the Internet have been studied before and we will present some of the previous findings before going into our own empirical research.

E-participation is generally seen as the use of ICT-tools to involve citizens in finding solutions for social problems (www.burger.overheid.nl). This description focuses primarily on what we call policy participation because the political/normative desirability of change is not questioned and the problems focused on are not directly related to social participation. We see e-participation as referring to all the ways in which citizens interact with one another or with other parties on the Internet. This participation takes place in the virtual world, but can have concrete effects on the lived or 'real' world (Gulved, 2002).

The question can be asked how the different forms of public participation, as identified above, will develop in the information age. In other words, what effect or influence does the Internet have on public participation? For a long time the digital divide dominated the discussion about the meaning of Internet for participation (Bekkers, 2004; Frissen, 2007). However, the importance of the digital divide in the sense of the social divide between the people who are information rich and poor within a nation (Norris, 2000) has been diminishing. Among Dutch youth for example one can no longer speak of a digital divide, for 97% have access to a computer and the Internet (SCP, 2005). Youngsters are 'digital natives' and for them the

Internet has become the most important medium of communication, more important for example than television (Frissen, 2007). This means that we can further specify the question regarding the meaning of Internet for participation. Which forms of participation take place on the Internet and what meaning should we attribute to this participation?

Based on a secondary analysis of research on ICT and political participation, Bovens (2003) concludes that the importance of ICT on this form of participation is minimal. There is no 'digital Athens' in the making. He perceives the rising of an 'enclave democracy' in which there is engagement with political issues, but this engagement is between people who already think alike and focus on specific issues. However, developments in the senatorial campaign of Howard Dean in 2004 do indicate that the Internet can lead to greater engagement (Hindman, 2005). In the recent presidential campaign of Barrack Obama the Internet also played a significant role. What is interesting about political participation on the Internet is that it does not only relate to existing political institutions, but that it can create new institutions such as the European Social Consulta (which, by the way, only existed for a short period of time). What is more, online participation can be used to organise offline participation (Bennett, 2007). For example, in 2004 a total of twenty million people were mobilised within six months for demonstrations against the war in Iraq.

When looking at policy participation, what could the impact of ICT be? Little research in this field has been conducted. Research by Meijer, Homburg and Bekkers (2007) does indicate that policy participation regarding surveillance (in Dutch: toezicht en handhaving) is still very limited. They show that hardly any possibilities for policy participation have been created (by government) and as far as these do exist the public interest is marginal.

What could be the impact of the Internet on social participation? Bekkers (2004, pg. 68) indicates that three 'camps' can be identified regarding the perceived impact of ICT on social participation (see also Norris, 2000; Linders and Goossen, 2004). One camp argues that the Internet improves social participation because new connections between people can be made and already existing relations can be maintained. Another camp believes that people are spending an increasing amount of time on the Internet and thereby less time with family, friends and neighbours. The third camp points out – mainly inspired by Wellman (1999) – that social participation obtains another form on the Internet because a digital community is developing on the Net. Here we would also like to identify a fourth camp which does not believe new connections are made, but that the Internet mainly leads to bonding in the sense of 'digital balkanization' (Putnam, 2000), meaning that primarily likeminded people meet each other on the Net and strengthen the bonds among one another (see also Papacharissi, 2002; Anduiza, Cantijoch and Gallego, 2007).

With regards to all these forms of participation the relevant question is how representative the users of all different (Web 2.0) Internet applications are with regard to the whole population. The general remark can be made that people will make use certain forma of Internet applications if this fits their 'normal' offline behaviour (Frissen, 2007): people who do not normally take part in public discussions offline will probably not start doing this in an online forum either. In the words of Norris (2000) there is a 'democratic divide', meaning that there is a difference between those who do, and do not, use the panoply of digital resources to engage, mobilize and participate in public life. People who participate are thus not representative. Moreover, the people within a nation who have access to the Internet are also not representative of the population. However, it should be noted that people who normally take part in, for example, political activities are not necessarily representative of the population either.

A remark that is often made about participation on the Internet is that its quality is low due to the ease with which one can participate. Two reactions are in order. First of all, being physically present at a discussion does not guarantee that the participation is of high quality in the sense that discussions are held in a rational-critical manner so as to reach a consensus of opinion (Habermas, 1991). The Internet could contribute to the quality of a discussion because it gives people time to consider their responses and possibly look up relevant information. Secondly, discussions on the Internet can also be evaluated in ways other than looking at quality. Perhaps it is not only the content of a discussion that is important, but also the fact that the Internet enables people to be in constant communication with one another. When we, for example, look at MSN, the contents of what is being discussed can, from an external perspective, be seen as having little quality. However, the fact that people are constantly online and talking to their contacts is in itself an interesting phenomenon. Constantly being in contact with each other and knowing what your peers are doing means that social ties are continually being confirmed and new (loose) ties may be created.

This short exploration of the meaning of ICT – and in particular the Internet – for political, policy and social participation shows us that the perceptions are very diverse. These differences can be ascribed to different conceptualisations of participation and also to choices for the practices that are being studied. What is more is that the Internet and its use are constantly changing and every analysis is therefore of temporary value. Nevertheless, the previous research has informed our present study in that it has helped to map and categorize the various citizens to citizens initiatives on the Internet.

4. Research methods

The goal of this research is to develop categories of public participation on the Internet and to reflect on the possible implications of the researched initiatives for the different forms of participation. The three different forms of participation were deduced from existing theory on public participation. Based on the theoretical conceptualizations, we formulated the following operational definitions:

- *Political participation*. The website is devoted to the influencing of decision-making and agenda-setting by political institutions or is about citizens' opinions about their role in the political process.
- *Policy participation*. The website is devoted to activities influencing the realization of governmental policy goals by supporting government and direct action towards third parties.
- *Social participation*. The website helps in the construction of social capital. Connections within and between social networks are supported by interactions on the website.

Based on these definitions we identified initiatives to be researched. We are well aware that these definitions do not give an unconditional footing for the identification of websites. One of the goals of this explorative research was therefore to give empirical substance to these categories. The basic idea behind our argument is that theoretical subcategories can be constructed on the basis of empirical findings.

Sites were identified in the following ways:

- *Internet search for relevant sites.* A few key search words were: forum government, forum overheid (forum government), political discussion, politieke discussie (political discussion), uitleg belastingen (explanation taxes). On the following dates Google was used to search for sites based, amongst others, on these search words: 18 October 2007, 20 October 2007, 30 October 2007, 2 November 2007 and 23 November 2007.
- *The identification of relevant sites in newspapers.* In the period October – December 2007 the Dutch newspapers the Volkskrant and the NRC Handelsblad were screened for relevant sites.
- *Asking experts in the field of ICT and politics for relevant sites.* The international network of contacts of the researchers formed the starting point for approaching experts. The following experts have presented us with relevant websites: Arre Zuurmond (Zenc en TU Delft, Lilia Efimova (Telematica Instituut), Robert Slagter (Telematica Instituut), Marcel Thaens (Ordina en EUR), Gert den Toom (UU), Dennis de Kool (EUR), Rebecca Moody (EUR), Charlie Schweik (University of Massachusetts, Amherst), Michael Ash (University of Massachusetts, Amherst).
- *Participating in lectures and congresses on this subject.* The authors participated in the e-participation summit in Amsterdam (15 november 2007) and attended a lecture by professor V. Frissen (Digitale Diaspora (Digital Diasporas) in The Hague on the 16th of November 2007).
- *A workshop on this subject was organized.* On the 27th of November 2007 a workshop on this subject was organized at the Telematica Insitute in Enschede (the Netherlands). Participants from the Telematica Institute were: Wolfgang Ebbers, Mark Melenhorst, Wil Janssen, Marcel Bijlsma, Mettina Veenstra. Participants from the Utrecht School of Governance were: Albert Meijer, Nils Burger, Stephan Grimmelikhuijsen en Gijs-Jan Brandsma. Participants from the University of Twente were: Jörgen Svensson, Lex van Velsen. In the workshop they were all explicitly asked to name examples of relevant sites.

The aim of the exploration was not to describe all the e-participation sites but rather to identify the best known initiatives and to show the variation between initiatives. The variation was primarily achieved by looking at different forms of participation and different geographical levels of participation. The explorative research was ended when additional efforts to find new subcategories no longer led to new results and all new found websites could be placed within the subcategories we had found (cf. Doreian and Woodard, 1992). In other words: the categories became saturated (Corbin and Strauss, 2008).

The description and analysis of the sites took place based on the following criteria: type of public participation (policy, political or social), geographical level (local, national or international), founder of the website (citizens, government, media, political parties, NGOs, companies), offerings of the website (forum, information, voting, evaluating, virtual world, social networking, exchanging multimedia files, download files), goal of the website (inform, debate, organize protest, entertainment, support, improve service delivery, create social coherence, trade), moderation (no, little, great deal), approximation of number of visitors (if available) (few, moderate, many), depth of argumentation (little, moderate, much), publicness (fully public, free subscription required, not public) and anonymity (fully anonymous, partly anonymous, not anonymous).

These criteria were, apart from the different forms of participation, not pre-established, but were developed during the research. We found the criteria useful for comparing sites and explaining differences between them. We used the descriptions to give an elaborate overview of forms of e-participation. This overview was subsequently analyzed to bring out the subcategories of the three forms of public participation.

4.1. Empirical Analysis of Types of Policy Participation

We found a broad set of 22 initiatives that we qualified as policy participation. These initiatives take place at the local and the national level: no forms of policy participation were identified at the international level which is not surprising since little policy implementation is carried out by international actors.

The following categories of policy participation were constructed on the basis of an analysis of the objective and use of the websites:

- *Citizens pressure government to implement policies accurately.* The well-known British example 'Fix My Street' fits within this category. Citizens can use this website to send a signal to local governments that they should come and fix something in their street. An interesting finding was that this website and a similar Dutch initiative were both set up with government funding.
- *Citizens support each other in issues related to government policies.* The Dutch website Forum Werk (Labour Forum) is an interesting community of people discussing issues related to finding a job or getting different kinds of government support. Similar initiatives have been found relating to tax, immigration and safety policies. These initiatives provide a way to strengthen people's civic competence.
- *Citizens expose offenders of government regulation.* The website 'Voorkom die bon' (Avoid that ticket) allows users to list people who were calling on their mobile phone while driving and not using a hands-free set for their phone. Using your mobile phone without a hands-free set is forbidden under Dutch traffic regulation and annoys other drivers since it can lead to irresponsible driving. One should note that this website has been set up by a company that sells these hands-free sets.
- *Citizens report offenders to government.* Meldpunt Kinderporno (Child Porn Report) is an initiative of citizens that want to stop the spread of child porn on the Internet. Citizens can report information about child porn on the Internet anonymously to this website. The owners of the website evaluate the information and, if it points to illegal activities, the mention is forwarded to Dutch or international law authorities.
- *Citizens undermine the implementation of government policies.* Flitsers (Speed Cameras) is a website that provides citizens with information about speed cameras on the Dutch motorways. Citizens can use this information to make sure they only speed in areas where there are no cameras and, hence, they can avoid tickets for speeding. This website undermines the police system for motorway speeding by exposing it.

These categories show that there are several ways in which policy participation supports the implementation of government policies. Citizens can give information to government agencies or expose offenders; they can also help each other and hence reduce the pressure on agency information services; they can send signals to agencies to improve the quality of their work. The categories also show that policy participation can be annoying for agencies since they are constantly pushed into improving their performance and some initiatives even undermine their policies. A common feature of these initiatives is that they are all concrete: they relate directly to citizens' life worlds.

Most of these initiatives form an addition rather than a replication of offline practices of policy participation. A first key difference between these initiatives and offline practices is that all actions can easily be made transparent to a general public. Citizens could send a letter to their local government before with complaints about their street, but through the Internet the general public can also read these complaints and follow whether governments take timely and appropriate action. Naming and shaming of offenders could take place through traditional media but this has become much easier now that reports about offenses, such as calling without a hands-free set in the car, can be published on the Internet without any cost or effort. A second key difference is that the Internet makes it possible to interact around forms of policy participation and hence form digital communities. Citizens could have formed communities before based on issues such as finding work or filling in tax forms, but the costs and effort of forming such a community in the offline world are high. The Internet enables citizens to form easy accessible and open communities around policy participation.

The reporting of offenders to government can be regarded as a replication of offline forms of policy participation. The Internet makes reporting easy and the Internet is the right medium for this type of offense, child porn on the Internet, but apart from that there are no fundamental differences from traditional means to report offenders through the telephone or mail.

Some of these forms of policy participation raise important normative questions. The 'Voorkom die bon' (Avoid that ticket) website is a form of exposing of citizens by other citizens. Is that acceptable? Or should the privacy of the offenders be respected? Another set of questions concerns the uneven effects of certain initiatives. If certain initiatives are only used by Internet savvy users, the result could be that government will be more responsive only to certain groups in society. People that don't have Internet access can't use the Fix My Street website and therefore may have less means to attract the attention of government agencies to the problems in their street.

4.2. Types of political participation

We qualified a broad set of 26 initiatives as forms of political participation. These initiatives take place at all levels: local, national and international. The variety of websites is enormous and our selection can never be considered to provide a comprehensive overview of all forms of political participation. Nevertheless, we did manage to construct a set of categories on the basis of our sample which provides a first idea of the variation in types of political participation.

- *Citizens protest against a specific proposal or policy.* A large group of websites is devoted to organizing protests against certain proposal or policies. A (typically) Dutch example of these websites is Red de Paddo (Safe the Magic Mushroom) which is devoted to organizing protests against a proposal to make the selling of magic mushrooms illegal. An international example is Bilaterals.org which aims to stimulate awareness of and protests against bilateral agreements between countries when these agreements could have a negative impact on less powerful groups within a country and the environment in general. These websites mainly have a single-issue character: they focus on one issue and this issue may be short-lived.

- *Citizens use a website to organize political action.* These websites also focus on specific issues but the primary goal of the website is not to debate issues or provide information but rather to organize a collective effort. The 'Petitions' website in the UK is such an example. Citizens can propose a petition and aim to attract enough votes to make the petition successful. 'Make Poverty History' is another example. The initiative was launched to influence world leaders gathering at the G8 meeting in Edinburgh (July 2005). The website of Make Poverty History has made selling the well-known white armband with the text 'Make Poverty History' one of its main goals. Both initiatives use the potential of the Internet to organize masses of people around the world (see also Bennett, 2007).

- *Citizens hold a plea for broad political changes.* The difference between this type of website and the previous type is that these initiatives are not connected to specific decisions or policies. They organize citizens in their pleas and actions for a world with peace, no poverty, a clean environment, and so forth. A well-known international example is Stand Against Poverty which aims to make people stand up and speak out to demand a more urgent political response to the growing crisis of global poverty and inequality.

- *Citizens discuss political issues within their own social networks.* Not all websites aim to achieve some kind of change through protests or actions. Many websites merely provide platforms for discussing political issues within certain social networks. An example is the leftist website Red Pepper, 'a magazine of political rebellion and dissent', which provides information about access to discussions on feminism, environmental issues, etc. Another example is the extreme right website Stormfront which enables members to discuss issues such as, primarily, immigration and integration. An interesting feature of these websites is that especially websites on the political extremes seem to lead to lively debates and discussions.
- *Citizens discuss political issues in the public sphere.* Although most political C2C initiatives connect like-minded spirits, some important initiatives are about bringing different people together to discuss political issues. These initiatives are sometimes connected to news programs on television. 'Een Vandaag' is a Dutch news program which triggers heated debates on its website. Other debates have a local character (e.g. Groups Google Stad Utrecht about the Dutch city of Utrecht) or focus on specific political questions (e.g. Talk Politics European Union). Successful websites, however, are connected to mass media or are well-known information websites. Less known websites seem to result in debates of kindred minds.
- *Citizens provide assessment tools for voting decisions.* Several websites on the Internet help citizens choose between political parties and candidates. 'Wie Kies Jij' (Who do you choose?) is a website that presents users with a list of ten questions that can help them choose the candidate of a party that suits their preferences best. There is a wide variety of these websites and they have already been investigated by several researchers (Boogers and Voerman, 2003).

These categories provide an interesting overview of forms of political involvement. They show that political participation can range from discussing issues with members of the same political party to voting on electronic petitions and finding out what the right candidate for you might be. The list also shows that extremists have found the Internet to be a useful platform but political participation is not only about discussing issues with people that have the same opinion. The trend of 'Balkanization' of political discussions and interactions (Putnam, 2000; Bovens, 2003) is not confirmed by our research since it shows that some important initiatives create platforms for debates between various groups which otherwise might not have directly interacted with one another.

Some of these online forms of political participation can largely be regarded as replications of offline practices. Websites are used to protest against specific proposals and policies or hold a plea for broad political changes. These initiatives do not seem to be much different from similar initiatives through traditional media. An interesting difference, though, is that websites operate on an international scale whereas there are very few traditional media that have global coverage. The organization of collective effort through websites is also a replication of the use of traditional media to organize protest, but the major difference seems to be that the cost of the use of the Internet is much lower than the cost of using traditional media (Bekkers, 2004).

The forms of political interaction identified, within a certain group and within the public sphere at large, also seem to be replications of offline interactions. An interesting difference, though, is that the Internet enables small and dispersed groups to form political communities on the Internet. One could claim that this is the political version of the 'long tail' (Anderson, 2004) possibilities the Internet has to offer: individuals or small groups of people whose interests can be seen as representing a niche are, through the Internet, able to interact with each other on a world-wide scale without being hindered by time, space or high cost.

The last form of online political participation we identified, citizens providing assessment tools for voting decisions, has few equivalents in the offline world. This initiative builds upon similar initiatives in the commercial world that provide consumers tools to choose between various alternatives. The Internet provides an interesting addition to consumer democracies by providing cheap and accessible tools for comparison of political candidates and parties.

Do these forms of political participation contribute to a 'strong democracy'? Many of these C2C initiatives seem to strengthen the capacity of citizens to organize political action and channel debate. In that sense, these initiatives indeed contribute to democratic processes by involving more citizens and by creating more venues for political participation. Some of the initiatives also show the risks that political participation poses to democracy. Terrorist websites were not included in our sample but some of the extremist websites also present a risk to core elements of our modern day concept of democracy (e.g. protection of minorities). A further in-depth investigation and analysis of these initiatives is needed to understand and evaluate the impact on democracy.

4.3. Types of Social Participation

We qualified a set of 20 initiatives as forms of social participation. Social participation takes place at the local, national and international level and varies from discussing issues online with the people in your street to building networks of friends around the world. Again we want to emphasize that our overview can never claim to be exhaustive and we do not aim to achieve more than to provide a first map of the diversity of social participation on the Internet. We constructed seven categories of social participation.

- *Citizens maintain contacts with other citizens in the same area.* These initiatives form a digital extension to social networks in neighbourhoods but may also help people to build new networks. 'Bergpolderweg' is a Dutch website which tries to bring together citizens in an area of the city of Rotterdam. The amount of people who participate in these local initiatives is very limited. This can probably be ascribed to the fact that they are not well-known to the larger public.

- *Citizens maintain network contacts within their social networks (bonding).* Various forms of bonding take place on the Internet. Bonding may be organized around student clubs (such as the Dutch student club Biton) but also, more interestingly, around ethnic or religious backgrounds. Maroc.nl and Hindi.punt.nl are interesting and well-visited websites of, respectively, Moroccan and Hindustan communities in the Netherlands. Various issues are discussed on these websites, ranging from questions within the private realm, for example about dating non Hindu girls to more public question about the Koran and political issues.

- *Citizens build networks of friends.* Social networking websites are at the core of Web 2.0. Citizens use websites such as Facebook to contact their friends but also to extend their social networks. Extensions are especially interesting when it comes to more functional social networking sites such as LinkedIn. These extensions can be expected to take the form of bonding but further research will need to be done to see whether forms of bridging with people from other social networks also takes place on these websites.
- *Citizens help each other through support or concrete advice.* The variety of support websites on the Internet is enormous. There is a wide variety of patient groups and groups of people who support each other with all kinds of psychological problems. Some interesting examples are parents supporting each other with advice (Ouders Online (Parents Online)), anorexia patients supporting each other (Anangel), visitors to prostitutes exchanging information about the price and quality of prostitutes (Hookers.nl). Some of these websites have a limited number of participants but the meaning of these sites to them seems to be substantial (judging by the number and length of the posts).
- *Citizens exchange (digital) goods and services.* The Internet is a giant market place and often citizens provide each other with goods at a low price or even for free. Internationally, e-Bay is the market leader when it comes to citizens buying and selling products to each other and 'Marktplaats' dominates commercial exchanges in the Netherlands. The photo website Flickr is also an interesting example of citizens exchanging products. These websites provide social capital since they enable citizens to help each other. Additionally, some of these interactions may result in the extension of social networks.
- *Citizens develop public goods together.* This is probably one of the most interesting new forms of social participation since there are not many equivalents in the offline world. The LINUX and Wikipedia examples are very well known and show how citizens around the world can cooperate to develop products and information services. The literature on these forms of cooperation is extensive but rarely focuses on the con-

tribution of these initiatives to social capital as a by product of cooperation.

- *Citizens form social networks in a virtual world.* Second Life is the best known example of a virtual world where people meet and interact. The interesting thing is that people do not meet 'as themselves' but rather as 'avatars'. These avatars create new connections and result in what could be called 'virtual social capital'. This virtual social capital creates cohesion in the virtual world and helps the avatars to achieve things. The question whether virtual social capital is isolated from or connected with offline social capital provides the starting point for interesting research.

This list of forms of social participation on the Internet illustrates that there is a great deal of diversity; varying from digitally meeting people from you neighbourhood to new interactions in a virtual world. This shows that social participation on the Internet may be a simple replication of offline interactions in digital form, but that some forms also constitute a totally new form of interacting with others (in whatever form). Whereas the use of the Internet for neighbourhood interactions eventually aims to contribute to more social capital in the offline world, interactions in Second Life create forms of virtual social capital. It would be interesting to analyze the meaning of virtual social capital of frequent visitors to virtual worlds such as Second Life.

The distinction between replication of offline practices on the one hand and additional digital practices on the other becomes especially relevant when it comes to the social networking sites. These sites are a replication of offline practices when sites such as Facebook are used to connect to people who meet offline. However, these websites are also used to form new social networks and therefore they also form an addition to offline practices. This is an interesting difference with other media such as the telephone and letters which are (almost) exclusively used to contact people for face-to-face meetings. When Facebook would be used to form social networks across traditional boundaries between groups, it could be an important medium for 'bridging'.

Interesting forms of mutual support are identified on the Internet which partly form a replication of offline practices (e.g. patient groups) but also form a relevant addition. 'Hookers' is an interesting initiative since one could not imagine an initiative with a similar amount of active users in the offline world. The anonymous character of the Internet facilitates interactions on themes that are not commonly accepted in society.

The production of public goods is also an interesting feature of the Internet. Offline production of common goods does take place on a small scale, e.g. when neighbours collectively take care of a garden in a public place, but offline examples on a global scale do not exist (as far as we know). Wikipedia and LINUX form fascinating examples of citizens not only providing each other with information and support but actually developing products which can potentially make life easier for everybody.

When we take this analysis back to Putnam's 'bonding' and 'bridging' (2000) an interesting question can be raised. It is clear that the Internet supports 'bonding' but we still do not know to what extent 'bridging' takes place. To assess the contribution of these C2C initiatives to 'bridging' we need to find out to what extent social networks across different groups are being created and, also, we need to find out to what extent various digital interactions (selling products at e-Bay, working on Linux, meeting people in Second Life) actually contributes to offline social capital.

4.4. Result of This Mapping Exercise

This mapping exercise has resulted in the overview of categories of public participation shown in Figure 2.

Policy participation
- Citizens pressure government to implement policies accurately
- Citizens support each other in issues related to government policies
- Citizens expose offenders of government regulation
- Citizens report offenders to government
- Citizens undermine the implementation of government policies

Political participation
- Citizens protest against a specific proposal or policy
- Citizens use a website to organize political action
- Citizens hold a plea for broad political changes
- Citizens discuss political issues within their own social networks
- Citizens discuss political issues in the public sphere
- Citizens provide assessment tools for voting decisions

Social participation
- Citizens maintain contacts with other citizens in the same area
- Citizens maintain network contacts within their social networks (bonding)
- Citizens build networks of friends
- Citizens help each other through support or concrete advice
- Citizens exchange (digital) goods and service
- Citizens develop public goods together
- Citizens form social networks in virtual world

Figure 2: Overview of Categories of Public Participation

This map – or perhaps we should call it a tree – can facilitate discussions about public participation on the Internet by enabling researchers and practitioners to stipulate explicitly which types of public participation they are investigating or supporting. This map can also help researchers to make decisions about research design and the selection of cases for in-depth studies of public participation.

Moreover, the mapping exercise results in a discussion of the extent to which The Internet replicates offline practices or forms a new addition to practices of public participation. Although many replications of offline practices were found, the findings also showed that certain characteristics of the Internet may lead to new practices of public participation. We identified 'transparency' and 'interaction' as important features facilitating new forms of policy participation; the 'long tail' and 'calculability' were identified as interesting features of the Internet facilitating new forms of political participation; the 'long tail', anonymity and 'vituality' were identified as important characteristics of the Internet facilitating new forms of social participation.

On the basis of this mapping exercise we were able to raise relevant normative and empirical questions concerning policy, political and social participation on the Internet. We posed normative questions about privacy and representation regarding policy participation, we wondered to what extent new forms of political participation contribute to a strong democracy and we asked empirical question regarding the extent to which digital forms of social participation contribute to 'bridging'. In that sense, this mapping exercise forms the first step in a broader investigation of public participation on the Internet and sets out directions for subsequent research.

5. Reflections on Public Participation

New forms of public participation are being created on the Internet. Citizens find ways to use the Internet to realize common goals and strengthen the common good and, therefore, C2C is a crucial component of new forms of e-governance. These forms, as we have shown, are both replications of and additions to traditional forms of public participation. In terms of the structuration framework we presented: social structures both form new practices and are formed by these new practices. On the basis of our explorative research, we presented a map of forms of public participation on the Internet and this map forms the answer to our research question. In this concluding paragraph, we will reflect upon the meaning of these new forms of public participation for the administration, politics and society. In these reflections we focus upon the possible beneficial effects of participation for government and society in terms of increasing 'strong democracy', improving the implementation of government policies and supporting social capital in society.

How can these new forms of political participation on the Internet strengthen democracy? Representation is an important shortcoming of all identified initiatives and the quality of debates generally does not reach as high a level as debates in newspapers. There is no direct and urgent reason for governments to react to these forms of political participation. That does not mean that these websites have no democratic value. An interesting opportunity these websites offer is that they enable governments to gauge sentiments in society. A common shortcoming of modern governments is that they often seem to have lost touch with citizens. A digital 'thermometer' can be used by politicians to get a better feeling of how citizens care and think about what goes on in the public sector. Governments do not necessarily have to react instantaneously to these sentiments but can use them as additional input for decision-making processes. Politicians and administrators can assess debates critically, interpret the value of the various positions and evaluate the possible meaning for policies. Especially when it comes to groups of citizens that are difficult to reach, such as drug users or visitors to prostitutes, a digital thermometer may enhance the sensibility of governments to society and thus enhance the governments' legitimacy.

Can these new forms of participation on the Internet support policy implementation? The overview shows that, as we already know from theory, the implementation of policies does not only depend on government efforts but should be conceptualized as the outcome of interactions between various actors. Some citizen initiatives clearly support the attainment of government objectives but others undermine government policies or apply means to support government objectives that are questionable. The Internet offers new opportunities to create alliances in favour of government policies but also against them. Governments will have to get involved in strategic games on the Internet to mould strong alliances and, at the same time, they need to develop responses to alliances which undermine the attainment of policy objectives.

Do these new forms of public participation help to build social capital in society? The importance of websites such as Hyves, YouTube and Wikipedia should not be neglected since these initiatives create frameworks for everyone. These common frameworks can facilitate other social interactions and make it easier for different groups in society to interact. At the same time, the level of interaction on these websites is limited and hence the contribution to building social capital may be limited. Based on our research we have found that initiatives with more interactions generally have a more stratified group of users and contribute more to 'bonding' than to 'bridging'.

These three forms of public participation have been discussed separately but they overlap since they all concern aspects of governance. History seems to repeat itself. Different forms of participation took place in Habermas' coffee houses in the late 19th century where citizens would discuss their social lives but also public and political affairs. Websites can be seen as the coffee houses of the information age and also integrate various forms of participation. YouTube, to name an example, contains private and political movie clips and combines social and political interests of citizens. Citizens visit YouTube to see the latest music clips and see the films that were posted by their friends but, while visiting the website, they may also start watching political movie clips and even films about policy implementation. A quick search led to the example of a film about all the garbage in New Bedford (Massachusetts - http://nl.youtube.com/watch?v=w7qn05koQhQ [14 Jan 2008]). A new domain of public participation is being constructed by citizens to fit the new routines of the information society.

References

Anderson, C. (2004) 'The Long Tail', *Wired Magizine* [Electronic], vol. 12, no. 10, Available: http://www.wired.com/wired/archive/12.10/tail.html [24 Jul 2007].

Anduiza, E., Cantijoch, M. and Gallego, A. (2007) 'Political Participation and the Internet: Descriptive Hypotheses and Causal Mechanisms', *Conference proceedings*, Changing politics through digital networks: The role of ICT's in the formation of new social en political actors and actions, Florence.

Arnstein, S. (1969) 'A ladder of citizen participation', *Journal of the American Institute of Planners*, vol. 34, no. 4, pp. 216 -224.

Axelrod, M. (1956) 'Urban Structure and Social Participation', *American Sociological Review*, vol. 21, no. 1, pp. 13-18.

Barber, B. (1984) *Strong Democracy: participatory democracy for a new age*, Berkeley: University of California Press.

Bekkers, V.J.J.M. (1994) *Nieuwe vormen van sturing en informatisering*, Delft: Eburon.

Bekkers, V.J.J.M. (2004) 'Virtual policy communities and responsive governance: Redesigning on-line debates', *Information Polity*, vol. 9, no. 3/4, pp. 193-203.

Bennett, L. (2007) 'The Digital Structure of Collective Action: Individuals, Organizations, and Networks in Protests Against the Iraq War', *Conference proceedings*, ,Changing politics through digital networks: The role of ICT's in the formation of new social en political actors and actions, Florence.

Boogers, M. and Voerman, G. (2003) 'Surfing Citizens and Floating Voters: Results of an Online Survey of Visitors to Political Web Sites during the Dutch 2002 General Elections Campaign', *Information Polity*, vol. 8, no. 1/2, pp. 17-27.

Bovens, M. (2003) *De digitale republiek. Democratie en rechtsstaat in de informatiemaatschappij*, Amsterdam: Amsterdam University Press.

Calenda, D. and Meijer, A. (2009). 'Young people, the Internet and Political Participation: Findings of a web survey in Italy, Spain and The Netherlands' Information, Communication and Society (to be published).

Coleman, D., Morrison, S.E. and Svennenig, M. (2007) 'New Media & Political' Efficacy, *Conference proceedings*, Changing politics through digital networks: The role of ICT's in the formation of new social en political actors and actions, Florence.

Corbin, J. and Strauss, A. (2008) *Basics of Qualitative Research*, 3rd edition, Los Angeles: SAGE Publications.

Deibert, R.D. (1997) *Parchment, Printing and Hypermedia*. New York: Columbia University Press.

Desai, U. (1989) 'Public Participation in Environmental Policy Implementation: Case of the Surface Mining Control and Reclamation Act', *The American Review of Public Administration*, vol. 19, no. 1, pp. 49-65.

DeSanctis, G. and Poole, M.S. (1994) 'Capturing the Complexity in Adnaced technology Use: Adaptive Structuration Theory', *Organization Science*, vol. 5, no. 2, pp. 121 – 147.

Doreian, P. and Woodard, K.L. (1992) 'Fixed list versus snowball selection of social networks', *Social Science Research,* vol. 21, pp. 216–233.

Edwards, A. (2003) *De gefaciliteerde democratie. Internet, de burger en zijn intermediairen*, Utrecht: Lemma.

Frissen, P.H.A. (1999) *Politics, Governance, Technology, A Postmodern Narrative on the*

Frissen, V. (2007) 'Digitale Diaspora', *Lecture*, The Hage, the 16th of November 2007.

Giddens, A. (1984) *The constitution of society: outline of the theory of structure,* Berkeley CA: University of California Press.

Gotved, S. (2002) 'Spatial Dimensions in Online Communities', *Space and Culture,* vol. 5, no. 4, pp. 405–14.

Habermas, J. (1991) *The Structural Transformation of the Public Sphere: An Inquiry into a category of Bourgeois Society,* Cambridge MA: MIT Press.

Hindman, M. (2005) 'The Real Lessons of Howard Dean: Reflections on the First Digital Campaign', *Perspectives on Politics*, vol. 3, no. 1, pp. 121-128.

Hutchby, I. (2001). *Conversation and Technology. From the Telephone to the Internet*. Cambridge, UK: Polity.

Hutchby, I. (2003). Affordances and the Analysis of Technologically Mediated Interaction: A Response to Brian Rappert, *Sociology,* Vol. 37, Nr. 3, pp. 581-589.

Linders, L. and Goossens, N. (2004) 'Bruggen bouwen met virtuele middelen', in Haan, de J. and Klumper, O. (ed.) *Jaarboek ICT en samenleving 2004. Beleid in praktijk*, Amsterdam: Boom.

Locke, L. (2007) 'The Future of Facebook', *Time Magazine*, 17 July, Available: http://www.time.com/time/business/article/0,8599,1644040,00.html [8 Dec 2007].

Macintosh, A. and Whyte, A. (2006) 'Evaluating how eparticipation changes local democracy', *e-Government Workshop*, London, Available: http://www.iseing.org/egov/eGOV06 [28 Sep 2008].

Meijer, A., Homburg, V. and Bekkers, V. (2007) 'Toezicht 2.0. Onderzoek naar toezicht, transparantie, burgers en compliance in het informatietijdperk', Unpublished Report for the Alliance ICT & Good Governance.

Norris, P. (2000) *Digital Divide: Civic Engagement, Information Poverty and the Internet Worldwide*, New York: Cambridge University Press.

O'Reilly, T. (2005) *What Is Web 2.0: Design Patterns and Business Models for the Next Generation of Software*, [Online], Available: www.oreillynet.com/lpt/a/6228 [20 Feb 2008].

Orlikowski, W.J. (1992) 'The Duality of Technology: Rethinking the Concept of Technology in Organizations', *Organization Science*, vol. 3, no. 3, August, pp. 398-427.

Papacharissi, Z. (2002) 'The Virtual Sphere: The internet as a public sphere', *New Media and Society*, vol. 4, no. 1, pp. 9-27.

Pascu, C., Osimo, D., Ulbrich, M., Turlea, G. and Burgelman, J.C. (2007) 'The potential disruptive impact of Internet 2 based technologies', First Monday [Electronic], vol. 12, no. 3, March, Available: http://www.firstmonday.org/issues/issue12_3/pascu/index.html [7 Jun 2008].

Putnam, R.D. (2000) *Bowling alone. The collapse and revival of American community*, New York: Simon & Schuster.

Rapoza, J. (2006) 'What Web 2.0 means to you', *eWeek*, vol. 23, no. 1, pp. 38.

Rhodes, R. (1997) *Understanding Governance: Policy Networks, Governance, Reflexivity and Accountability*, Milton Keynes: Open University Press.

Rowe, G. and Frewer, L.J. (2000) 'Public Participation Methods: A Framework for Evaluation', *Science, Technology & Human Values*, vol. 25, no. 1, pp. 3-29.

Sellen, A.J. and Harper, R.H.R. (2002). *The Myth of the Paperless Office*, Cambridge: MIT Press.

Smith, L.G. (1983) *Impact assessment and sustainable resource management*. Harlow UK: Longman.

Sociaal Cultureel Planbureau (SCP), (2005) *Jaarrapport Integratie 2005*, Den Haag: SCP Publications.

Virtual State, Cheltenham: Edward Elgar.

Wellman, B. (ed.) (1999) *Networks in the Global Village: Life in Contemporary Communities*, Boulder: Westview Press.

Conceptualising Citizen's Trust in e-Government: Application of Q Methodology

Hisham Alsaghier, Marilyn Ford, Anne Nguyen and Rene Hexel
Griffith University, Brisbane, Australia
h.alsaghier@griffith.edu.au
m.ford@griffith.edu.au
a.nguyen@giffith.edu.au
r.hexel@griffith.edu.au
Originally published in EJEG(2009) Volume 7, issue 4.

Editorial Commentary

Several of the chapters included in this book explicitly identify trust as an issue of concern in e-Government. Those that don't refer to trust explicitly, almost invariably contain some implicit reference to trust. Alsaghier et al argue that trust plays a vital role in helping citizens overcome any issues they may have with perceived risk. Consequently, they are of the opinion that we need to develop a much clearer understanding of the role of trust and that we need to understand how to build trust if e-Government is to deliver its potential. Enhancing citizen acceptance of e-Government will depend on governments' ability to build trust and if governments want to build trust they need to understand what trust is. The authors develop an eclectic view of trust and seek to integrate concepts drawn from the disciplines of psychology and sociology and from the domains of e-commerce and HCI (Human Computer Interaction). The authors define trust in e-Government as an individual's belief that the government body will perform an action that is important to the individual without the individual having control over the government body's execution of that action. There is a huge body of literature that emphasises the importance of impersonal trust in making social networks work - the absence of trust will preclude the growth of cooperative behaviour. The authors argue that if the public do not have trust in e-Government then e-Government will not work: trust is thus a necessary condition for e-Government.

Alsaghier et. al. develop a model that measures, inter alia, an individual's disposition to trust (some people are naturally more trusting than others); their familiarity with the "online world"; their trust in institutions; the quality of, for example, websites; the ease of use of e-Government web-based facilities; a user's perceived sense of risk and an individual's level of trust in e-Government. While the authors' research is still developing, their work provides useful insights into trust in e-Government and it also provides a potential methodology for measuring the effects of various concepts and constructs on users' ability to trust e-Government and use it more extensively.

Abstract: In e-Government contexts, trust plays a vital role in helping citizens overcome perceived risks. Trust makes citizens comfortable sharing personal information, make online government transactions, and acting on e-Government advice. Thus, trust is a significant notion that should be critically investigated to help both researchers and practitioners understand citizens' acceptance of e-Government. Prior research in trust has focused mainly on consumer trust in e-Commerce. Most existing literatures on trust in e-Government focus on technical perspectives such as Public Key Infrastructure (PKI). This paper contributes to the literature by proposing a conceptual model of citizens' trust in e-Government. The model proposed is comprised of constructs from multiple disciplines: psychology, sociology, e-commerce, and Human-Computer interaction (HCI). The research is also aimed at developing variables in order to measure the theoretical constructs in the proposed model. This pool of items is generated from a literature review. Q-Methodology has been utilised to validate the measurement items. The outcome of two Q-sorting rounds resulted in developing a survey instrument for the proposed model with excellent validity and reliability.

Keywords: e-Government, trust, perceived risk, citizens' participation, technology acceptance model

1. Introduction

Electronic commerce or, in short, e-commerce and its sophisticated technologies have enabled governments and companies to provide products and services for their citizens and customers through web sites. Online services are cheaper, more convenient, and easy to provide. Electronic Government or e-Government has been classified as one instance of ecommence (Schneider, 2003). Many governments around the world have launched their e-Government initiatives to provide citizens and organisations with more convenient ways for accessing government information and services (Turban, King, Lee, Warkentin, & Chung, 2002). Previous research has been carried out to evaluate the quality and quantity of the e-Government services provided and the overall adoption of e-Government. One factor that plays a vital role in e-commerce adoption, especially e-Government, is a mature trust between the citizen and his/her government. Although trust has been recently studied in e-commerce, there is a lack of research that investigates the trust phenomenon in e-Government. Most of the existing online trust literatures focus on e-commerce and in particular, Business-to-Consumer (B2C) e-commerce.

The purpose of this paper is twofold. The first is to identify the factors that most likely affect citizens' trust in e-Government. This is contextualised by investigating the elements and components that transact trust beliefs in electronic services, whether these elements and components are related to technical aspects, such as HCI, or to business, psychological, sociological, or cultural perspectives. The second purpose is to develop an instrument to measure the theoretical constructs in the proposed model.

2. Literature Review and Theoretical Background

2.1. Overview of e-Government

There are a number of e-Government definitions in the existing literature. Most revolve around the concepts of government's employment of technology, in particular web-based applications, to improve access and delivery of government services to citizens, business partners, and other government agencies. The World Bank defines trust as, "...the use by government agencies of information technologies (such as Wide Area Networks the Internet, and mobile computing) that have ability to transform relations with citizens, businesses, and other arms of government." (World Bank Group, 2007).

2.1.1. Stages of e-Government Development

There are various stages of e-Government development. According to Howard (2001) and Lau (2001), there are four major stages of e-Government development:

- **Information Publishing**: this is a basic form of e-Government where government posts information on official government websites. The presented information may include information about available public services, government contracts, and government events.
- **Two-way Communication**: in this stage citizens communicate with the government through the Internet and make simple requests. Usually, the information requested is not processed immediately online but sent to the client by ground mail or email.
- **Transaction**: this stage is more sophisticated than previous stages, and indicates that citizens are able to conduct transactions online. Driving licence renewing is one example of such transactions.
- **Integration**: this is the most sophisticated stage of e-Government development. In this stage, all government services provided from different departments and agencies are integrated together and accessed through a single website called the e-Government portal.

2.1.2. e-Government Sectors

The nature of e-Government adoption depends on the degree to which several parties are engaged, including: citizens, businesses, and other government agencies. Therefore, the applications of e-Government are categorised according to users' needs and the capacity of ICT. The different users and beneficiaries of e-Government shape the characteristic of e-Government applications. e-Government applications are classified according to the governmental relationships with a variety of constituents.

e-Government has been divided into the following four sectors according to whom participates: Government to Government (G2G) for all operations inside or between government agencies; Government to Business (G2B) for all interested participants in institutions or private companies and the government; and Government to Citizen (G2C) which refers to all dealings between citizens and the government (DeBenedictis, Howell, Figueroa, & Boggs, 2002). Some observers, such as Ndou (2004), further identify a fourth sector, Government to Employees (G2E).

Government-to-Citizen (G2C)

The G2C sector refers to all dealings between citizens and the government over online media (DeBenedictis et al., 2002). G2C e-Government is designed to facilitate citizen interaction with the government and is perceived to be the primary goal of e-Government (Seifert, 2008). Using G2C e-Government, citizen transactions with government, such as license renewal, can be less time consuming and easier to carry out.

The citizen demand for G2C e-Government is expected to increase significantly over the next ten years as the youth, who are now growing up in the information age with personal computers and the Internet as a routine presence in their live, become adults (Seifert, 2008). One example of a G2C initiative is GoBenefits.gov, which is an American governmental web site that provides a single point of access for citizens to locate and determine potential eligibility for government benefits and services.

Government-to-Business (G2B)
The G2B sector deals mainly with the sale of surplus government goods to the public and the procurement of goods and services. Recently, G2B initiatives received a significant amount of attention as a result of high enthusiasm in the business sector and the potential for reducing costs through improved procurement practices and increased competition (Seifert & Petersen, 2002). When implemented effectively, G2B e-Government has the potential to streamline and improve the consistency of personnel-intensive tasks (Seifert, 2008).

e-Procurement is the main application of G2B e-Government that allows government agencies to reap the benefits being realized in the private sector though electronic means (Fang, 2002). One example of a G2B initiative is FedBizOpps.gov which is a web site administered by the General Services Administration (GSA), an independent agency of the United States government established to manage and support basic functions of federal agencies. FedBizOpps.gov is designed to serve as a central location for agencies to post procurement notices.

Government-to-Government (G2G)
The G2G sector represents the backbone of e-Government in which governments (federal, state, and local) integrate their internal systems and procedures into a central system (Seifert, 2008). The main aim of G2G e-Government is to facilitate processes if inter-government organisations by streamlining collaboration and coordination.

G2G e-Government involves sharing data and conducting electronic transactions between governmental actors. The main motivating force behind the G2G sector includes the growing attention being paid to improve efficiency by saving transactions cost, increasing the speed of transactions, reducing the number of personnel necessary to complete a task, and improving the consistency of outcomes (Seifert, 2008). Examples of G2G e-Government include e-Identity, e-Security services, Electronic Document Management, and Process Management Services.

2.2. Research Model

In the context of the Government-to-Citizen category of e-Government, there are two major objectives: providing citizens with effective information access, and providing citizens with access to the full range of e-Government services online (National Research Council, 2002). The basic idea behind e-Government is to allow citizens to interact with their government through the internet; for example, they ask questions and receive answers, get updated government regulations, obtain government official documents, fill applications, pay tax and bills, receive payments, and forth. The two forms of citizen engagement in e-Government are receiving e-Government information and requesting e-Government service (Warkentin, Gefen, Pavlou, & Rose, 2002).

The research model described in Figure 1 targets the way citizens' trust can affect their intention to engage in e-Government. The model consists of nine constructs that delineate the conceptual model of citizens' trust in e-Government. It attempts to formulate an important number of factors that have been observed to affect citizens' trust in e-Government. These factors have been integrated from different models of trust that exist in the literature. The following provides a theoretical review of how each construct was derived.

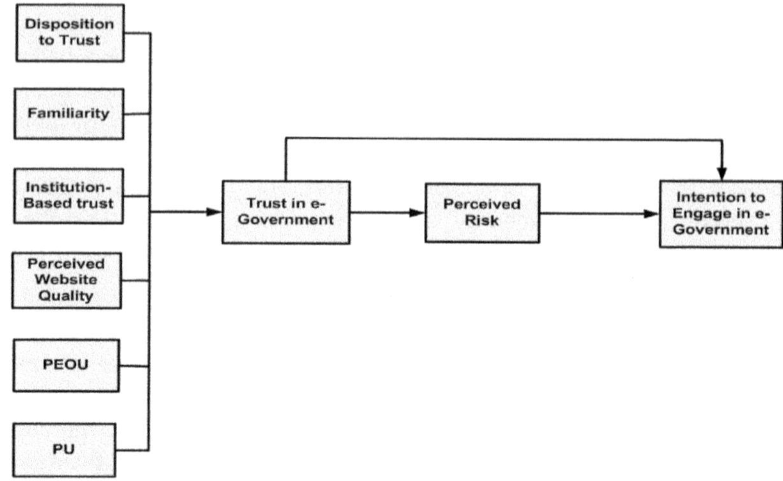

Figure 1: Theoretical research model

2.2.1. Trust in e-Government

In this research, trust is defined as an individual's (trustor, hence citizen) belief or expectation that another party (trustee, hence e-Government) will perform a particular action important to the trustor in the absence of trustor's control over trustee's performance (Mayer, Davis, & Schoorman, 1995). Hence, trust indicates that trustor will rely on trust behaviour (Rotter, 1971b). Trust occurrs in an uncertain environment (Schlenker, Helm, & Tedeschi, 1973) where the risk exists (Lewis & Weigert, 1985) and the trustor is vulnerable to unfulfilled expectations or harmful outcomes (Zand, 1972). People use trust as a mental mechanism to reduce the complexity and uncertainty of living in a complex environment (Luhmann, 1979).

Trust has been cited as an important and crucial requirement for economic and social interactions (Baier, 1986; Barber, 1983; Dasgupta, 1998; Lewis & Weigert, 1985; Luhmann, 1979; Mayer et al., 1995; McAllister, 1995; Rotter, 1971a). trust has been also observed as a key value in the context of e-commerce (Gefen, 2000; Gefen & Straub, 2004), and in e-Government (Galindo, 2002). Furthermore, trust enables cooperative behaviour (Gambetta, 1988). Hence, trust beliefs lead for trust behaviour. In this model trust in e-Government will lead citizens to engage in e-Government (Warkentin et al., 2002).

H1: citizen trust in e-Government positively influences intensions to engage in e-Government.

2.2.2. Disposition to Trust

Individuals have differences in terms of tendency to trust another party (Rotter, 1971a) whether this party is a person, a group, an organisation, or a business. Disposition to trust, "...is a propensity or tendency to believe in the positive attributes of others in general." (McKnight, Kacmar, & Choudhury, 2004 p. 36). Disposition to trust has been identified as a construct for trust in many trust models (McKnight, Choudhury, & Kacmar, 2002; McKnight & Chervany, 2001; McKnight et. al., 2004). McKnight and Chervany (2001) proposed two constructs for disposition to trust: *Faith in Humanity* and *Trusting Stance*. Faith in humanity is founded on assumptions that others are usually upright, well meaning, and dependable. Trusting stance indicates that one believes that, regardless of others' reliability, one will obtain better outcomes by dealing with other people - i.e. trust others until they prove the trustor is wrong. Research has shown that disposition to trust has a significant impact on trust in online contexts (McKnight et. al., 2002; McKnight et. al., 2004; Pavlou & Gefen, 2004). Trust in the web institution is positively affected by disposition to trust because people who trust others generally will trust institutions involving people (McKnight et. al., 2004) such as online vendors. Thus, disposition to trust is positively associated with consumer's trust in e-commerce (Kim & Kim, 2005). In the e-Government context, disposition to trust has been argued to increase trust in e-Government (Warkentin et. al., 2002). This leads to the following hypothesis:

H2: Citizens' disposition to trust is positively associated with trust in e-Government.

2.2.3. Familiarity

Familiarity is stage where people use their previous experience (Luhmann, 1979), interactions, and learning to understand what, where, why, and when people do what they do (Gefen, 2000). It has been argued that familiarity is a precondition for trust (Luhmann, 1979), that trust occurrs in a familiar world, and the familiar features of the world may be changed which in turn may impact the possibility of developing trust in human relations (Luhmann, 1988). Luhmann's note about the impact of changing levels of familiarity on trust is useful in understanding e-Government trust because the e-Government environment is different from the tradition government environment. Therefore, most of citizens are not familiar with e-Government environments, especially in the early stage of e-Government adoption, which will influence citizens' trust in e-Government.

H3: Citizens' familiarity with e-Government positively affects trust in e-Government.

2.2.4. Institution-Based Trust

Institution-based trust is considered as the trustor's confidence that situational structures exist which facilitate outcome success of trusting behavior (Pavlou, Tan, & Gefen, 2003) and, more impotently, that impose sanctions when trust is breached (Humphery & Schmitz, 1998; Lane & Bachmann, 1996). Following McKnight et. al. (2002, pg. 339), institution-based trust is defined as "...the belief that needed structural conditions are present (e.g., in the Internet) to enhance the probability of achieving a successful outcome in an endeavour like e-commerce". Institution-based trust is generated when the trustor believes that safety, guarantee, insurance and other performance structures are presented to secure a situation (Pavlou et. al., 2003; Shapiro, 1987). In an economic context, Institution-based trust "...proved to be the most resilient,..., expanded and elaborated [trust creating mode]..." in impersonal economic environment (Zucker, 1986, pg. 96). In an e-commerce context, institution-based trust has been argued to be best suited for online marketplaces because secure online transactions (between the buyer and seller) are conducted under the aegis of third parties who constitute an *institutional context* (Pavlou & Gefen, 2004).

McKnight et. al. (2002) defined two dimensions (sub-constructs) of institution-based trust: *structural assurance* and *situation normality*. Structural assurance is related to structures that existed to promote success such as guarantees, regulations and legal resources. Situation normality is the belief that success is expected as the environment is normal and in appropriate order. An example of situation normality in an internet environment is the expectation that communication infrastructure is secure, i.e. security mechanisms and techniques (encryption) are employed to secure the communication channel. Accordingly, the following hypotheses are proposed:

H4a: Structure assurance trust positively affects citizens' trust in e-Government.

H4b: Situation normality trust positively affects citizens' trust in e-Government.

3. Perceived website quality

Several research studies have been conducted to identify the design elements that communicate trust in e-commerce web sites. The Studio Archetype and Sapient study (1999) is a significant research project that has investigated trust in e-commerce from an HCI perspective. They identified different types of forms that communicate consumers' trust in an e-commerce website. *Navigation* and *presentation* of websites are two factors that have been identified as very important design elements that facilitate user trust in the websites. Based on this empirical evidence (Studio Archetype/Sapient & Cheskin Research, 1999), the following hypotheses are proposed:

H5a: Easiness of navigation of e-Government website positively affects citizens' trust in e-Government.

H5b: e-Government website presentation positively affects citizens' trust in e-Government.

3.1. Technology Acceptance Model (TAM)

Other important components that are assumed to affect citizens' trust in e-Government are: *Perceived Usefulness (PU)* and *Perceived Ease of Use (PEOU)*. PU and PEUO are two important components in the Technology Acceptance Model (TAM) (Davis, 1989; Davis, Bagozzi, & Warshaw, 1989). TAM is an adaptation of the theory of reasoned action (TRA) (Fishbein & Ajzen, 1975). PU is the degree to which the user believes that the use of the system enhances his or her task performance. PEOU is the degree to which the user believes that using the system is easy and difficulty-free. TAM has been applied to the usability of e-commerce websites (Gefen, Karahanna, & Straub, 2003); as wll, several researchers have hypothesised that PEOU and PU positively affect trust in e-vendors (Chau, Hu, Lee, & Au, 2007; Koufaris, Kambil, & Labarbera, 2001; Pavlou, 2003; Tang & Chi, 2005). In the e-Government context, the following hypotheses are proposed:

H6a: PEOU of an e-Government website positively influences citizens' trust in e-Government.

H6b: PU of an e-Government website positively influences citizens' trust in e-Government,

3.2. Perceived Risk

Risk is closely connected with trust; if there is no risk, there is no need for trust (Luhmann, 1988). Therefore, trust is manifested in the presence of risk where the possible damage is greater than the possible advantage that is sought (Deutsch, 1960). Trust "...derives from the calculus of gains and losses, weighed by perceived risks..." (Rousseau, Sitkin, Burt, & Camerer, 1998, pg. 398). However, "...placing trust means suspending, discounting, bracketing the risk, acting as if the risk were not existent" (Sztompka, 2003 p. 31). Therefore, trust affects risk which in turns affects behaviour, i.e. perceived risk moderates the relations between trusting belief and intention to trust behaviour (Gefen, Rao, & Tractinsky, 2003). Accordingly, the following hypotheses are proposed:

H7a: Citizens' trust in e-Government negatively affects perceived risk.

H7b: Perceived risk negatively affects intention to engage in e-Government.

3.3. Instrument Development

The constructs are based on a comprehensive review of the literature and grounded in existing theories. Multi-item scales were developed or adapted from the literature in order to measure the constructs. The application of multi-item or summated scales is useful for investigating latent constructs (Borsboom, Mellenbergh, & Heerden, 2003; Colton & Covert, 2007) and, if properly developed, multi-item scales will provide meaningful measurements which will be accurate and interpretable (Peterson, 2000). Therefore, the constructs in this research are composed of three or more items (Cronbach & Meehl, 1955). As delineated in the research model (Figure 1), there are 9 major constructs. We developed the measurement scale for the *intention to engage in e-Government* construct. Items to measure the other constructs were adapted from previous empirical research. The adapted items were considerably modified. The following is a discussion of the literature that supports the items in each construct.

3.4. Items generation

Table 1: Pool of items entered in the Q-sort analysis

Construct ID	Construct	Subconstruct/ Dimension	Number of Items
1	Disposition to Trust	Benevolence	3
		Integrity	3
		Competence	3
		Trusting Stance	3
2	Familiarity		4
3	Institution-Based Trust	Structure Assurance Trust	4
		Situation Normality	11
4	Website Design	Navigation	4
		Presentation	5
5	Perceived Ease of Use		5
6	Perceived Usefulness		6
7	Trust in e-Government	Competence	6
		Integrity	7
		Benevolence	4
8	Perceived Risk	Security risk	4
		Performance risk	5
		Time Risk	2
9	Intention to engage in e-Government		8
Total			87

The items for the *"Trust in E-Government"* construct were adapted from: empirical research on consumer trust in the internet (Corbitta, Thanasankit, & Yi, 2003; Sirkka L. Jarvenpaa, Tractinsky, & Vitale, 2000), the empirical research on interdisciplinary typology of trust for e-Commerce (McKnight et. al., 2002; McKnight & Chervany, 2001), and the literature of trust building technology in the electronic market (Ba & Pavlou, 2002). The items for *"Disposition of Trust"* were synthesized from an empirical study on the trust measurement in e-Commerce (McKnight et al., 2002), and the literature on the consumer trust relationship in e-Commerce (McKnight & Chervany, 2001). The items for *"Perceived Risk"* were drawn from empirical studies on conceptualization of trust, risk and their relationship in e-Commerce (Gefen, Rao et. al., 2003; Sirkka L. Jarvenpaa et. al., 2000), from an empirical work that has investigated perceived risks as barriers to Internet and e-commerce usage (Liebermann & Stashevsky, 2002), and from an empirical investigation on the effect of perceived risk on purchase intention in the Internet (Kim, Kim, & Leong, 2005).The items for the *"Familiarity"* construct were primarily based on empirical study on the impact of familiarity on the consumer trust in e-Commerce (Gefen, 2000), and on the description of the meaning of familiarly in the literature (Luhmann, 1988; Zhang, Ghorbani, & Cohen, 2007). The items for the *"Trust in e-Government"* construct were adapted from empirical research on the trust measurement in e-Commerce (McKnight et al., 2002), from an empirical study on the role of trust in e-Commerce (Gefen, 2000), and from an empirical investigation of citizens' trust in government and its linkage with their satisfaction with e-Government (Welch, Hinnant, & Moon, 2005). The items for *"Institution-Based Trust"* (Situation Normality and Structure Assurance) were drawn from previous empirical research on institution-based trust and its effect on trust in the online environment (McKnight et. al., 2002), and from a theoretical exploration of institute-based trust (Zucker, 1986). The items for *"Perceived Website Quality"* (Navigation and Presentation) were adapted from an empirical study that has identified e-Commerce virtual design elements that effect consumers' trust (Stephens, 2004). The items for *"Perceived Usefulness"* and *"Perceived Ease of Use"* were adapted from empirical research that have investigated the relation between trust and technology acceptance model in the online environment (Gefen, Karahanna et. al., 2003).

Table 1 shows the number of items in each contrast and sub-construct in the theoretical research model.

3.5. Scale Development: Q-Sort Method

The Q-Sort method is derived from Q-Methodology, a factor analysis technique, which was developed by Stephenson (1953). It has been used by psychology and social sciences to investigate people's subjectivity, i.e. their viewpoints. Unlike R-factor analysis which studies the correlation between variables, Q-methodology examines the correlation between individuals (Brown, 1997). In Q-methodology, the items are the sample in the Q-sort and the people who complete the Q-sort are the experimental condition (Cross, 2004). Therefore, Q-methodology examines the correlations between subjects across a sample of items. One of the main applications of Q-methodology is to assess reliability and construct validity of questionnaire items that are being prepared for survey research (Nahm, Solis-Galvan, Rao, & Ragu-Nathan, 2002). Nahm et. al. (2002) demonstrated how the Q-sort method can be used to pre-test items after they have been developed or generated based on a literature review and before questionnaire items are administrated in a survey. The method consists of two stages (Nahm et al., 2002). In the first stage, two independent judges are asked to sort the items of the questionnaire according to different constructs. Based on this, the agreement between the two judges (inter-judge agreement) is calculated. In the second stage, items that were classified incorrectly and were found ambiguous in the first stage are reworded or deleted. The two-stage process is repeated continuously until a satisfactory level of agreement is reached.

In this study, items were placed in a common pool and subjected to two sorting rounds by two independent judges in each round. The participants in the Q-sort process (judges) were chosen so they represented the target population of the research and were experts in the field. Two of the participants were directors in the e-Government program in Saudi Arabia, one participant was a consultant in the e-Government program in Saudi Arabia, and one participant was a manager of IT departments in a government ministry. Participants were grouped in pairs. Each pair composed two independent judges in each round. The judges were asked to sort a list of items into groups, each group representing one of the 9 constructs. The differences and similarities among sorted items were used as an indicator for construct validity.

3.5.1. Q-sorting Procedures

The research model and its 9 constructs with their definition were presented to the judges. Items generated to measure the constructs were printed on individual 3"x5" cards. After randomly shuffling the cards (items), each judge was given the deck and asked to sort the cards into categories. Each category represented one of the 9 constructs. In addition to the nine constructs, a *"Not Applicable"* category was included to make sure the judges did not force any items into a particular category. Each round consisted of different pairs of judges. Judges were allowed to ask question either related to the sorting procedure or related to the research model and constructs.

3.5.2. Q-sort Evaluation

In order to evaluate and assess both the validity and reliability of the instrument, three evaluation criteria were used to assess the Q-sort: the inter-judge agreement level, Cohen's Kappa Index (Cohen, 1960), and Moore and Benbasat's "Hit Ratio" (Moore & Benbasat, 1991). The inter-judge agreement level is calculated by counting how many items that both judges agreed to place into a particular category. Then, the number of agreed upon items is divided by the total number of items to obtain the percentage of the inter-judge agreement. The second measure is Cohen's Kappa index which is "...the proportion of joint judgement in which there is agreement after chance is excluded" (Nahm et. al., 2002, p. 115). For instance, assume that two judges independently classified a set of N components as either accepted or rejected; after the classification is finished we can construct the following table (Nahm et. al., 2002):

		Judge 1		
		Acceptable	Rejectable	Totals
Judge 2	Acceptable	X_{11}	X_{12}	X_{1+}
	Rejectable	X_{21}	X_{22}	X_{2+}
	Totals	X_{+1}	X_{+2}	N

Cohen's Kappa index can be calculated as follows:

$$k = \frac{N_i * X_{ii} - \sum_i (X_{i+} X_{+i})}{N^2 - \sum_i (X_{i+} X_{+i})}$$

Where:

N_i: total number of items

x_{ii}: number of items agreed on by two judges

X_{i+}: number of items in the ith row

X_{+i}: number of items in the ith column

Previous research has considered a score of Kabb index greater than 0.65 to be acceptable (S. L. Jarvenpaa, 1989; Landis & Koch, 1977; Todd & Benbasat, 1993).

The third measure is Moore and Benbasat's "Hit Ratio" which measures how many items were correctly placed in the intended category by the judges. The "Hit Ratio" is computed by counting all items that were correctly sorted into intended theoretical constructs by each judge, and then dividing them by twice the total number of items.

3.5.3. First sorting round

The first round consisted of 87 items for the nine constructs. The judges in this round were a director in the e-Government program in Saudi Arabia and a manager of IT department in a government ministry. In this round, the inter-judge raw agreement scores averaged 80% (Table 2) and the initial overall placement ratio of items within the target constructs was 75% (Table 3) as 131 of 174 items were correctly classified.

Table 2: Inter-judge scores: first sorting round

	Judge 1										
	Construct	1	2	3	4	5	6	7	8	9	NA
Judge 2	1	10									
	2		4								
	3		1	4				1			
	4				6	3					
	5					3					
	6						4				2
	7			3				11	1		
	8								9		
	9							1		7	
	NA										0
	Total Items: 87	**Number of Agreement: 70**						**Agreement Ratio: 80%**			

Table 3: Items placement ratios: first sorting round

	Actual Categories												
	Construct	1	2	3	4	5	6	7	8	9	NA	Total	%
Theoretical Categories	1	22									2	24	92%
	2		8									8	100%
	3		2	17				11				30	57%
	4				12	6						18	67%
	5				1	8	1					10	80%
	6						8				4	12	67%
	7			8				24	2			34	71%
	8		2	2					18			22	82%
	9							2		14		16	88%
	Total Items Placement: 174				**Number of Hits: 131**				**Overall Hit Ratio: 75%**				

The results of the first round indicate some confusion concerning some of the constructs. In order to understand this confusion, the off-diagonal items were examined to look for clusters. On the Institution-Based Trust construct, 11 of the 13 misclassified items are in the Trust in e-Government construct. This is expected since in both constructs there are items that are related to trust beliefs. A similar effect appears in the Trust in e-Government construct, where 8 of the 10 misclassified items are in the Institution-Based Trust construct. This misplacement of the items confirms the confusion between the Trust in e-Government construct and the Institution-Based Trust construct, enforcing the need for further clarification between these two constructs in the next round. Another cluster appears in the Perceived Website Quality construct, where 6 misclassified items were placed in the Perceived Ease of Use construct. This is understandable from the fact that the quality of a website promotes and enhances the ease of use. On the Perceived Risk construct, there are two clusters; one on Familiarity (2 out of 4 misclassified items were placed in this construct) and one on Institution-Based Trust (2 out of 4 misclassified items were placed in this construct). Similarly, two misclassified items in the Trust in e-Government construct were placed in the Perceived Risk construct. This confusion may be due to the strong link between risk perception and trust, which argued for further clarification of the related measures in the next round. On the Intention to Engage in e-Government construct, two misclassified items were placed in the Trust in e-Government construct. Another cluster found in the Institution-Based Trust, where 2 out of 13 misclassified items were placed under the Familiarity construct. On the Perceived Ease of Use construct, there were two clusters; one on the Perceived Website Quality construct (1 out of 2 misclassified items was placed in this construct) and one on the Perceived Usefulness construct (1 out of 2 misclassified items was placed in this construct). Finally, 6 items were classified as not applicable; 2 items from Disposition to Trust construct and 4 from the Perceived Usefulness construct.

Cohen's Kappa for this round was computed as:

$$K = \frac{87 * 70 - 131}{87^2 - 131} = 0.80$$

Following the guidelines of Landis and Koch (1977) for interpreting the Cohen's Kappa, the value of 0.80 indicates an excellent level of agreement beyond chance for the judges in the first round. This value is identical to the value of raw agreement (Table 2). The item placement ratios averaged 75%. The lowest item placement ratio value was 57% for the Institution-Based Trust construct, indicating a low degree of constructs validity. Also, the Perceived Website Quality, Perceived Usefulness, and the Trust in e-Government constructs had a low value of item placement ratio: 67%, 67%, and 71% respectively. On the other hand, several constructs, namely Familiarity, Disposition to Trust, Intention to Engage in e-Government, Perceived Risk, and Perceived Ease of Use obtained 100%, 92%, 88%, 82%, and 80% of item placement ratio respectively, indicating a high degree of constructs validity.

In order to identify the cause of misclassifications in round one, each judge's individual classification for each item was examined. An examination of the off-diagonal entries in the placement matrix (Table 3) was conducted. The ambiguous items that had been fitted in more than one category or fitted in no category were careful analysed. The analysis led to the rewording of ambiguous items including 11 items belonging to Institution-Based Trust, 3 items belonging to Perceived Website Quality construct, 2 items belonging to Perceived Risk construct, one item belonging to Trust in e-Government construct, and one item belonging to Intention to Engage in e-Government construct. The analysis also led to deleting the too indeterminate items including 5 items belonging to Trust in e-Government, 2 items belonging to Disposition to Trust, 2 items belonging to Perceived Usefulness, and 2 items belonging to Perceived Ease of Use. Overall, 11 items were deleted and 18 items were reworded. One additional item suggested by two judges was added to the Perceived Ease of Use construct.

3.5.4. Second Sorting Round

The second round consisted of 77 items for the nine constructs. The judges in this round were a director in the e-Government program in Saudi Arabia and a consultant in the e-Government program in Saudi Arabia. In this round, the inter-judge raw agreement scores averaged 91% (

Table 4), an 11% improvement of the previous round. The overall placement ratio of items within the target constructs was 88% (Table 5), a 13% improvement from round one, as 131 of 174 items were correctly classified.

In the second round, the changes effected on items in round one had resulted in a good improvement of the measures. However, a further examination of the off-diagonal entries in the placement matrix (Table 5) is needed in order to improve potential reliability and construct validity.

Table 4: Inter-judge scores: second sorting round

	Judge 1										
	Construct	1	2	3	4	5	6	7	8	9	NA
Judge 2	1	9									
	2		4								
	3			12				1			
	4				7						
	5				1	4					
	6						4				
	7							9	1	1	
	8								10		
	9									7	
	NA										0
	Total Items: 77	Number of Agreement: 70						Agreement Ratio: 91%			

Table 5: Items placement ratios: second sorting round

	Actual Categories												
	Construct	1	2	3	4	5	6	7	8	9	NA	Total	%
Theoretical Categories	1	18									1	19	95%
	2		8									8	100%
	3			27				6			2	35	77%
	4				15							15	100%
	5				3	8						11	73%
	6						8				2	10	80%
	7							18	2	2		22	82%
	8								20			20	100%
	9									14		14	100%
	Total Items Placement: 154				Number of Hits: 136					Overall Hit Ratio: 88%			

The analysis of the placement matrix showed that there was a relatively small cluster around the Institution-Based Trust construct. A closer investigation of the items causing this cluster indicates that those items have words such as “confidence” and “rely” which are related to trust, causing a slight confusion between Institution-Based Trust and Trust in e-Government constructs. The analysis led to rewording the items so the difference between trust in the Internet in general (Institution-Based Trust) and trust in e-Government in particular, were distinguishable. Additionally, 3 misclassified items in the Perceived Website Quality construct were placed in the Perceived Ease of Use construct. A closer look at the items causing the confusion revealed that items with words like "easier" and "easy" caused a slight confusion between the Perceived Website Quality and Perceived Ease of Use constructs. The analysis led to rewording two items in Perceived Ease of Use so it was clearly distinguished from the ease of searching and requesting e-Government services and the features and characteristics of e-Government websites quality.

Cohen's Kappa for this round was computed as:

$$K = \frac{77 * 70 - 136}{77^2 - 136} = 0.91$$

Following the guidelines of Landis and Koch (1977) for interpreting the Cohen's Kappa, the value of 0.91, an 11% improvement from round one, indicates an excellent level of agreement beyond chance for the judges in the second round. At this point, we decided to stop Q sorting round two, with Cohen's Kappa of 0.91, the average placement ratio of 88%, and the inter-judge raw agreement of 91%, indicating a high level of reliability and construct validity. See Appendix A for the complete items list.

4. Summary and conclusions

In this paper a conceptual model of citizens' trust in e-Government is proposed. The model consists of nine theoretical constructs which delineate the concept of citizens' trust in e-Government. An instrument to measure these constructs is developed also in this research. A pool of 87 items was generated. Q-methodology was then employed to ensure construct validity and reliability. Two Q-sorting rounds were conduced to validate the instrument. After the analysis of the Q-sorting, 77 items remained and are reported in Appendix A. This instrument can be used to investigate citizens' trust in e-Government. The future direction for this research is to administer a large scale survey for users of e-Government.

5. Appendix A. measures

Disposition to Trust

1. In general, people really do care about the well-being of others.
2. The typical person is sincerely concerned about the problems of others.
3. Most of the time, people care enough to try to be helpful, rather than just looking out for themselves.
4. In general, most folks keep their promises.
5. I think people generally try to back up their words with their actions.
6. Most people are honest in their dealings with others.
7. A large majority of professional people are competent in their area of expertise.
8. I usually trust people until they give me a reason not to trust them.
9. I generally give people the benefit of the doubt when I first meet them.
10. My typical approach is to trust new acquaintances until they prove I should not trust them.

Familiarity

1. I am familiar with looking for government services on the Internet.
2. I am familiar with conducting online translation with government on the Internet.
3. I am familiar with the e-Government web sites.
4. I am familiar with communicating with government agencies and departments through their official web sites.

Institution-Based Trust

1. I feel good about how things go when I do purchasing or other activities on the Internet.
2. I am comfortable making purchases on the Internet.
3. I feel that most Internet vendors would act in a customers' best interest.
4. If a customer required help, most Internet vendors would do their best to help.
5. Most Internet vendors are interested in customer well-being, not just their own well-being.
6. I am comfortable relying on Internet vendors to meet their obligations.
7. I feel fine doing business on the Internet since Internet vendors generally fulfil their agreements.
8. I always feel confident that I can rely on Internet vendors to do their part when I interact with them.
9. In general, most Internet vendors are competent at serving their customers.
10. Most Internet vendors do a capable job at meeting customer needs.
11. I feel that most Internet vendors are good at what they do.
12. The Internet has enough safeguards to make me feel comfortable using it to transact personal business.
13. I feel assured that legal and technological structures adequately protect me from problems on the Internet.
14. I feel confident that encryption and other technological advances on the Internet make it safe for me to do business there.
15. In general, the Internet is now a robust and safe environment in which to transact business.

Website-Quality

1. Most of the e-Government web sites are easy to navigate.
2. Most of the e-Government web sites' contents are easily accessible.
3. Most of the e-Government web sites are intuitive.
4. Most of e-Government web sites provide sufficient information to search for the relevant government services.
5. Most of the e-Government web sites are easy to read.
6. Most of e-Government web sites are visually pleasing.
7. Most of e-Government web sites are consistent throughout the site.
8. Most of e-Government web sites are professionally designed.
9. Most of the e-Government web sites show how users can contact and communicate with them.

PEOU

1. Most of the e-Government web sites are easy to use.
2. It is easy to learn how to interact with e-Government web sites.
3. Most of e-Government web sites are flexible to interact with.
4. Communication with the state government is easier through its official websites.

PU

1. I perceived that using the e-Government web sites enables citizens to search for government services and conduct government transactions faster.
2. I perceived that using the e-Government web sites can enhance the effectiveness of citizens' transactions with government.
3. Most of e-Government web sites are useful for searching government services.
4. Most of e-Government web sites are useful for conducting government transactions.

Trust in e-Government

1. I believe that e-Government web sites are competent and effective in providing government services.
2. Citizens can always predict performance of most e-Government web sites from their past experience with the web sites.
3. Most e-Government web sites exhibit care, concern, honesty and goodwill to their citizens, thus providing a basis to advance the citizens relationship.
4. I believe most e-Government web sites will perform to the outmost of the citizens' benefit.
5. I believe that most e-Government web sites are truthful in their dealings with the citizens.
6. I would characterize e-Government as honest.
7. I believe that most e-Government web sites would keep their commitments.
8. I believe that e-Government web sites are sincere and genuine.
9. I believe that e-Government web sites are trustworthy.
10. I believe that most e-Government web sites would act in the citizens' best interest.
11. If the citizens required help, e-Government web sites would do their best to help them.
12. I believe that e-Government web sites are interested in the citizens well-being, not just their own.

Perceived Risk

1. Using e-Government web sites to transact with government departments and agencies I perceive that it is not secure to send sensitive information.
2. When using credit card to pay for government services though e-Government web sites I feel that credit card details are likely to be stolen.
3. I would feel insecure sending sensitive information via e-Government web sites.
4. Overall, it is not safe to transmit sensitive information over e-Government web sites.
5. As I consider transacting with government departments and agencies via e-Government web sites, I worry about whether they will perform as they are supposed to.
6. If I were to transact with government departments and agencies via e-Government web sites, I would be concerned that they would not provide the level of benefits that I would be expecting.
7. I am not confident about the ability of e-Government web sites to perform as expected.
8. Considering the possible problems associated with e-Government web sites performance, a lot of risk would be involved with searching and requesting government services via e-Government web sites.
9. It would be to risky to rely on the information provided in e-Government web sites.
10. Using e-Government web sites to search and request government services could lead to an inefficient use of my time.
11. Using e-Government web sites to search and request government services will take too much time or be a waste of time.

Intention to Engage in e-Government

1. How likely is it that you would request government services via e-Government web sites?
2. How likely is it that you would continue visiting e-Government web sites?
3. I would be willing to provide credit card information to pay for government services via e-Government web sites.
4. I can always rely on information provided in e-Government websites.
5. I would be willing to provide my government identification number to e-Government web sites.
6. I would be willing to provide information like my name, address, and phone number to e-Government websites.
7. I would be willing to pay to access information on e-Government web sites.
8. I will follow the procedures and advices provided in e-Government web sites.

References

Ba, S., & Pavlou, P. A. (2002). Evidence of the Effect of Trust Building Technology in Electronic Markets: Price Premiums and Buyer Behavior. *MIS Quarterly, 26*(3), 243-268.

Baier, A. (1986). Trust and Antitrust. *Ethics, 96*(2), 231-260.

Barber, B. (1983). *Logic and Limits of Trust*. New Jersey: Rutgers University.

Borsboom, D., Mellenbergh, G. J., & Heerden, J. v. (2003). The Theoretical Status of Latent Variables. *Psychological Review, 110*(2), 203-219.

Brown, S. R. (1997). The History and Principles of Q methodology in Psychology and the Social Sciences. Retrieved 19/04/2007, from http://facstaff.uww.edu/cottlec/QArchive/Bps.htm

Chau, P. Y. K., Hu, P. J.-H., Lee, B. L. P., & Au, A. K. K. (2007). Examining customers' trust in online vendors and dropouts: An empirical study. *Electronic Commerce Research and Applications, Forthcoming*.

Cohen, J. (1960). A Coefficient of Agreement for Nominal Scales. *Educational and Psychological Measurement, 20*(1), 37-46.

Colton, D., & Covert, R. W. (2007). *Designing and constructing instruments for social research and evaluation*. San Francisco, CA: Jossey-Bass.

Corbitta, B. J., Thanasankit, T., & Yi, H. (2003). Trust and e-commerce: a study of consumer perceptions. *Electronic Commerce Research and Applications, 2*(3), 203-125.

Cronbach, L. J., & Meehl, P. E. (1955). Construct Validity in Psychological Tests. *Psychological Bulletin, 52*(4), 281-302.

Cross, R. M. (2004). Exploring attitudes: the case for Q methodology. *Health Education Research, 20*(2), 206-213.

Dasgupta, P. (1998). Trust as a Commodity. In D. Gambetta (Ed.), *Trust: Making and Breaking Cooperative Relations* (electronic edition ed.): Basil Blackwell Ltd.

Davis, F. D. (1989). Perceived Usefulness, Perceived Ease of Use, and User Acceptance of Information Technology. *MIS Quarterly, 13*(3), 319-340.

Davis, F. D., Bagozzi, R. P., & Warshaw, P. R. (1989). User Acceptance of Computer Technology: A Comparison of Two Theoretical Models. *Management Science, 35*(8), 982-1003.

DeBenedictis, A., Howell, W., Figueroa, R., & Boggs, R. A. (2002). E-Government defined: an overview of the next big information technology challenge. *Issues in Information Systems, 3*, 130-136.

Deutsch, M. (1960). The Effect of Motivational Orientation Upon Trust and Suspicion. *Human Relations, 13*, 123-139.

Fang, Z. (2002). E-Government in Digital Era: Concept, Practice, and Development. *International Journal of The Computer, The Internet and Management, 10*(2), 1-22.

Fishbein, M., & Ajzen, I. (1975). *Belief, Attitude, Intention, and Behavior: An Introduction to Theory and Research*. Reading, MA: Addison-Wesley.

Galindo, F. (2002). e-Government Trust Providers. In A. Gronlund (Ed.), *Electronic Government: Design, Applications and Management*. London: Idea Group Publishing.

Gambetta, D. (1988). Can We Trust Trust? In D. Gambetta (Ed.), *Trust: Making and Breaking Cooperative Relations*: Basil Blackwell Ltd.

Gefen, D. (2000). E-commerce: the role of familiarity and trust. *The international Journal of Management Science, 28*, 725-737.

Gefen, D., Karahanna, E., & Straub, D. (2003). Trust and TAM in online shopping: an integrated model. *MIS Quarterly, 27*(1), 51-90.

Gefen, D., Rao, V. S., & Tractinsky, N. (2003). *The Conceptualization of Trust, Risk and Their Relationship in Electronic Commerce: The Need for Clarifications.* Paper presented at the Proceedings of the 36th Hawaii International Conference on System Sciences, Hawaii, USA.

Gefen, D., & Straub, D. W. (2004). Consumer trust in B2C e-Commerce and the importance of social presence: experiments in e-Products and e-Services. *The international Journal of Management Science, 32*, 407-424.

Howard, M. (2001). E-Government across the globe: How Will "e" Change Government? *Government finance Review, 17*(4), 6-9.

Humphery, J., & Schmitz, H. (1998). Trust and Inter Firm Relations in Developing and Transition Economies. *Journal of Development Studies, 34*(4), 32-61.

Jarvenpaa, S. L. (1989). The Effect of Task Demands and Graphical Format on Information Processing Strategies. *Management Science, 35*(3), 285-303.

Jarvenpaa, S. L., Tractinsky, N., & Vitale, M. (2000). Consumer trust in an Internet store. *Information Technology and Management, 1*, 45-71.

Kim, L. H., Kim, D. J., & Leong, J. K. (2005). The Effect of Perceived Risk on Purchase Intention in Purchasing Airline Tickets Online. *Journal of Hospitality & Leisure Marketing, 13*(2), 33-53.

Kim, Y. H., & Kim, D. J. (2005). *A study of Online Transaction Self-Efficacy, Consumer Trust, and Uncertainty Reduction in Electronic Commerce Transaction.* Paper presented at the Proceedings of the 38th Hawaii International Conference on System Sciences.

Koufaris, M., Kambil, A., & Labarbera, P. A. (2001). Consumer Behavior in Web-Based Commerce: An Empirical Study. *International Journal of Electronic Commerce 6*(2), 115-138.

Landis, R., & Koch, G. G. (1977). The Measurement of Observer Agreement for Categorical Data. *Biometrics, 33*(1), 159-174.

Lane, C., & Bachmann, R. (1996). The Social Constitution of Trust: Supplier Relations in Britain and Germany. *Organisation Studies, 17*(3), 365-395.

Lau, E. (2001). Online government: A Surfer's Guide. *Organization for Economic Development, 224*, 46-47.

Lewis, J. D., & Weigert, A. J. (1985). Trust as a Social Reality. *Social Forces, 63*(4), 967-985.

Liebermann, Y., & Stashevsky, S. (2002). Perceived risks as barriers to Internet and e-commerce usage. *Qualitative Market Research: An International Journal, 5*(4), 291-300.

Luhmann, N. (1979). *Trust and Power*. Great Britain: John Wiley & Sons Ltd.

Luhmann, N. (1988). Familiarity, Confidence, Trust: Problems and Alternatives. In D. Gambetta (Ed.), *Trust: Making and Breaking Cooperative Relations*: Basil Blackwell Ltd.

Mayer, R. C., Davis, J. H., & Schoorman, F. D. (1995). An Integrative Model of Organizational Trust. *The Academy of Management Review, 20*(3), 709-734.

McAllister, D. J. (1995). Affect- and Cognition-Based Trust as Foundations for Interpersonal Cooperation. *The Academy of Management Journal, 38*(1), 24-59.

McKnight, D., Choudhury, V., & Kacmar, C. (2002). Developing and Validating Trust Measures for e-Commerce: An Integrative Typology. *Information Systems Research, 13*(3), 334-359.

McKnight, D. H., & Chervany, N. L. (2001). *Conceptualizing Trust: A Typology and E-Commerce Customer Relationships Model.* Paper presented at the 34th Hawaii International Conference on System Sciences.

McKnight, D. H., Kacmar, C. J., & Choudhury, V. (2004). Dispositional Trust and Distrust Distinctions in Predicting High- and Low-Risk Internet Expert Advice Site Perceptions. *e-Service Journal 3*(2), 35-55.

Moore, G. C., & Benbasat, I. (1991). Development of an Instrument to Measure the Perceptions of Adopting an Information Technology Innovation. *Information Systems Research, 2*(3), 192-222.

Nahm, A. Y., Solis-Galvan, L. E., Rao, S. S., & Ragu-Nathan, T. S. (2002). The Q-Sort Method: Assessing Reliability and Construct Validity of Questionnaire Items at a Pre-Testing Stage. *Journal of Modern Applied Statistical Methods, 1*(1), 114-125.

National Research Council. (2002). *Information Technology research, innovation, and e-governemnt* Washington, DC: National Academy Press.

Ndou, V. D. (2004). E-Government for Developing Countries: Opportunities and Challenges. *Electronic Journal of Information Systems in Developing Countries, 18*(1), 1-24.

Pavlou, P. A. (2003). Consumer Acceptance of Electronic Commerce—Integrating Trust and Risk with the Technology Acceptance Model. *International Journal of Electronic Commerce, 73*, 69-103.

Pavlou, P. A., & Gefen, D. (2004). Building Effective Online Marketplaces with Instituation-Based Trust. *Information Systems Research, 15*(1), 37-59.

Pavlou, P. A., Tan, Y.-H., & Gefen, D. (2003). *The Transitional Role of Institutional Trust in Online Interorganizational Relationships.* Paper presented at the Proceedings of the 36th Hawaii International Conference on System Sciences (HICSS'03).

Peterson, R. A. (2000). *Constructing effective questionnaires* Thousand Oaks: Sage Publications.

Rotter, J. B. (1971a). Generalized expectancies for interpersonal trust. *American Psychologist, 26*(5), 443-452.

Rotter, J. B. (1971b). Generalized expectancies for interpersonal trust. *American Psychologist, 26*(5).

Rousseau, D. M., Sitkin, S. B., Burt, R. S., & Camerer, C. (1998). Not so Different after All: A Cross-Discipline View of Trust. *The Academy of Management Review, 23*(3), 393-404.

Schlenker, B. R., Helm, B., & Tedeschi, J. T. (1973). The Effects of Personality and Situational Variables on Behavioral Trust. *Journal of Personality and Social Psychology, 25*(3), 419-427.

Schneider, G. P. (2003). *Electronic Commerce* (4 ed.). Boston, MA: Thomson Learning Inc.

Seifert, J. W. (2008). A Primer on E-Government: Sectors, Stages, Opportunities, and Challenges of Online Governance. In R. B. Ventura (Ed.), *E-Government in High Gear*. New York: Nova Science Publishers.

Seifert, J. W., & Petersen, R. E. (2002). The Promise of All Things E? Expectations and Challenges of Emergent Electronic Government. *Perspectives on Global Development and Technology, 1*(2), 193-212.

Shapiro, S. P. (1987). The Social Control of Impersonal Trust. *The American Journal of Sociology, 93*(3), 623-658.

Stephens, R. T. (2004). *A Framework for the Identification of Electronic Commerce Visual Design Elements that Enable Trust within the Small Hotel Industry.* Unpublished PhD Thesis, Nova Southeastern University, Fort Lauderdale, Florida.

Stephenson, W. (1953). *The study of behaviour: Q-technique and its methodology.* Chicago: University of Chicago Press.

Studio Archetype/Sapient, & Cheskin Research. (1999). *ECommerce Trust Study* o. Document Number)

Sztompka, P. (2003). *Trust : A Sociological Theory*. Cambridge: Cambridge University Press.

Tang, T.-W., & Chi, W.-H. (2005). *The Role of Trust In Customer Online Shopping Behavior: Perspective of Technology Acceptance Model.* Paper presented at the Proccedings of NAACSOS Conference 2005 Indiana, USA.

Todd, P., & Benbasat, I. (1993). An Experimental Investigation of theRelationship between Decision Makers, Decision Aids and Decision Making Effort. *Information Systems Research, 31*(2), 80-100.

Turban, E., King, D., Lee, J., Warkentin, M., & Chung, H. M. (2002). *Electronic Commerce : A Managerial Perspective* (2nd ed.). Upper Saddle, New Jersey: Prentice Hall.

Warkentin, M., Gefen, D., Pavlou, P. A., & Rose, G. M. (2002). Encouraging Citizen Adoption of e-Government by Building Trust. *Electronic Markets, 12*(3), 157-162.

Welch, E. W., Hinnant, C. C., & Moon, M. J. (2005). Linking Citizen Satisfaction with E-Government and Trust in Government. *Journal of Public Administration Research and Theory, 15*(3), 371-391.

World Bank Group. (2007). e-Government. Retrieved 12/11/2006

Zand, D. E. (1972). Trust and Mangagerial Problem Solving. *Administrative Science Quarterly, 17*(2), 229-239.

Zhang, J., Ghorbani, A. A., & Cohen, R. (2007). A familiarity-based trust model for effective selection of sellers in multiagent e-commerce systems. *International Journal of Information Security 6*(5), 333-344.

Zucker, L. G. (1986). Production of Trust: Institutional Sources of Economic Structure. In B. M. Staw & L. L. Cummings (Eds.), *Research in Organizational Behavior* (Vol. 8, pp. 53-111). London, England: JAI Press Inc.

e-Government and Technology Acceptance: The Case of the Implementation of Section 508 Guidelines for Websites

Paul Jaeger and Miriam Matteson
University of Maryland, USA
pjaeger@umd.edu
Originally published in EJEG (2009) Volume 7, issue 1.

Editorial Commentary

When accessing a government website to find information or to conduct a transaction, how many of us stop to think what assumptions web site developers have made about the skills and abilities (or disabilities) of the members of the public that will be accessing those sites? This is a critical issue in the public sector given that the public sector tends to cater most intensively for people with specific needs, specific problems and badly developed skill sets that may limit their ability to make as good a use of the Internet as more skilled people. One wonders, for example, what reading age is required for a user adequately to understand the content of a given web page. Jaeger and Matteson discuss recent developments in the USA where the massive growth in e-Government has affect the nature of the relationship of the government and its citizens. Here they use the Technology Acceptance Model (TAM) to explore if e-Government has become more accessible to those citizens with disabilities. While their paper focuses specifically on e-Government accessibility for the disabled, they argue that their model and methodology is equally applicable for assessing e-Government accessibility either more widely or for other "marginal" groups in society. Worryingly, the authors reveal that most of the e-Government websites they examined did not comply with the requirements of Section 508 of the Rehabilitation Act. This failure, they argue, rendered most e-Government websites inaccessible to some or all citizens with disabilities. Perhaps more important was their observation that an organisation's assessment of the accessibility of its own website was often more positive than the authors' assessment of the accessibility of the site. Perhaps we need to be even more diligent in the development of e-Government strategies that are inclusive and reflect the needs, skills and abilities of all citizens rather than the interests of the better off, the better educated and the more technologically capable.

Abstract: This paper examines the relevance of the Technology Acceptance Model for e-Government websites at federal government level in the United States through an exploratory research study. Various unfunded government mandates over the past several years have required agencies to create websites, put services on the sites, and make them accessible to citizens, and the federal e-Government now includes tens of thousands of sites. Section 508 of the Rehabilitation Act, for example, was passed to ensure e-Government sites would be accessible to persons with disabilities. By studying the implementation of the requirements of Section 508 through a number of data collection techniques and in terms of the Technology Acceptance Model, this paper seeks to use this particular law as an example through which to better understand the processes by which government agencies adopt e-Government requirements and the actions that government managers can take to improve the implementation of such adoption.

Keywords: e-Government, technology acceptance model, accessibility, Section 508, disability, public servants, websites

1. Introduction: e-Government technologies and guidelines

Governments internationally are showing a strong preference for delivering services via the Internet, particularly as a means of boosting cost-efficiency and reducing time spent on direct interactions with citizens (Ebbers, Pieterson, & Noordman 2008). The United States has created a larger e-Government network than any other nation. While e-Government includes a wide-range of functions such as e-voting, e-procurement, data collection, management and analysis, inter-agency collaboration, intra- and inter-agency communication, e-learning, for agency staff, human resource management, a key focus of the President's e-Government Management Agenda (http://www.whitehouse.gov/omb/egov/) is on interactions between the government and citizens and many government agencies are viewing e-Government as their primary method for interacting with citizens. As such, it is extremely important for e-Government research to focus on issues of how e-Government is meeting the needs of citizens.

Citizens still show a strong preference for phone-based or in person interactions with government representatives when they have questions or are seeking services, though individuals with higher levels of education are typically more open to using online interactions with government (Ebbers, Pieterson, & Noordman 2008; Steib & Navarro 2006). e-Government services generally are limited by difficulties in searching for and locating the desired information, as well as lack of availability of computers and Internet access for many segments of the general population (Singh, & Sahu 2008). Such problems are exacerbated by a general lack of familiarity with the structure of government and attitudes toward technology and government among many citizens (Jaeger & Thompson 2003, 2004). While the e-Government Act of 2002 and President's e-Government Management Agenda have emphasized the transformative effect of e-Government, thus far it has primarily been used as a way to make information available, provide forms and electronic filing, and distribute the viewpoints of government agencies (Jaeger 2005). As commercial sites are developing faster and provide more innovative services than e-Government sites, public satisfaction with government websites is declining (Barr 2007).

For these and other reasons, the majority of citizens, even those with a high speed Internet connection at home, seeking government information and services, prefer to speak to a person directly in their contacts with the government (Horrigan 2004). As a result of these tensions between policy, implementation, and public perception, e-Government exists as an option, but not the preferred option, of most citizens. There is a range of reasons that may deter some users—infrequent need for them, lack of interactivity, lack of availability of services or information that people really want. However, a key part of the problem is that e-Government websites are not being designed to fully implement user-oriented standards.

This paper examines this problem as a matter of technology acceptance, specifically the process by which and the extent to which agencies accept and implement standards for e-Government websites. This problem will be examined through the lens of Section 508 of the Rehabilitation Act (29 U.S.C. § 794d), which provides a set of standards to ensure e-Government website are accessible to persons with disabilities. As e-Government websites are intended to serve as the electronic face of government and provide the majority of government services, determining how to better increase the adoption of standards for e-Government sites by government agencies is essential to improving the usage of and user experiences with e-Government websites.

2. Accessibility and e-Government

Accessibility is equal access to information and communication technologies (ICTs) for persons with disabilities. "Accessibility allows individuals with disabilities—regardless of the type of disability they have—to use ICTs, such as websites, in a manner that is equal to the use enjoyed by others" (Jaeger 2008: 24). This equal access is of utmost importance to persons with disabilities in a society where functions of government, business, and personal life are increasingly online. In the United States, 54 million people have a disability, while the number of persons with disabilities worldwide is more than 550 million, and that number will continue to grow as the baby boom generation ages (Jaeger & Bowman 2005). For ICTs to be accessible, they should: 1) provide equal or equivalent access to all users, and 2) work compatibly with assistive technologies, such as narrators, scanners, enlargement, voice-activated technologies, and many other devices that persons with disabilities may employ.

The United States federal government has created numerous laws related to accessibility of ICTs (Jaeger 2004a, 2004b). For websites, the most prominent law is Section 508 of the Rehabilitation Act, which mandates specific design requirements that reduce barriers to access for different types of disabilities and promote compatibility with assistive technologies that users may be employing. Section 508 has a detailed set of technological and accessibility requirements as well as guidance for implementation (www.section508.gov). Federal e-Government websites, in spite of the requirements of Section 508, are still often inaccessible to persons with disabilities long after the Section 508 requirements were supposed to have been implemented in 2001 (Jaeger 2004b, 2006). Some persons with disabilities have come to distrust e-Government as a result of these accessibility issues (Cullen & Hernon 2006).

Accessibility in the online environment is a relatively new development as a focus of research and is also a highly complex topic that involves policy, technical, and user issues (Jacko & Hanson 2002; Stephanidis & Savidis 2001). This combination of newness and complexity has thus kept most investigations of online accessibility at a very practical level, including most studies of the accessibility of e-Government websites. As a result, no conceptual frameworks have been established for the standards for evaluation of the accessibility of e-Government websites. Having a conceptual framework through which to evaluate the implementation of Section 508 standards on e-Government websites would be beneficial to government employees, researchers, and citizens with disabilities. This exploratory paper proposes that an extant conceptual framework is potentially useful to the study of the accessibility of e-Government websites in terms of the implementation of Section 508 requirements.

3. The Technology Acceptance Model

The Technology Acceptance Model (TAM) was originally introduced and studied as a means of understanding how users adopt and use new technology by evaluating the factors that influenced the decision to accept a new technology (Davis 1989). TAM is based on the belief "that perceived ease of use and usefulness can predict attitudes toward technology" (Lederer et al. 2000: 269). Perceived usefulness of a technology and perceived ease of use of a technology combine to create an attitude about the technology, influencing decisions of whether to adopt the technology. Figure 1 shows the most basic form of TAM. Perceived ease of use and perceived usefulness are shaped by external factors unique to the situation, while the behavioral decisions ultimately dictate whether and how a technology is used (Davis, Bagozzi, & Warshaw 1989).

Since its introduction, TAM has been tested in many studies and has been used to evaluate numerous different technologies, including email, voice mail, and many others (i.e., Dasgupta, Granger, & McGarry 2002; Gefen & Straub 1997; Straub, Keil, & Brenner 1997). Some recent studies of TAM have extended the application of the model to areas beyond a single technology, such as the study of online educational settings or the World Wide Web (i.e., Dishaw & Strong 1999; Saade & Bahli 2005; Venkatesh & Davis 2000).

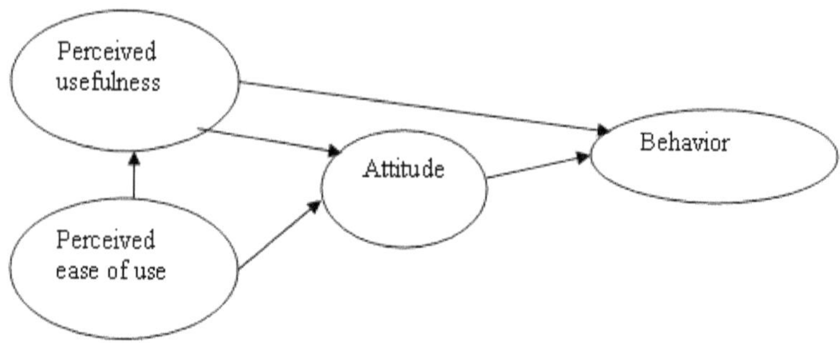

Figure 1: Basic Technology Acceptance Model.

One of the extensions of TAM has been to explore decisions by organizations comprised of groups of users, instead of individual users, to adopt new technologies. These studies have examined TAM in relation to organizational adoptions of new technologies in contexts such as e-commerce, police investigations, sales force coordination, and telemedicine (Chau & Hu 2002; Colvin & Goh 205; Grandon & Pearson 2004; Olson & Boyer 2003; Robinson, Marshall, & Stamps 2005; Yu et al. 2005). Such studies have focused on technology in numerous different forms, including software, hardware, websites, technology standards, and Internet-based activities. These types of studies of TAM within the context of organizations demonstrate the potential applicability of TAM to the acceptance of new technologies by government agencies.

Grandon and Pearson (2004), for example, explore how small and medium sized businesses accept the use of e-commerce as a part of their business activities. That study found the acceptance of e-commerce by the organizations was based on perception of the value of e-commerce in an organization, in light of certain external and internal factors, and the level of success of the adoption was influenced by a number of internal factors. The acceptance of the new technology was influenced by agency mission, actual cost, perceived cost, agency priorities, and staff interest, among others. This approach appears to have utility when applied to the process through which government agencies adopt new technologies and apply them.

4. TAM and e-Government websites

The conceptual framework tested in this study was based on the idea of a modified TAM for organizational acceptance of new technology, similar to those like the Grandon and Pearson (2004) study detailed above. The organizations studied were United States federal government agencies and the new technology at issue was accessible websites that comply with the standards of Section 508. The TAM (and its related variants) were originally developed and intended to be applied to assess the reaction and behavior of individual users of a technology. This study conceived of the federal agencies as users of the standards of Section 508 and the accessibility standards as a new technology that they were supposed to adopt. Federal agencies with e-Government websites are providers of technologies to citizens, such as websites, but they are also users of technologies, such as the elements they must use to create and provide websites. It is in this later sense that this study approached the federal agencies, with the essential problem in this research being how agencies choose to adopt or not adopt the Section 508 accessibility standards for their websites. As such, the TAM provides a unique conceptual approach to the study of the organizational acceptance of the accessibility standards by federal agencies.

Figure 2 illustrates the preliminary conceptual framework for this study. The two upper layers of the model are contextual, while the three lower layers represent the accessibility research conducted in this study. The contextual layers are derived from extant research and professional literature about the policy environment for e-Government and issues of accessibility. The three lower layers of the framework display the research focus of this study—the mandate to implement the standards of Section 508, the ways the standards could be implemented, and the actual level of compliance that is achieved.

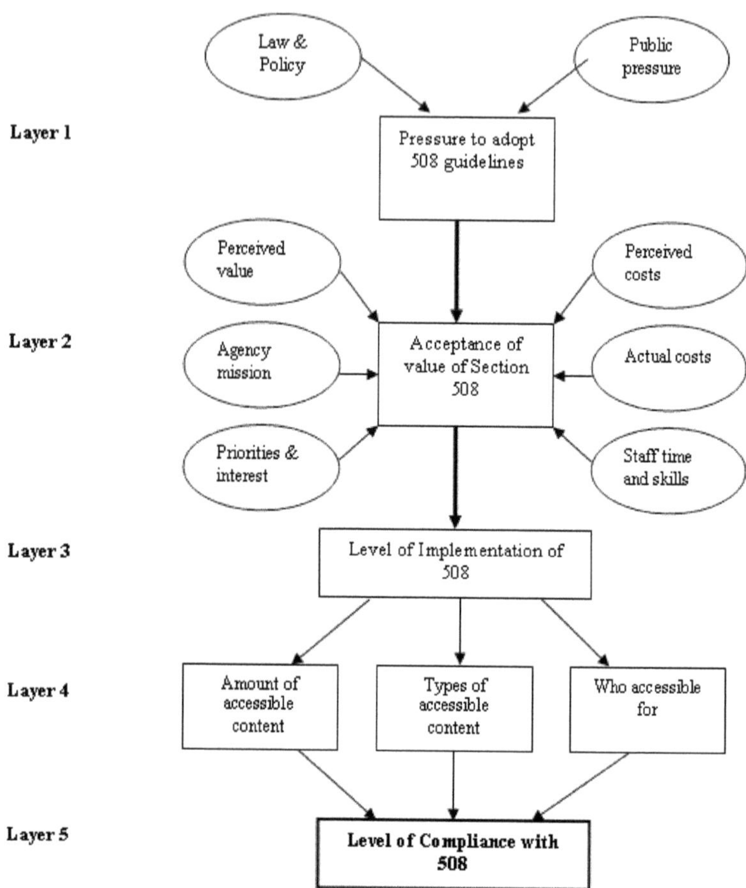

Figure 2: Conceptual framework for the study, based on modified TAM for organizations.

The top layer of the Figure 2 shows the external pressures to adopt Section 508 standards for federal e-Government websites. Various law and policy instruments, including Section 508, create legal standards for accessible websites, while various types of public pressures, such as complaints, news reports, lawsuits, and research studies may create further pressure by bringing attention to the issue (Jaeger 2004a). These pressures drive the acceptance of Section 508 standards for websites as a value to which agencies adhere.

As the second layer of the figure shows, there are many internal issues related to perceived usefulness and perceived ease of adoption of Section 508 standards for websites. Issues related to culture can have a significant impact on decisions to accept and implement a technology (Straub, Keil, & Brenner 1997). Feedback within an agency has been shown to play an important role in the development of online government services (Mahler & Regan 2002). These specific internal issues are drawn from the review of relevant research literature as key factors that can influence agency decisions regarding how to adopt Section 508 standards (see Jaeger 2004a, 2004b, 2006, 2008). On the left side of the figure are the internal factors related to perceived usefulness of adoption of Section 508 standards to websites—perceived value, agency mission, and priorities and interests of the agency. On the right hand side of the middle level of the figure are the internal factors related to perceived ease of adoption of Section 508 standards for websites—perceived costs, actual costs, and staff time and awareness.

The third layer of Figure 2 examines the influences of the varying contextual factors that will shape the ultimate level of compliance with Section 508 on an agency website. The fourth layer of Figure 2 represents the extent to which the standards of Section 508 are implemented on an agency website. The amount of accessible content, the types of content that are accessible, and the types of disabilities that content is accessible for will all be influenced by decisions made regarding implementation of Section 508 standards on e-Government websites.

The fifth layer of Figure 2 focuses on compliance with the Section 508 standards for federal e-Government websites. Ultimately, the amount of accessible content, the types of accessible content, and the types of disabilities for which content is accessible demonstrate the extent to which an agency website complies with the standards of Section 508. If an agency considers adoption to be difficult or of limited value, the levels of compliance with Section 508 standards will likely be low. In contrast, if an agency considers adoption a high priority or of significant value, then the levels of compliance with Section 508 standards will be high.

5. The study of TAM and 508 standards

This framework was examined in a multi-method, user-centered study of e-Government websites for compliance with the Section 508 of the Rehabilitation Act standards for accessibility (Jaeger 2006, 2008). This study employed five data collection methods in the assessment of e-Government websites in terms of the implementation of Section 508 of the Rehabilitation Act. Selected federal e-Government websites were evaluated using policy analysis, expert testing, user testing, and automated testing, along with a survey administered to federal webmasters that assessed their views on accessibility. In the evaluation of e-Government sites, the use of a multi-method approach is optimal (Thompson, McClure, & Jaeger 2003).

The policy analysis was conducted through extensive review of legal and policy documents. The expert testing involved the evaluation by persons knowledgeable about the design of accessible websites to provide a technical evaluation of the accessibility. The user testing under the guidance of a researcher was used to provide detailed information from the perspective of users. Table 1 lists sample questions used in expert and user testing.

Table 1: Sample questions from expert testing and user testing

Sample Expert Testing Questions:

1. Provides an audio/video/textual equivalent for every element related to content and services?
2. Alternative formats of elements of multimedia presentations synchronize to the appropriate parts of the presentation?
3. All information conveyed through color also conveyed without color?
4. Provides clear navigation mechanisms?
5. Does not rely on moving pictures or flash to convey content?
6. Ensures user control of time-sensitive content changes?

Sample User Testing Questions:

1. Are you able to navigate the site without difficulty? If not, what accessibility problems did you face in navigating?
2. Are you able to use particular applications (i.e., download forms, view audio or video, fill out forms) on the site without difficulty? If not, what accessibility problems did you face in using these applications?
3. Do you feel that the site as a whole is working well with the assistive technology you are using? Please specify.
4. Do you notice problems that might affect people with other types of disabilities? Please specify.

Automated testing—the use of software designed to test accessibility of websites—was used, but proved to provide no additional information to the expert and user testing. Appendix A provides a detailed description of the data collection methods.

The study also employed questionnaires to government webmasters about agency perceptions of accessibility. The questionnaires were sent to a diverse set of prominent government agencies that work with directly citizens. This survey received a response rate of 60%. Table 2 lists sample questions from the survey of government webmasters.

Table 2: Sample questions for government webmasters.

1. Do you feel that the accessibility of your website for persons with disabilities is a priority within your agency?
2. When working to make your website accessible for persons with disabilities, where do you turn for resources and guidelines?
3. Do you perform accessibility testing on your website to test how well it can be used by persons with disabilities? If so, at what point in the website development process is this testing done?
4. What factors (i.e., staff time, staff skills, funding, agency mission, etc.) influence the priority accorded to the accessibility of your website for persons with disabilities?
5. Have you received any feedback from users of your site regarding its accessibility? If so, were the comments generally positive or negative?
6. If you feel that the accessibility of your website could be improved, what resources would you find beneficial in working to improve it?

The primary finding from the study was that most e-Government websites do not comply with all of the requirements of Section 508 of the Rehabilitation Act, rendering most e-Government websites inaccessible to some or all persons with disabilities (Jaeger, 2006, 2008). Key accessibility barriers that were recurring problems across all of the sites tested included:

- Compatibility problems with screen enlargement;
- Compatibility problems with screen readers;
- Compatibility problems with alternate color schemes;
- Use of flash and moving images to convey content;
- Cluttered layout and organization;
- Audio content does not have a text equivalent;
- Graphics lack Alt tags;
- Difficult drop-down, mouse-over menus; and

- Problems with consistency and clarity of context, orientation, and navigation.

Further, the webmaster survey revealed that agency perceptions of the accessibility of these websites often did not match the actual levels of accessibility on the sites (Jaeger 2006, 2008).

The three lower levels of the proposed framework were studied through several methods of accessibility testing. Accessibility testing by users with a range of different disabilities, experts in accessibility testing, and automated tools evaluated the ways in which and the extent to which Section 508 standards have been implemented on the sites.

In addition to the testing, the questionnaires to government webmasters examined the context in which agencies are implementing accessibility on their websites. The law and policy analysis was used to examine the initial pressures to implement Section 508 standards, while the webmaster questionnaires explored the factors that influence agency perspectives and decision-making processes related to Section 508. As such, the webmaster questionnaires served to directly connect the findings of the accessibility testing to information about the agency perspectives and decision-making processes related to implementing accessible websites, explicitly linking the accessibility methods to the larger contextual issues.

The tentative conceptual framework presented in Figure 2 served as an initial guide for this study. Given the newness of accessibility research and the lack of established conceptual frameworks for studies of e-Government accessibility, this proposed framework of a TAM at least provided an exploratory conceptual basis from which to begin research.

6. Findings and modification of the TAM

The top layer, which posits that law and policy combine with public pressure to create the impetus for an agency to adopt the Section 508 standards on its website, seems sound in light of the findings of the study. The literature review and the policy analysis revealed an intertwined relationship between the development of the laws and policies and the support by the public and by particular stakeholder groups for such laws and policies. The passage and implementation of the primary disability rights laws were inextricably linked to public support and political protests by interested groups (Jaeger 2004a; Jaeger & Bowman 2005). Without sufficient public support and stakeholder intervention, the passage of the Rehabilitation Act, Individuals with Disabilities Education Act, or the Americans with Disabilities Act would not have been assured. As the policy analysis demonstrated, the passage of Section 508 of the Rehabilitation Act and the promulgation of standards were greeted with significant support from an array of stakeholder groups. Further, disability rights groups and government organizations like the Access Board and the National Council on Disability have continued to lobby for better implementation of Section 508. The data from the user testing and expert testing affirm the accuracy of the top layer of the framework, as the websites that faired the best in all of the testing were primarily agencies that focus on issues related to disability. These agencies would be most likely to be interested in and affected by public pressure from stakeholder groups on issues of disability.

The bottom three layers of the conceptual framework can also be assessed in light of the data from the study. The user testing and the expert testing methods were both focused on gathering data about the level of implementation of the standards of Section 508, the success of that implementation, and the ultimate level of compliance with the Section 508 standards on a site. From the data collected, it seems that the lower three levels of the framework represent what appears to be happening on the websites. On sites where the methods of accessibility testing found poor design in terms of persons with disabilities, the problems clearly were not the result of failed efforts to provide accessibility, but were instead the result of limited attempts to provide accessibility. These sites lacked significant evidence of attempts to meet many of the Section 508 standards, demonstrating a decision to make a minimal effort to implement the standards. In these cases, the resulting sites had limited levels of accessible content, with many different types of content being inaccessible for persons with a range of different disabilities. This finding was independently reached through the user and expert methods of accessibility testing.

The opposite situations—where the design of the website evidenced meaningful attempts to provide accessibility and, thus, the intent to implement the standards of Section 508—the sites were well designed for accessibility and faired much better in the accessibility testing. In the sites that were generally better designed for accessibility, the flaws were often implementations of the standards that were not completely correct. The sites designed with a noticeable intent to comply with the standards received much better results in the expert testing and the user testing. The primary reason for these better results was that the sites provided much higher levels of accessible content, access to most or all types of content, and accessibility for users with most or all disabilities.

For both of the sites that were poorly designed for accessibility and the sites that were well designed for accessibility, the lower three layers of the conceptual framework seemed to accurately represent the situation. However, the second layer of the conceptual framework proved more difficult to assess, due to the complexity of this level of the framework and to the limitations of the responses to the webmaster questionnaire. It is also the layer that is most tied to the TAM, as it reveals the decision making process in the agency related to acceptance.

Based on the findings of the policy analysis, the second layer seems reasonable, and the findings from the user and expert accessibility testing do not call any elements of the second layer into question. However, results of the webmaster questionnaire, the data collection method most relevant to assessing this layer of the framework, are less helpful than hoped in relation to the framework. When asked about the factors that influenced decisions related to the implementation of the Section 508 standards and when asked about the prioritization of accessibility within the agency, many responses focused on the importance of providing accessibility without giving many details related to agency process or decision-making.

Even though the top layer and the lowest three layers of the framework seem accurate based on the data gathered in the study, the questions about the second layer also raise questions about the interactions of the other layers and their relationships to one another that will need to be answered in further studies. Nevertheless, the data from this study have identified four important elements not included in the initial conceptual framework:

- User feedback – Comments from users with disabilities would influence compliance with Section 508 standards at many agencies.

- Education and training – Many federal web developers are receiving insufficient training about designing, testing, and monitoring for accessibility.
- Monitoring and enforcement – The current citizen-based monitoring and enforcement structure needs to be accounted for in the conceptual framework.
- Political climate – Accessibility is not a political priority to many agencies.

Figure 3 is a revised version of the conceptual framework that incorporates these factors.

One way to address the need for information about the second layer would be a study targeted directly at web developers at government agencies. Such a study, however, would need to have a much larger sample than the one in this study. Further research will also need to account for and evaluate the suggested additions to the revised conceptual framework. One clear finding, however, is that agency management plays an enormously important role in the adoption of Section 508 requirements.

To further test the fitness of TAM as a conceptual framework for the implementation of Section 508 and other e-Government standards, future work in this area should consider the role that management plays in implementing requirements for e-Government websites. Managerial leadership and political support can be central to e-Government development (Chou, Chen & Pu 2008; Ho & Ni 2004). In specific terms of the adoption of Section 508 standards, managerial leadership and political support may offer the best means of increasing adoption of Section 508 standards among federal agencies.

Managerial influence can be explored as an external variable in the TAM, which influences the perceived usefulness and the perceived ease of use of the technology (Bhattacherjee & Sanford 2006). Alternatively, managerial influence might appear as a direct effect on a user's behavioral intention to accept the new technology. Although this relationship is not captured in the TAM, support for it can be found in other technology acceptance theories, such as the Theory of Reasoned Action (TRA) (Fishbein & Ajzen 1975); Theory of Planned Behavior (TPB) (Ajzen 1991); and the Unified Theory of Acceptance and Use of Technology (UTAUT) (Venkatesh et al. 2003). In the case of government agencies implementing Section 508 provisions for websites, agency managers may be perceived as "important others" by employees responsible for implementing the changes, and thus managerial influence might affect an employee's behavioral intent to implement the provisions.

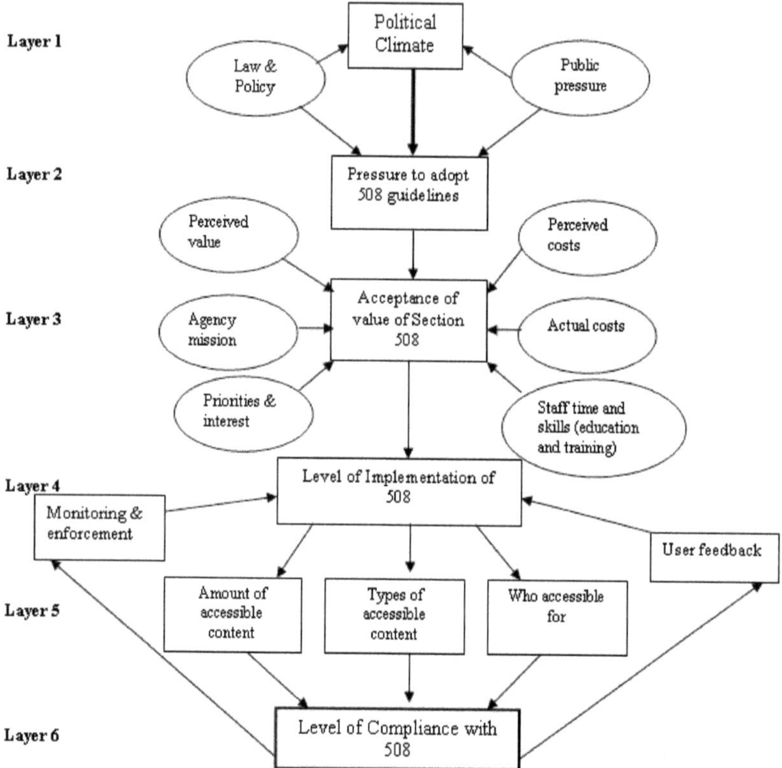

Figure 3: Revised conceptual framework of TAM for Section 508 standards on government websites.

7. Conclusion: The implications of TAM and Section 508

While this paper has focused on adoption of the Section 508 standards on e-Government websites, the general ideas and approaches explored in this paper may have relevance to the adoption of e-Government standards more widely. Given the importance placed on e-Government as a means of communicating with and providing services to citizens, improving the adoption and implementation of standards is essential for e-Government to meet the stated administrative goals. This paper has identified potential areas for further research, and further research is definitely needed to ascertain the relevance of the TAM to e-Government and the process of adoption of e-Government standards to websites. The proposed model needs to be tested with other e-Government standards, and individual factors suggested in this study will need to be tested to understand the role they play in the process. These ideas need to be researched in the context of other e-Governments—international, state, and local. The particular roles of management in the adoption of e-Government standards seem to merit specific attention. Ultimately, such research could improve understanding of the ways residents and public servants use e-Government technologies (Chang et al. 2005).

Results from TAM studies might also be useful to helping to determine the best methods for addressing the issues at hand. In terms of compliance with Section 508, TAM studies might help determine the best means for raising compliance with Section 508 requirements, such as the creation of an independent division monitoring conformance of e-services to Section 508 regulations; making conformance report an essential part of e-Government project deliverables; or the adoption of technological products and frameworks known to assist accessible content and service development. However, TAM alone will not be able to explain issues of technology adoption related to e-Government. Additional factors, such as costs and technology maturity, should be considered as well.

The United States and many other local, state, federal, and supra-national governments rely on their online presence for activities ranging from information provision to complex service delivery. Given the growing importance of e-Government and the continually increasing amounts of government information and services available primarily or exclusively on the web, the process of adoption by government agencies of e-Government standards is a significant issue that merits considerable further study. Hopefully, the ideas, approaches, and models suggested in this paper will serve to foster more research in this area.

Appendix A: Data Collection Approach

The study that inspired the discussion in this paper was conducted in 2005 and 2006 (Jaeger 2006; 2008). While the data collection techniques are not central to the concepts explored in the paper, the framework of the study provides context to this discussion. The study employed five data collection methods in the assessment of the implementation of Section 508 on e-Government websites: policy analysis, expert testing, user testing, automated testing, and a survey administered to federal webmasters that assessed their views on accessibility. The study examined major e-Government sites of the United States federal government and the sites of federal agencies with a mission related to service for persons with disabilities. These two types of sites were selected to compare the levels of attention accessibility standards received on prominent e-Government sites and on sites oriented toward persons with disabilities.

The study first engaged in the policy analysis to identify the range of federal laws, policy documents, instruments, and standards that related to the accessibility of government websites. The policy analysis was designed to provide context and serve as the basis for the development of testing protocols and questionnaires.

The expert testing was next conducted. Expert testing is the evaluation by persons knowledgeable about the design of websites based on an established protocol. The protocol was pre-tested before use, and experts were recruited from a population of web developers and researchers. The expert evaluators were persons who could identify the barriers to accessibility in design and understood the legal requirements for accessibility and how they should be properly implemented.

These questions were drawn from the specific Section 508 requirements and are necessary for achieving a broad understanding of the accessibility of the site. The testing was conducted to ensure as wide an analysis as possible. Sites were tested through multiple browsers and for compatibility with a range of technologies related to different types of disabilities, including narrators and screen readers, screen enlargement software, magnifiers, alternate color schemes, and alternate navigation devices, among others. Expert testing was conducted until no new issues were identified in subsequent tests.

Expert testing is particularly important because it is very unlikely that the evaluation of an e-Government site could be conducted so thoroughly as to include user tests that represented people who have all the different types and levels of disabilities that must be accounted for in designing for accessibility. Though the expert testing did not reach the same depth or granularity in identifying problems for any particular disability as a user with that disability would, expert testing did identify the major accessibility issues on each site.

User testing, the testing of a website by users under the guidance of a researcher, was conducted next and provided a great depth of information from the perspective of each user who is tested. The user tests were conducted with both guided and think-aloud protocols to get the broadest range of insights possible. The instruments were pre-tested before use, and subjects were recruited through disability organizations. Subjects were recruited to represent a wide range of types and levels of severities of disabilities, spanning quadriplegia to complete sight loss. Users with visual and mobility disabilities were targeted in this study because those groups among all types of disabilities face the most significant barriers to equal access to online content.

People with different levels of severity of the same kind of disability will often experience different accessibility issues on the same site. A person involved in user testing can best provide information related to the experiences of people like themselves. As with the expert tests, user tests were conducted until no new information about the sites was identified in subsequent tests. User tests took, on average, one to two hours to complete.

The results of the automated testing were muted in comparison to the results of the expert and user testing. Not only did a range of commonly used automated testing programs reveal no additional insights beyond the expert testing and user testing, the automated programs found far fewer issues than most individual expert and user participants. While the automated programs were useful to corroborate the findings of the other forms of data collection, they did not contribute any independent data.

After the three types of testing had been completed, a questionnaire was sent to the webmasters of all of the sites being studied to gauge their perceptions of the accessibility of their websites and the emphasis given to website accessibility within their agencies. The questions for the survey were developed based on the findings from the four previous forms of data collection. The responses to the questionnaire revealed the agencies' perceptions of the accessibility of their websites, which often did not match the findings from the user testing and the expert testing.

References

Ajzen, I. (1991) "The theory of planned behavior", *Organizational Behavior and Human Decision Processes*, vol. 50, pp. 179-211.

Barr, S. (2007). "Public less satisfied with government websites", [online], *Washington Post,* http://www.washingtonpost.com/wp-dyn/content/article/2007/03/20/AR2007032001338.html.

Chang, I. C., Li, Y.-C., Hung, W.-F. & Hwang, H.-G. (2005) "An empirical study on the impact of quality antecedents on tax payers' acceptance of Internet tax-filing systems", *Government Information Quarterly*, vol. 22, pp. 389-410.

Chau, P. Y. K. & Hu, P. J-H. (2002) "Investigating healthcare professionals' decisions to accept telemedicine: An empirical test of competing theories", *Information & Management*, vol. 39, pp. 297-311.

Chou, T.-C., Chen, J.-R., & Pu, C.-K. (2008) "Exploring the collective actions of public servants in e-Government development", *Decision Support Systems,* vol. 45, pp. 251-265.

Colvin, C. A. & Goh, A. (2005) "Validation of the technology acceptance model for police", *Journal of Criminal Justice*, vol. 33, pp. 89-95.

Cullen, R. & Hernon, P. (2006) "More citizen perspectives on e-Government", in Hernon, P., Cullen, R. & Relyea, H. C., (eds.), *Comparative Perspectives on e-Government: Serving today and building for tomorrow*, Lanham, MD: Scarecrow Press.

Dasgupta, S., Granger, M. & McGarry, N. (2002) "User acceptance of e-collaboration technology: An extension of the technology acceptance model", *Group Decision and Negotiation*, vol. 11, pp. 87-100.

Davis, F. D. (1989) "Perceived usefulness, perceived ease of use, and user acceptance of information technology", *MIS Quarterly*, vol. 13, pp. 319-339.

Davis, F. D., Bagozzi, R. P. & Warshaw, P. R. (1989) "User acceptance of computer technology: A comparison of two theoretical models", *Management Science*, vol. 35, pp. 983-1003.

Dishaw, M.T. & Strong, D.M. (1999) "Extending the technology acceptance model with task-technology fit constructs", *Information & Management*, vol. 36, pp.9-21.

Ebbers, W. E., Pieterson, W. J. & Noordman, H. N. (2008) "Electronic government: Rethinking channel management strategies", *Government Information Quarterly*, vol. 25, pp. 181-201.

e-Government Act of 2002, P.L. 107-347.

Fishbein, M. & Ajzen, I. (1975) *Belief, attitude, intention and behavior: An introduction to theory and research*, Reading, MA: Addison-Wesley.

Gefen, D. & Straub, D. W. (1997) "Gender differences in the perception and use of e-mail: An extension of the technology acceptance model", *MIS Quarterly*, vol. 21, pp. 389-400.

Grandon, E. E. & Pearson, J. M. (2004) "Electronic commerce adoption: An empirical study of small and medium U.S. businesses", *Information & Management*, vol. 42, pp. 197-216.

Ho, A. T-K. & Ni, A. Y. (2004) "Explaining the adoption of e-Government features: A case study of Iowa County Treasurers' offices", *American Review of Public Administration*, vol. 34, pp. 164-180.

Horrigan, J. B. (2004) *How Americans get in touch with government*, Washington DC: Pew Internet & American Life Project.

Jacko, J. A. & Hanson, V. L. (2002) "Universal access and inclusion in design", *Universal Access in the Information Society*, vol. 2, pp. 1-2.

Jaeger, P. T. (2004a) "Beyond Section 508: The spectrum of legal requirements for accessible e-Government websites in the United States", *Journal of Government Information*, vol. 30, pp. 518-533.

Jaeger, P. T. (2004b) "The social impact of an accessible E-democracy: The importance of disability rights laws in the development of the federal e-Government", *Journal of Disability Policy Studies*, vol. 15, pp. 19-26.

Jaeger, P. T. (2005) "Deliberative democracy and the conceptual foundations of electronic government", *Government Information Quarterly*, vol. 22, pp. 702-719.

Jaeger, P. T. (2006) "Assessing Section 508 compliance on federal e-Government websites: A multi-method, user-centered evaluation of accessibility for persons with disabilities", *Government Information Quarterly*, vol. 23, pp. 169-190.

Jaeger, P. T. (2008) "User-centered policy evaluations of Section 508 of the Rehabilitation Act: Evaluating e-Government websites for accessibility", *Journal of Disability Policy Studies,* vol. 19, pp. 24-33.

Jaeger, P. T. & Bowman, C. A. (2005) *Understanding disability: Inclusion, access, diversity, & civil rights*, Westport, CT: Praeger.

Jaeger, P. T. & Thompson, K. M. (2003) "e-Government around the world: Lessons, challenges, and new directions", *Government Information Quarterly*, vol. 20, pp. 389-394.

Jaeger, P. T. & Thompson, K. M. (2004) "Social information behavior and the democratic process: Information poverty, normative behavior, and electronic government in the United States", *Library & Information Science Research*, vol. 26, pp. 94-107.

Lederer, A. L., Maupin, D. J., Sena, M. P. & Zhuang, Y. (2000) "The technology acceptance model and the World Wide Web", *Decision Support Systems*, vol. 29, pp. 269-282

Mahler, J. & Regan, P. M. (2002) "Learning to govern online: Federal agency Internet use", *American Review of Public Administration*, vol. 32, pp. 326-349.

Olson, J. R. & Boyer, K. K. (2003) "Factors influencing the utilization of Internet purchasing in small organizations", *Journal of Operations Management*, vol. 21, pp. 225-245.

Reddick, C. G. (2005) "Citizen interaction with e-Government: From the streets to servers?", *Government Information Quarterly*, vol. 22, pp. 338-357.

Robinson, L., Marshall, G. W. & Stamps, M. B. (2005) "Sales force use of technology: Antecedents to technology acceptance", *Journal of Business Research*, vol. 58, pp. 1623-1631.

Saade, R. & Bahli, B. (2005) "The impact of cognitive absorption on perceived usefulness and perceived ease of use in online learning: An extension of the technology acceptance model", *Information & Management*, vol. 42, pp. 317-327.

Section 508 of the Rehabilitation Act. 29 U.S.C. § 794d.

Singh, A. K. & Sahu, R. (2008). "Integrating Internet, telephones, and call centers for delivering better quality e-governance to all citizens", *Government Information Quarterly*, vol. 25, 477-490.

Stephanidis, C. & Savidis, A. (2001) "Universal access in the information society: Methods, tools, and interactive technologies", *Universal Access in the Information Society*, vol. 1, pp. 40-55.

Straub, D., Keil, M. & Brenner, W. (1997), "Testing the technology acceptance model across cultures: A three country study", *Information & Management*, vol. 33, pp. 1-11.

Streib, G. & Navarro, I. (2006), "Citizen demand for interactive e-Government: The case of Georgia consumer services", *American Review of Public Administration*, vol. 36, pp. 288-300.

Thompson, K. M., McClure, C. R. & Jaeger, P. T. (2003) "Evaluating federal websites: Improving e-Government for the people", in George, J. F. (ed.), *Computers in society: Privacy, ethics, and the Internet,* Upper Saddle River, NJ: Prentice Hall.

Vassilakis, C., Lepouras, G., Fraser, J., Haston, S. & Georgiadis, P. (2005) "Barriers to electronic service development", *E-Services Journal*, vol. 4, pp. 41–63.

Venkatesh, V., & Davis, F. D. (2000) "A theoretical extension of the technology acceptance model: Four longitudinal field studies", *Management Science*, vol. 46, pp. 186-204.

Venkatesh, V., Morris, M. G., Davis, G. B., & Davis, F. D. (2003) "User acceptance of information technology: Toward a unified view", *MIS Quarterly*, vol. 27, pp. 425-478.

White House (2003) *e-Government Strategy: Implementing the President's Management Agenda for e-Government*, Washington DC: Author.

Yu, J., Ha, I., Choi, M., & Rho, J. (2005) "Extending the TAM for a t-commerce", *Information & Management*, vol. 42, pp. 965-976.

www.ingramcontent.com/pod-product-compliance
Ingram Content Group UK Ltd.
Pitfield, Milton Keynes, MK11 3LW, UK
UKHW021052270726
13967UKWH00012B/579